SUSE Linux Enterprise Server 12 - Virtualization Guide

A catalogue record for this book is available from the Hong Kong Public Libraries.

Published in Hong Kong by Samurai Media Limited.

Email: info@samuraimedia.org

ISBN 978-988-8406-51-7

Contents

About This Manual

This manual offers an introduction to setting up and managing virtualization with KVM (Kernel-based Virtual Machine), Xen, and Linux Containers (LXC) on SUSE Linux Enterprise Server. The first part introduces the different virtualization solutions by describing their requirements, their installations and SUSE's support status. The second part deals with managing VM Guests and VM Host Servers with `libvirt`. The following parts describe various administration tasks and practices and the last three parts deal with hypervisor-specific topics.

Many chapters in this manual contain links to additional documentation resources. This includes additional documentation that is available on the system and documentation available on the Internet.

For an overview of the documentation available for your product and the latest documentation updates, refer to http://www.suse.com/doc.

1 Available Documentation

We provide HTML and PDF versions of our books in different languages. The following manuals for users and administrators are available for this product:

Article "Installation Quick Start"

> Lists the system requirements and guides you step-by-step through the installation of SUSE Linux Enterprise Server from DVD, or from an ISO image.

Book "Deployment Guide"

> Shows how to install single or multiple systems and how to exploit the product inherent capabilities for a deployment infrastructure. Choose from various approaches, ranging from a local installation or a network installation server to a mass deployment using a remote-controlled, highly-customized, and automated installation technique.

Book "Administration Guide"

> Covers system administration tasks like maintaining, monitoring and customizing an initially installed system.

Virtualization Guide

> Describes virtualization technology in general, and introduces libvirt—the unified interface to virtualization—and detailed information on specific hypervisors.

Book "Storage Administration Guide"

> Provides information about how to manage storage devices on a SUSE Linux Enterprise Server.

Book "AutoYaST"

> AutoYaST is a system for installing one or more SUSE Linux Enterprise systems automatically and without user intervention, using an AutoYaST profile that contains installation and configuration data. The manual guides you through the basic steps of auto-installation: preparation, installation, and configuration.

Book "Security Guide"

> Introduces basic concepts of system security, covering both local and network security aspects. Shows how to use the product inherent security software like AppArmor or the auditing system that reliably collects information about any security-relevant events.

Book "Security and Hardening Guide"

> Deals with the particulars of installing and setting up a secure SUSE Linux Enterprise Server, and additional post-installation processes required to further secure and harden that installation. Supports the administrator with security-related choices and decisions.

Book "System Analysis and Tuning Guide"

> An administrator's guide for problem detection, resolution and optimization. Find how to inspect and optimize your system by means of monitoring tools and how to efficiently manage resources. Also contains an overview of common problems and solutions and of additional help and documentation resources.

Book "GNOME User Guide"

> Introduces the GNOME desktop of SUSE Linux Enterprise Server. It guides you through using and configuring the desktop and helps you perform key tasks. It is intended mainly for end users who want to make efficient use of GNOME as their default desktop.

Find HTML versions of most product manuals in your installed system under `/usr/share/doc/manual` or in the help centers of your desktop. Find the latest documentation updates at http://www.suse.com/doc where you can download PDF or HTML versions of the manuals for your product.

2 Feedback

Several feedback channels are available:

Bugs and Enhancement Requests

For services and support options available for your product, refer to http://www.suse.com/support/.

To report bugs for a product component, go to https://scc.suse.com/support/requests, log in, and click *Create New*.

User Comments

We want to hear your comments about and suggestions for this manual and the other documentation included with this product. Use the User Comments feature at the bottom of each page in the online documentation or go to http://www.suse.com/doc/feedback.html and enter your comments there.

Mail

For feedback on the documentation of this product, you can also send a mail to doc-team@suse.de. Make sure to include the document title, the product version and the publication date of the documentation. To report errors or suggest enhancements, provide a concise description of the problem and refer to the respective section number and page (or URL).

3 Documentation Conventions

The following typographical conventions are used in this manual:

- /etc/passwd: directory names and file names

- *placeholder*: replace *placeholder* with the actual value

- PATH: the environment variable PATH

- ls, --help: commands, options, and parameters

- user: users or groups

- Alt , Alt – F1 : a key to press or a key combination; keys are shown in uppercase as on a keyboard

- *File, File › Save As*: menu items, buttons

- x86_64 › This paragraph is only relevant for the x86_64 architecture. The arrows mark the beginning and the end of the text block. ◁

  System z, POWER › This paragraph is only relevant for the architectures z Systems and POWER. The arrows mark the beginning and the end of the text block. ◁

- *Dancing Penguins* (Chapter *Penguins*, ↑Another Manual): This is a reference to a chapter in another manual.

I Introduction

1 Virtualization Technology

Virtualization is a technology that provides a way for a machine (Host) to run another operating system (guest virtual machines) on top of the host operating system.

1.1 Overview

SUSE Linux Enterprise includes the latest open source virtualization technologies, Xen and KVM. With these Hypervisors, SUSE Linux Enterprise can be used to provision, de-provision, install, monitor and manage multiple virtual machines (VM Guests) on a single physical system (for more information see *Hypervisor*.)

Out of the box, SUSE Linux Enterprise can create virtual machines running both modified, highly tuned, paravirtualized operating systems and fully virtualized unmodified operating systems. Full virtualization allows the guest OS to run unmodified and requires the presence of x86_64 processors (either Intel* Virtualization Technology (Intel VT) or AMD* Virtualization (AMD-V)).

The primary component of the operating system that enables virtualization is a Hypervisor (or virtual machine manager), which is a layer of software that runs directly on server hardware. It controls platform resources, sharing them among multiple VM Guests and their operating systems by presenting virtualized hardware interfaces to each VM Guest.

SUSE Linux Enterprise is an enterprise-class Linux server operating system that offers two types of Hypervisors: Xen and KVM. Both Hypervisors support virtualization on 64-bit x86-based hardware architectures. Both Xen and KVM support full virtualization mode. In addition, Xen supports paravirtualized mode. SUSE Linux Enterprise with Xen or KVM acts as a virtualization host server (*VHS*) that supports VM Guests with its own guest operating systems. The SUSE VM Guest architecture consists of a Hypervisor and management components that constitute the VHS, which runs many application-hosting VM Guests.

In Xen, the management components run in a privileged VM Guest often called *Dom0*. In KVM, where the Linux kernel acts as the hypervisor, the management components run directly on the VHS.

1.2 Virtualization Capabilities

Virtualization design provides many capabilities to your organization. Virtualization of operating systems is used in many different computing areas:

- Server consolidation: Many servers can be replaced by one big physical server, so hardware is consolidated, and Guest Operating Systems are converted to virtual machine. It provides the ability to run legacy software on new hardware.

- Isolation: guest operating system can be fully isolated from the Host running it. So if the virtual machine is corrupted, the Host system is not harmed.

- Migration: A process to move a running virtual machine to another physical machine. Live migration is an extended feature that allows this move without disconnection of the client or the application.

- Disaster recovery: *Virtualized* guests are less dependent on the hardware, and the Host server provides snapshot features to be able to restore a known running system without any corruption.

- Dynamic load balancing: A migration feature that brings a simple way to load-balance your service across your infrastructure.

1.3 Virtualization Benefits

Virtualization brings a lot of advantages while providing the same service as a hardware server. First, it reduces the cost of your infrastructure. Servers are mainly used to provide a service to a customer, and a virtualized operating system can provide the same service, with:

- Less hardware: You can run several operating system on one host, so all hardware maintenance will be reduced.

- Less power/cooling: Less hardware means you do not need to invest more in electric power, backup power, and cooling if you need more service.

- Save space: Your data center space will be saved because you do not need more hardware servers (less servers than service running).

- Less management: Using a VM Guest simplifies the administration of your infrastructure.

- Agility and productivity: Virtualization provides *migration* capabilities, *live migration* and *snapshots*. These features reduce downtime, and bring an easy way to move your service from one place to another without any service interruption.

1.4 Understanding Virtualization Modes

Guest operating systems are hosted on virtual machines in either full virtualization (FV) mode or paravirtual (PV) mode. Each virtualization mode has advantages and disadvantages.

- Full virtualization mode lets virtual machines run unmodified operating systems, such as Windows* Server 2003, but requires the computer running as the VM Host Server to support *hardware-assisted* virtualization technology, such as AMD* Virtualization or Intel* Virtualization Technology.
  Some guest operating systems hosted in full virtualization mode can be configured to run the Novell* Virtual Machine Drivers instead of drivers originating from the operating system. Running virtual machine drivers improves performance dramatically on guest operating systems, such as Windows Server 2003. For more information, see *Appendix A, Virtual Machine Drivers*.

- Paravirtual mode does not require the host computer to support *hardware-assisted* virtualization technology, but does require the guest operating system to be modified for the virtualization environment. Typically, operating systems running in paravirtual mode enjoy better performance than those requiring full virtualization mode.
  Operating systems currently modified to run in paravirtual mode are called *paravirtualized operating systems* and include SUSE Linux Enterprise Server and NetWare® 6.5 SP8.

1.5 I/O Virtualization

VM Guests not only share CPU and memory resources of the host system, but also the I/O sub-
system. Because software I/O virtualization techniques deliver less performance than bare met-
al, hardware solutions that deliver almost "native" performance have been developed recently.
SUSE Linux Enterprise Server supports the following I/O virtualization techniques:

Full Virtualization

> Fully Virtualized (FV) drivers emulate widely supported real devices, which can be used
> with an existing driver in the VM Guest. Since the physical device on the VM Host Server
> may differ from the emulated one, the hypervisor needs to process all I/O operations before
> handing them over to the physical device. Therefore all I/O operations need to traverse
> two software layers, a process that not only significantly impacts I/O performance, but
> also consumes CPU time.

Paravirtualization

> Paravirtualization (PV) allows direct communication between the hypervisor and the VM
> Guest. With less overhead involved, performance is much better than with full virtualiza-
> tion. However, paravirtualization requires either the guest operating system to be modified
> to support the paravirtualization API or paravirtualized drivers. See *Section 7.1.1, "Availabil-
> ity of Paravirtualized Drivers"* for a list of guest operating systems supporting paravirtualiza-
> tion.

VFIO

> VFIO stands for *Virtual Function I/O* and is a new user-level driver framework for Linux.
> It replaces the traditional KVM PCI Pass-Through device assignment. The VFIO driver ex-
> poses direct device access to userspace in a secure memory (*IOMMU*) protected environ-
> ment. With VFIO, a VM Guest can directly access hardware devices on the VM Host Server
> (pass-through), avoiding performance issues caused by emulation in performance critical
> paths. This method does not allow to share devices—each device can only be assigned to
> a single VM Guest. VFIO needs to be supported by the VM Host Server CPU, chipset and
> the BIOS/EFI.
>
> Compared to the legacy KVM PCI device assignment, VFIO has the following advantages:
>
> - Resource access is compatible with secure boot.
>
> - Device is isolated and its memory access protected.

- Offers a userspace device driver with more flexible device ownership model.

- Is independent of KVM technology, and not bound to x86 architecture only.

SR-IOV

The latest I/O virtualization technique, Single Root I/O Virtualization SR-IOV combines the benefits of the aforementioned techniques—performance and the ability to share a device with several VM Guests. SR-IOV requires special I/O devices, that are capable of replicating resources so they appear as multiple separate devices. Each such "pseudo" device can be directly used by a single guest. However, for network cards for example the number of concurrent queues that can be used is limited, potentially reducing performance for the VM Guest compared to paravirtualized drivers. On the VM Host Server, SR-IOV must be supported by the I/O device, the CPU and chipset, the BIOS/EFI and the hypervisor—for setup instructions see *Section 13.14, "Adding a PCI Device to a VM Guest"*.

KVM PCI Pass-Through (deprecated)

This method of assigning PCI devices to VM Guests is deprecated and has been replaced by VFIO. KVM PCI Pass-Through is still supported by SUSE, but using VFIO instead is strongly recommended. Support for KVM PCI Pass-Through will be removed from future versions of SUSE Linux Enterprise Server.

> **(!) Important: Requirements for VFIO and SR-IOV**
>
> To be able to use the VFIO and SR-IOV features, the VM Host Server needs to fulfill the following requirements:
>
> - IOMMU needs to be enabled in the BIOS/EFI.
>
> - For Intel CPUs, the Kernel parameter `intel_iommu=on` needs to be provided on the Kernel command line. Refer to *Book "Administration Guide", Chapter 11 "The Boot Loader GRUB 2", Section 11.3.3.2 "Kernel Parameters Tab"* for details.
>
> - The VFIO infrastructure needs to be available. This can be achieved by loading the Kernel module `vfio_pci`. Refer to *Book "Administration Guide", Chapter 9 "The* `systemd` *Daemon", Section 9.6.4 "Loading Kernel Modules"* for details.

2 Introduction to Xen Virtualization

This chapter introduces and explains the components and technologies you need to understand to set up and manage a Xen-based virtualization environment.

2.1 Basic Components

The basic components of a Xen-based virtualization environment are the *Xen hypervisor*, the *Dom0*, any number of other *VM Guests*, and the tools, commands, and configuration files that let you manage virtualization. Collectively, the physical computer running all these components is called a *VM Host Server* because together these components form a platform for hosting virtual machines.

The Xen Hypervisor

The Xen hypervisor, sometimes simply called a virtual machine monitor, is an open source software program that coordinates the low-level interaction between virtual machines and physical hardware.

The Dom0

The virtual machine host environment, also called *Dom0* or controlling domain, is composed of several components, such as:

- The SUSE Linux operating system, which gives the administrator a graphical and command line environment to manage the virtual machine host components and its virtual machines.

   Note

  The term "Dom0" refers to a special domain that provides the management environment. This may be run either in graphical or in command line mode.

- The xl toolstack based on the xenlight library (libxl). Use it to manage Xen guest domains.

- QEMU—an open source software that emulates a full computer system, including a processor and various peripherals. It provides the ability to host operating systems in both full virtualization or paravirtualization mode.

Xen-Based Virtual Machines

A Xen-based virtual machine, also called a *VM Guest* or *DomU*, consists of the following components:

- At least one virtual disk that contains a bootable operating system. The virtual disk can be based on a file, partition, volume, or other type of block device.

- A configuration file for each guest domain. It is a text file following the syntax described in the manual page `man 5 xl.conf`.

- Several network devices, connected to the virtual network provided by the controlling domain.

Management Tools, Commands, and Configuration Files

There is a combination of GUI tools, commands, and configuration files to help you manage and customize your virtualization environment.

2.2   Xen Virtualization Architecture

The following graphic depicts a virtual machine host with four virtual machines. The Xen hypervisor is shown as running directly on the physical hardware platform. Note that the controlling domain is also a virtual machine, although it has several additional management tasks compared to all the other virtual machines.

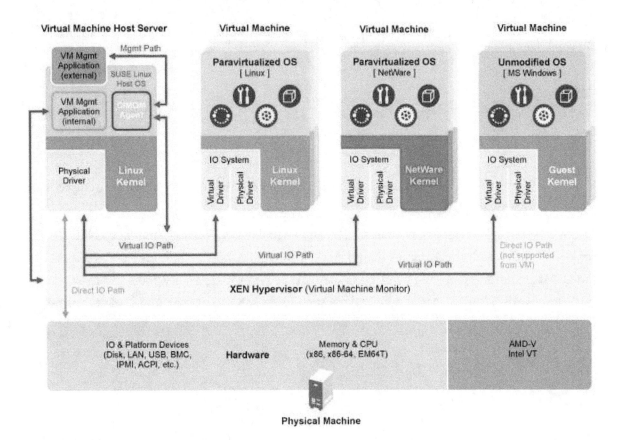

FIGURE 2.1: XEN VIRTUALIZATION ARCHITECTURE

On the left, the virtual machine host's Dom0 is shown running the SUSE Linux operating system. The two virtual machines shown in the middle are running paravirtualized operating systems. The virtual machine on the right shows a fully virtual machine running an unmodified operating system, such as the latest version of Microsoft Windows/Server.

3 Introduction to KVM Virtualization

3.1 Basic Components

KVM is a full virtualization solution for the AMD64/Intel 64 and the z Systems architectures supporting hardware virtualization.

VM Guests (virtual machines), virtual storage, and virtual networks can be managed with QEMU tools directly, or with the `libvirt`-based stack. The QEMU tools include **qemu-system-ARCH**, the QEMU monitor, **qemu-img**, and **qemu-ndb**. A `libvirt`-based stack includes `libvirt` itself, along with `libvirt`-based applications such as **virsh**, **virt-manager**, **virt-install**, and **virt-viewer**.

3.2 KVM Virtualization Architecture

This full virtualization solution consists of two main components: a set of Kernel modules (`kvm.ko`, `kvm-intel.ko`, and `kvm-amd.ko`) providing the core virtualization infrastructure and processor-specific drivers, and a userspace program (`qemu-system-ARCH`) that provides emulation for virtual devices and control mechanisms to manage VM Guests (virtual machines). The term KVM more properly refers to the Kernel level virtualization functionality, but is in practice more commonly used to reference the userspace component.

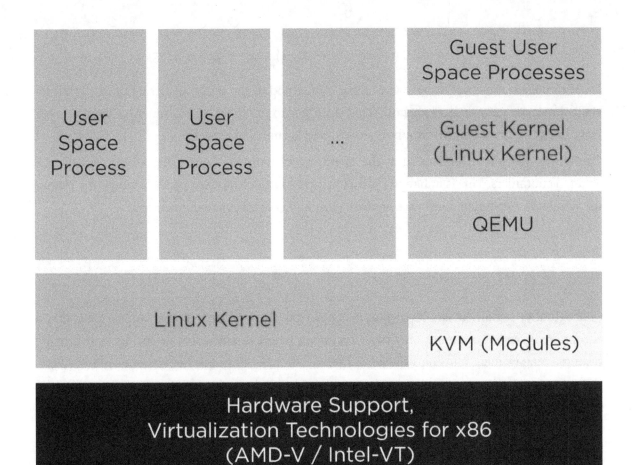

FIGURE 3.1: KVM VIRTUALIZATION ARCHITECTURE

 Note: Hyper-V Emulation Support

QEMU can provide certain Hyper-V hypercalls for Windows* guests to partly emulate a Hyper-V environment. This can be used to achieve better behavior for Windows* guests that are Hyper-V enabled.

4 Introduction to Linux Containers

Linux containers are a lightweight virtualization method to run multiple virtual units ("containers") simultaneously on a single host. This is similar to the *chroot* environment. Containers are isolated with kernel Control Groups (*cgroups*) and kernel Namespaces.

Containers provide virtualization at the operating system level where the *kernel* controls the isolated containers. This is unlike full virtualization solutions like Xen or KVM where the *processor* simulates a complete hardware environment and controls virtual machines.

4.1 Overview

Conceptually, containers can be seen as an improved *chroot* technique. The difference is that a chroot environment separates only the file system, whereas containers go further and provide resource management and control via *cgroups*.

BENEFITS OF CONTAINERS

- Isolating applications and operating systems through containers.

- Providing nearly native performance as container manages allocation of resources in real-time.

- Controlling network interfaces and applying resources inside containers through *cgroups*.

LIMITATIONS OF CONTAINERS

- All containers run inside the host system's kernel and not with a different kernel.

- Only allows Linux "guest" operating systems.

- Security depends on the host system. Container is not secure. If you need a secure system, you can confine it using an AppArmor or SELinux profile.

5 Virtualization Tools

`libvirt` is a library that provides a common API for managing popular virtualization solutions, among them KVM, LXC, and Xen. The library provides a normalized management API for these virtualization solutions, allowing a stable, cross-hypervisor interface for higher-level management tools. The library also provides APIs for management of virtual networks and storage on the VM Host Server. The configuration of each VM Guest is stored in an XML file.

With `libvirt` you can also manage your VM Guests remotely. It supports TLS encryption, x509 certificates and authentication with SASL. This enables managing VM Host Servers centrally from a single workstation, alleviating the need to access each VM Host Server individually.

Using the `libvirt`-based tools is the recommended way of managing VM Guests. Interoperability between `libvirt` and `libvirt`-based applications has been tested and is an essential part of SUSE's support stance.

5.1 Virtualization Console Tools

The following libvirt-based tools for the command line are available on SUSE Linux Enterprise Server. All tools are provided by packages carrying the tool's name.

`virsh`

> A command line tool to manage VM Guests with similar functionality as the Virtual Machine Manager. Allows you to change a VM Guest's status (start, stop, pause, etc.), to set up new guests and devices, or to edit existing configurations. **`virsh`** is also useful to script VM Guest management operations.
>
> **`virsh`** takes the first argument as a command and further arguments as options to this command:
>
> ```
> virsh [-c URI] command domain-id [OPTIONS]
> ```
>
> Like **`zypper`**, **`virsh`** can also be called without a command. In this case it starts a shell waiting for your commands. This mode is useful when having to run subsequent commands:
>
> ```
> ~> virsh -c qemu+ssh://wilber@mercury.example.com/system
> ```

```
Enter passphrase for key '/home/wilber/.ssh/id_rsa':
Welcome to virsh, the virtualization interactive terminal.


Type:  'help' for help with commands
       'quit' to quit


virsh # hostname
mercury.example.com
```

virt-install

A command line tool for creating new VM Guests using the `libvirt` library. It supports graphical installations via VNC or *SPICE* protocols. Given suitable command line arguments, **virt-install** can run completely unattended. This allows for easy automation of guest installs. **virt-install** is the default installation tool used by the Virtual Machine Manager.

vm-install

A tool to set up a VM Guest, configure its devices and start the operating system installation. Starts a GUI wizard when called from a graphical user interface. When invoked on a terminal, starts the wizard in command line mode. **vm-install** can be selected as the installation tool when creating a new virtual machine in the Virtual Machine Manager.

5.2 Virtualization GUI Tools

The following libvirt-based graphical tools are available on SUSE Linux Enterprise Server. All tools are provided by packages carrying the tool's name.

Virtual Machine Manager (virt-manager)

The Virtual Machine Manager is a desktop tool for managing VM Guests. It provides the ability to control the life cycle of existing machines (start/shutdown, pause/resume, save/restore) and create new VM Guests. It allows managing various types of storage and virtual networks. It provides access to the graphical console of VM Guests with a built-in VNC viewer and can be used to view performance statistics. **virt-manager** supports connecting to a local `libvirtd`, managing a local VM Host Server, or a remote `libvirtd` managing a remote VM Host Server.

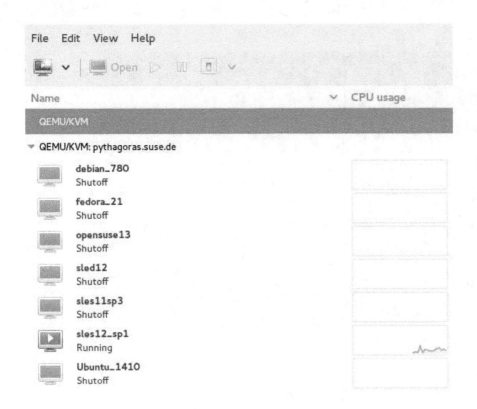

To start the Virtual Machine Manager, enter **virt-manager** at the command prompt.

virt-viewer

A viewer for the graphical console of a VM Guest. It uses SPICE (configured by default on the VM Guest) or VNC protocols and supports TLS and x509 certificates. VM Guests can be accessed by name, ID, or UUID. If the guest is not already running, the viewer can be told to wait until the guest starts, before attempting to connect to the console. **virt-viewer** is not installed by default and is available after installing the package `virt-viewer`.

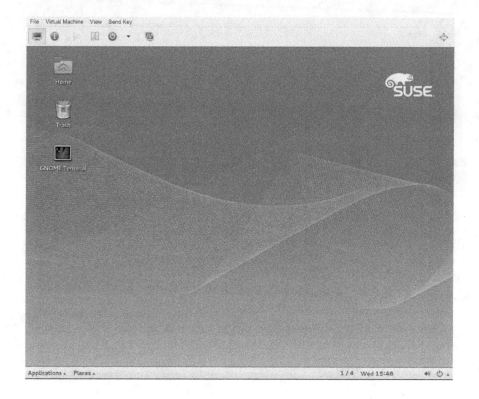

`yast2 vm`

A YaST module that simplifies the installation of virtualization tools and can set up a network bridge:

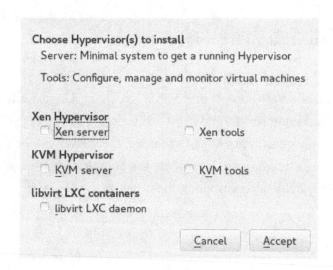

6 Installation of Virtualization Components

None of the virtualization tools is installed by default.

6.1 Installing KVM

To install KVM and KVM tools, proceed as follows:

1. Start YaST and choose *Virtualization* › *Installing Hypervisor and Tools.*

2. Select *KVM server* for a minimal installation of QEMU tools. Select *KVM tools* if a `libvirt`-based management stack is also desired. Confirm with *Accept.*

3. To enable normal networking for the VM Guest, using a network bridge is recommended. YaST offers to automatically configure a bridge on the VM Host Server. Agree to do so by choosing *Yes,* otherwise choose *No.*

4. After the setup has been finished, you can start setting up VM Guests. Rebooting the VM Host Server is not required.

6.2 Installing Xen

To install Xen and Xen tools, proceed as follows:

1. Start YaST and choose *Virtualization* › *Installing Hypervisor and Tools.*

2. Select *Xen server* for a minimal installation of Xen tools. Select *Xen tools* if a `libvirt`-based management stack is also desired. Confirm with *Accept.*

3. To enable normal networking for the VM Guest, using a network bridge is recommended. YaST offers to automatically configure a bridge on the VM Host Server. Agree to do so by choosing *Yes,* otherwise choose *No.*

4. After the setup has been finished, you need to reboot the machine with the *Xen kernel.*

6.3 Installing Containers

To install containers, proceed as follows:

1. Start YaST and choose *Virtualization › Installing Hypervisor and Tools*.

2. Select *libvirt lxc daemon* and confirm with *Accept*.

6.4 Patterns

It is possible using Zypper and patterns to install virtualization packages. Run the command `zypper in -t pattern` *PATTERN*. Available patterns are:

KVM

- `kvm_server`: sets up the KVM VM Host Server with QEMU tools for management

- `kvm_tools`: installs the `libvirt` tools for managing and monitoring VM Guests

Xen

- `xen_server`: sets up the Xen VM Host Server with Xen tools for management

- `xen_tools`: installs the libvirt tools for managing and monitoring VM Guests

Containers

There is no pattern for containers; install the *libvirt-daemon-lxc* package.

7 Supported Guests, Hosts and Features

Supported virtualization limits for Xen and KVM are outlined in the Release Notes [http://www.suse.com/releasenotes/].

7.1 Supported VM Guests

This section lists the support status for various guest operating systems virtualized on top of SUSE Linux Enterprise Server 12 SP1. All guest operating systems are supported both fully-virtualized ("FV" in the following table) and paravirtualized ("PV" in the following table) with two exceptions: Windows, which is only supported fully-virtualized, and OES and NetWare operating systems, which are only supported on Xen paravirtualized. All guest operating systems are supported both in 32-bit and 64-bit flavors, unless stated otherwise (see NetWare).

TABLE 7.1: PARAVIRTUALIZED OS SUPPORT

Operating System	FV Support (Xen/KVM)	PV Support (Xen)
SLES 12 SP1	Full	Full
SLES 12	Full	Full
SLES 11 SP4	Full	Full
SLES 11 SP3	Full	Full
SLES 10 SP4	Full	Full
SLED 12	Technology preview[1]	Technology preview[1]
SLED 12 SP1	Technology preview[1]	Technology preview[1]
OES 11 SP1	None	Full[2,3]
OES 11 SP2	None	Full[2,3]
Netware 6.5 SP8	None	Full (32-bit only)[2]
RHEL 5.11 +	Full/best effort[4]	Full/best effort[4]

Operating System	FV Support (Xen/KVM)	PV Support (Xen)
RHEL 6.7 +	Full/best effort[4]	Full/best effort[4]
RHEL 7.2 +	Full/best effort[4]	Full/best effort[4]
Windows Server 2003 SP2 +	Full	None
Windows Server 2008 SP2 +	Full	None
Windows Server 2008 R2 SP1 +	Full	None
Windows Server 2012 +	Full	None
Windows Server 2012 R2 +	Full	None
Windows 7 SP1 +	Best effort	None
Windows 8 +	Best effort	None
Windows 8.1 +	Best effort	None
Windows 10	Best effort	None

[1] Technology preview: The operating system has been tested to install and run successfully. Bugs can be reported and will be tracked by SUSE Technical Services, but no support commitments or service level agreements apply. Potential fixes and patches will be evaluated for future inclusion.

[2] You need a static IP address for each virtual machine running NetWare or OES.

[3] OES can only be installed from a network installation source.

[4] RedHat* guest operating systems are fully supported with *Expanded Support*. Otherwise, they will be supported on a best-effort basis (fixes if reasonable).

7.1.1 Availability of Paravirtualized Drivers

To improve the performance of the guest operating system, paravirtualized drivers are provided when available. Although they are not required, it is strongly recommended to use them. The paravirtualized drivers are available as follows:

SUSE Linux Enterprise Server 12 / 12 SP1

Included in kernel

SUSE Linux Enterprise Server 11 SP1 / SP2 / SP3

Included in kernel

SUSE Linux Enterprise Server 10 SP4

Included in kernel

RedHat

Available in RedHat Enterprise Linux 5.4 and newer

Windows

SUSE has developed virtio-based drivers for Windows, which are available in the Virtual Machine Driver Pack (VMDP). For more information, see http://www.suse.com/products/vmdriverpack/.

7.2 Supported VM Host Servers for SUSE Linux Enterprise Server 12 SP1 VM Guests

This section lists the support status of SUSE Linux Enterprise Server 12 SP1 running as a guest on top of various virtualization hosts (*Hypervisor*). Both 32-bit and 64-bit versions are supported for the host if available. The support status is defined as follows:

- Full support for all SUSE host systems and SUSE Linux Enterprise Server 12 SP1 VM Guests

- Full support for SUSE Linux Enterprise Server 12 SP1 VM Guests on third-party host systems

The following SUSE host operating systems are supported:

- SUSE Linux Enterprise Server 11 SP4 (KVM/Xen)

- SUSE Linux Enterprise Server 12 SP1 (KVM/Xen)

The following third party host operating systems are supported:

- KVM for IBM z Systems 1.1.0

- Oracle VM 3.2

- VMware ESX 5.1

- VMware ESXi 5.1

- Windows 2008 SP2+

- Windows 2008 R2 SP1+

- Windows 2012+

- Windows 2012 R2+

- Citrix XenServer 6.1

- Oracle VM 3.2

The following host operating systems will be supported when released:

- SUSE Linux Enterprise Server 12 SP2 (KVM/Xen)

- VMware ESX 5.2

- VMware ESXi 5.2

- Citrix XenServer 6.2

- Microsoft Windows Server OS future releases and service packs

- Oracle VM 3.3

7.3 KVM Hardware Requirements

Currently, SUSE only supports KVM full virtualization on AMD64/Intel 64 hosts and on z Systems (only as Technology Preview). On the AMD64/Intel 64 architecture, KVM is designed around hardware virtualization features included in AMD* (AMD-V) and Intel* (VT-x) CPUs. It supports virtualization features of chipsets, and PCI devices, such as an I/O Memory Mapping Unit (*IOMMU*) and Single Root I/O Virtualization (*SR-IOV*).

On the AMD64/Intel 64 architecture, you can test whether your CPU supports hardware virtualization with the following command:

```
egrep '(vmx|svm)' /proc/cpuinfo
```

If this command returns no output, your processor either does not support hardware virtualization, or this feature has been disabled in the BIOS or Firmware.

The following Web sites identify AMD64/Intel 64 processors that support hardware virtualization: http://ark.intel.com/Products/VirtualizationTechnology (for Intel CPUs), and http://products.amd.com/ (for AMD CPUs).

 Note: KVM Kernel Modules Not Loading

The KVM kernel modules only load if the CPU hardware virtualization features are available.

The general minimum hardware requirements for the VM Host Server are the same as outlined in *Book "Deployment Guide", Chapter 2 "Installation on AMD64 and Intel 64", Section 2.2 "System Requirements for Operating Linux"*. However, additional RAM for each virtualized guest is needed. It should at least be the same amount that is needed for a physical installation. It is also strongly recommended to have at least one processor core or hyper-thread for each running guest.

7.4 Feature Support

7.4.1 Host (Dom0)

TABLE 7.2: FEATURE SUPPORT—HOST (Dom0)

Features	Xen
Network and block device hotplugging	Yes
Physical *CPU hotplugging*	No
Virtual *CPU hotplugging*	Yes

Features	Xen
Virtual *CPU pinning*	Yes
Virtual *CPU capping*	Yes
Intel* VT-x2: FlexPriority, FlexMigrate (migration constraints apply to dissimilar CPU architectures)	Yes
Intel* VT-d2 (DMA remapping with interrupt filtering and queued invalidation)	Yes
AMD* IOMMU (I/O page table with guest-to-host physical address translation)	Yes

 Note: Adding or Removing Physical CPUs at Runtime Is Not Supported

The addition or removal of physical CPUs at runtime is not supported. However, virtual CPUs can be added or removed for each VM Guest.

7.4.2 Paravirtualized Guest

TABLE 7.3: FEATURE SUPPORT—PARAVIRTUALIZED GUEST

Features	Xen
Virtual network and virtual block device hotplugging	Yes
Virtual *CPU hotplugging*	Yes
Virtual *CPU over-commitment*	Yes
Dynamic virtual memory resize	Yes
VM save and restore	Yes (excludes SLES 9 SP4 in multiprocessor mode)

Features	Xen
VM live migration	Yes between like virtual host systems with similar resources (excludes SLES 9 SP4 in multiprocessor mode)
Advanced debugging with GDBC	Yes
Dom0 metrics visible to VM	Yes
Memory ballooning	Yes
PCI pass-through	Yes (guests excluded are Netware and SUSE Linux Enterprise Server 9 SP4)

For live migration, both source and target system architectures need to match; that is, the processors (AMD* or Intel*) must be the same. Unless CPU ID masking is used, such as with Intel FlexMigration, the target should feature the same processor revision or a more recent processor revision than the source. If VMs are moved among different systems, the same rules apply for each move. To avoid failing optimized code at runtime or application start-up, source and target CPUs need to expose the same processor extensions. Xen exposes the physical CPU extensions to the VMs transparently. To summarize, guests can be 32- or 64-bit, but the *VHS* must be identical.

 Note: Intel FlexMigration

For machines that support Intel FlexMigration, CPU-ID masking and faulting allow more flexibility in cross-CPU migration.

7.4.3 Fully Virtualized Guest

TABLE 7.4: FEATURE SUPPORT—FULLY VIRTUALIZED GUEST

Features	Xen	KVM
Virtual network and virtual block device hotplugging	Yes	Yes
Virtual *CPU hotplugging*	No	No

Features	Xen	KVM
Virtual *CPU over-commitment*	Yes	Yes
Dynamic virtual memory re-size	Yes	Yes
VM save and restore	Yes	Yes
VM Live Migration	Yes between like virtual host systems with similar re-sources (that is, from 32-bit to 32-bit, 64-bit to 64-bit)	Yes
VM snapshot	Yes	Yes
Advanced debugging with GDBC	Yes	Yes
Dom0 metrics visible to VM	Yes	Yes
PCI pass-through	Yes	Yes

 Note: Windows Guest

Hotplugging of virtual network and virtual block devices, and resizing, shrinking, and restoring dynamic virtual memory are supported in Xen and KVM only if PV drivers are being used (VMDP).

For KVM, a detailed description of supported limits, features, recommended settings and scenarios, and other useful information is maintained in `kvm-supported.txt`. This file is part of the KVM package and can be found in `/usr/share/doc/packages/kvm`.

II Managing Virtual Machines with `libvirt`

8 Starting and Stopping `libvirtd`

The communication between the virtualization solutions (KVM, Xen, LXC) and the libvirt API is managed by the daemon `libvirtd`, which needs to run on the VM Host Server. libvirt client applications such as virt-manager, possibly running on a remote machine, communicate with `libvirtd` running on the VM Host Server, which services the request using native hypervisor APIs. Use the following commands to start and stop `libvirtd` or check its status:

```
root # systemctl start libvirtd

root # systemctl status libvirtd
libvirtd.service - Virtualization daemon
Loaded: loaded (/usr/lib/systemd/system/libvirtd.service; enabled)
Active: active (running) since Mon 2014-05-12 08:49:40 EDT; 2s ago
[...]

root # systemctl stop libvirtd

root # systemctl status libvirtd
[...]
Active: inactive (dead) since Mon 2014-05-12 08:51:11 EDT; 4s ago
[...]
```

To automatically start `libvirtd` at boot time, either activate it using the YaST *Services Manager* module or by entering the following command:

```
root # systemctl enable libvirtd
```

9 Guest Installation

A VM Guest is comprised of an image containing an operating system and data files and a configuration file describing the VM Guest's virtual hardware resources. VM Guests are hosted on and controlled by the VM Host Server. This section provides generalized instructions for installing a VM Guest.

Virtual machines have few if any requirements above those required to run the operating system. If the operating system has not been optimized for the virtual machine host environment, the unmodified OS can run only on *hardware-assisted* virtualization computer hardware, in full virtualization mode, and requires specific device drivers to be loaded. The hardware that is presented to the VM Guest depends on the configuration of the host.

 Note: Virtual Machine Architectures

The virtual machine host runs only on AMD64 and Intel 64. Additionally, KVM for z Systems is included on SUSE Linux Enterprise Server as a technology preview. It does not run on other system architectures such as POWER. A 64-bit virtual machine host can, however, run both 32-bit and 64-bit VM Guests.

You should be aware of any licensing issues related to running a single licensed copy of an operating system on multiple virtual machines. Consult the operating system license agreement for more information.

9.1 GUI-Based Guest Installation

The *New VM* wizard helps you through the steps required to create a virtual machine and install its operating system. There are two ways to start it: Within Virtual Machine Manager either click the *Create New Virtual Machine* icon or choose *File › New Virtual Machine*. Alternatively, start YaST and choose *Virtualization › Create Virtual Machines for Xen and KVM*.

1. Start the *New VM* wizard either from YaST or Virtual Machine Manager.

2. Choose an installation source—either a locally available media or a network installation source. If you want to set up your VM Guest from an existing image, choose *import existing disk image*.

On a VM Host Server running the Xen hypervisor, you can choose whether to install a paravirtualized or a fully virtualized guest. The respective option is available under *Architecture Options*. Depending on this choice, not all installation options may be available.

3. Depending on your choice in the previous step, you need to provide the following data:

Local Installation Media

Specify the path on the VM Host Server to an iso image containing the installation data. If it is available as a volume in a libvirt storage pool, you can also select it via the *Browse* button (see *Chapter 12, Managing Storage* for more information). Alternatively, choose a physical CD-ROM or DVD inserted in the optical drive of the VM Host Server.

Network Installation

Provide the *URL* pointing to the installation source. Valid URL prefixes are, for example, `ftp://`, `http://`, `https://`, and `nfs://`. Under *URL Options* you may provide a path to an auto-installation file (AutoYaST or Kickstart, for example) and Kernel parameters. Having provided a URL, the operating system should be automatically detected correctly. If this is not the case, deselect *Automatically Detect Operating System Based on Install-Media* and manually select the *OS Type* and *Version*.

Network Boot (PXE)

When booting via PXE, you only need to provide the *OS Type* and the *Version*.

Import an Existing Image

To set up the VM Guest from an existing image, you need to specify the path on the VM Host Server to the image. If it is available as a volume in a libvirt storage pool, you can also select it via the *Browse* button (see *Chapter 12, Managing Storage* for more information).

4. Choose the memory size and number of CPUs for the new virtual machine.

5. This step is omitted if having chosen *Import an Existing Image* in the first step.
Set up a virtual hard disk for the VM Guest. Either create a new disk image or choose an existing one from a storage pool (see *Chapter 12, Managing Storage* for more information). If you choose to create a disk, a `qcow2` image will be created under `/var/lib/libvirt/(images.`
Setting up a disk is optional. In case you are running a live system directly from CD or DVD, for example, you can omit this step by deselecting *Enable Storage for this Virtual Machine*.

6. The last screen of the wizard lets you specify the name for the virtual machine. Options to specify the network device and the MAC address can be found under *Advanced Options*. If you need to customize the configuration in detail before the installation, activate the relevant check box. Exit the wizard with *Finish*. Depending on your choice, this will either start the installation or open the VM Guest configuration screen.

Tip: Passing Key Combinations to Virtual Machines

The installation starts in a Virtual Machine Manager console window. Some key combinations, such as `Ctrl`-`Alt`-`F1`, are recognized by the VM Host Server but are not passed to the virtual machine. To bypass the VM Host Server, Virtual Machine Manager provides the "sticky key" functionality. Pressing `Ctrl`, `Alt`, or `Shift` three times makes the key sticky, then you can press the remaining keys to pass the combination to the virtual machine.

For example, to pass `Ctrl`-`Alt`-`F2` to a Linux virtual machine, press `Ctrl` three times, then press `Alt`-`F2`. You can also press `Alt` three times, then press `Ctrl`-`F2`.

The sticky key functionality is available in the Virtual Machine Manager during and after installing a VM Guest.

9.2 Installing from the Command Line with `virt-install`

`virt-install` is a command line tool that helps you create new virtual machines using the `libvirt` library. It is useful if you cannot use the graphical user interface, or need to automatize the process of creating virtual machines.

`virt-install` is a complex script with a lot of command line switches. The following are required. For more information, see the man page of `virt-install` (1).

General Options

- `--name vm_guest_name`: Specify the name of the new virtual machine. The name must be unique across all guests known to the hypervisor on the same connection. It is used to create and name the guest's configuration file and you can access the guest with this name from **virsh**. Alphanumeric and `_-.:+` characters are allowed.

- `--memory required_memory`: Specify the amount of memory to allocate for the new virtual machine in megabytes.

- `--vcpus number_of_cpus`: Specify the number of virtual CPUs. For best performance, the number of virtual processors should be less than or equal to the number of physical processors.

Virtualization Type

- `--paravirt`: Set up a paravirtualized guest. This is the default if the VM Host Server supports paravirtualization and full virtualization.

- `--hvm`: Set up a fully virtualized guest.

- `--virt-type hypervisor`: Specify the hypervisor. Supported values are `kvm`, `xen`, or `lxc`.

Guest Storage

Specify one of `--disk`, `--filesystem` or `--nodisks` the type of the storage for the new virtual machine. For example, `--disk size=10` creates 10 GB disk in the default image location for the hypervisor and uses it for the VM Guest. `--filesystem /export/path/on/vmhost` specifies the directory on the VM Host Server to be exported to the guest. And `--nodisks` sets up a VM Guest without a local storage (good for Live CDs).

Installation Method

Specify the installation method using one of `--location`, `--cdrom`, `--pxe`, `--import`, or `--boot`.

Accessing the Installation

Use the `--graphics value` option to specify how to access the installation. SUSE Linux Enterprise Server supports the values `vnc` or `none`.

If using vnc **virt-install** tries to launch **virt-viewer**. If it is not installed or cannot be run, connect to the VM Guest manually with you preferred viewer. To explicitly prevent **virt-install** from launching the viewer use `--noautoconsole`. To define a password for accessing the VNC session, use the following syntax: `--graphics vnc,password=PASSWORD`.

In case you are using `--graphics none`, you can access the VM Guest through operating system supported services, such as SSH or VNC. Refer to the operating system installation manual on how to set up these services in the installation system.

EXAMPLE 9.1: EXAMPLE OF A virt-install COMMAND LINE

The following command line example creates a new SUSE Linux Enterprise Desktop 12 virtual machine with a virtio accelerated disk and network card. It creates a new 10 GB qcow2 disk image as a storage, the source installation media being the host CD-ROM drive. It will use VNC graphics, and it will auto-launch the graphical client.

KVM

```
virt-install --connect qemu:///system --virt-type kvm  --name sled12 \
--memory 1024 --disk size=10 --cdrom /dev/cdrom --graphics vnc \
--os-variant sled12
```

Xen

```
virt-install --connect xen:// --virt-type xen  --name sled12 \
--memory 1024 --disk size=10 --cdrom /dev/cdrom --graphics vnc \
--os-variant sled12
```

9.3 Advanced Guest Installation Scenarios

This section provides instructions for operations exceeding the scope of a normal installation, such as including modules and extensions packages.

9.3.1 Memory Ballooning with Windows Guests

Memory ballooning is a method to change the amount of memory used by VM Guest at runtime. Both the KVM and Xen hypervisors provide this method, but it needs to be supported by the guest as well.

While openSUSE and SLE-based guests support memory ballooning, Windows guests need the Virtual Machine Driver Pack (VMDP) [http://www.suse.com/products/vmdriverpack/] to provide ballooning. To set the maximum memory greater than the initial memory configured for Windows guests, follow these steps:

1. Install the Windows guest with the maximum memory equal or less than the initial value.

2. Install the Virtual Machine Driver Pack in the Windows guest to provide required drivers.

3. Shut down the Windows guest.

4. Reset the maximum memory of the Windows guest to the required value.

5. Start the Windows guest again.

9.3.2 Including Add-On Products in the Installation

Some operating systems such as SUSE Linux Enterprise Server offer to include add-on products in the installation process. In case the add-on product installation source is provided via network, no special VM Guest configuration is needed. If it is provided via CD/DVD or ISO image, it is necessary to provide the VM Guest installation system with both, the standard installation medium and an image for the add-on product.

In case you are using the GUI-based installation, select *Customize Configuration Before Install* in the last step of the wizard and add the add-on product ISO image via *Add Hardware › Storage*. Specify the path to the image and set the *Device Type* to *CD-ROM*.

If installing from the command line, you need to set up the virtual CD/DVD drives with the --disk parameter rather than with --cdrom. The device that is specified first is used for booting. The following example will install SUSE Linux Enterprise Server 12 plus SDK:

```
virt-install --name sles12+sdk --memory 1024 --disk size=10 \
--disk /virt/iso/SLES12.iso,device=cdrom \
--disk /virt/iso/SLES12_SDK.iso,device=cdrom \
```

```
--graphics vnc --os-variant sles12
```

10 Basic VM Guest Management

Most management tasks, such as starting or stopping a VM Guest, can either be done using the graphical application Virtual Machine Manager or on the command line using `virsh`. Connecting to the graphical console via VNC is only possible from a graphical user interface.

 Note: Managing VM Guests on a Remote VM Host Server

If started on a VM Host Server the `libvirt` tools Virtual Machine Manager `virsh` and `virt-viewer` can be used to manage VM Guests on the host. However, it is also possible to manage VM Guests on a remote VM Host Server. This requires to configure remote access for `libvirt` on the host. See *Chapter 11, Connecting and Authorizing* for instructions.

To connect to such a remote host with Virtual Machine Manager, you need to set up a connection as explained in *Section 11.2.2, "Managing Connections with Virtual Machine Manager"*. If connecting to a remote host using `virsh` or `virt-viewer`, you need to specify a connection URI with the parameter `-c` (for example `virsh -c qemu+tls://saturn.example.com/system` or `virsh -c xen+ssh://`). The form of connection URI depends on the connection type and the hypervisor—see *Section 11.2, "Connecting to a VM Host Server"* for details.

Examples in this chapter are all listed without a connection URI.

10.1 Listing VM Guests

The VM Guest listing shows all VM Guests managed by `libvirt` on a VM Host Server.

10.1.1 Listing VM Guests with Virtual Machine Manager

The main window of the Virtual Machine Manager lists all VM Guests for each VM Host Server it is connected to. Each VM Guest entry contains the machine's name, its status (*Running, Paused,* or *Shutoff*) displayed as icon and literally, and a CPU usage bar.

10.1.2 Listing VM Guests with `virsh`

Use the command **`virsh list`** to get a list of VM Guests:

List all running guests

```
virsh list
```

List all running and inactive guests

```
virsh --all
```

For more information and further options, see **`virsh help list`** or **`man 1 virsh`**.

10.2 Accessing the VM Guest via Console

VM Guests can be accessed via a VNC connection (graphical console) or, if supported by the guest operating system, via a serial console.

10.2.1 Opening a Graphical Console

Opening a graphical console to a VM Guest lets you interact with the machine like a physical host via a VNC connection. If accessing the VNC server requires authentication, you are prompted to enter a user name (if applicable) and a password.

When you click into the VNC console, the cursor is "grabbed" and cannot be used outside the console anymore. To release it, press `Alt`–`Ctrl`.

 Tip: Seamless (Absolute) Cursor Movement

> To prevent the console from grabbing the cursor and to enable seamless cursor movement, add a tablet input device to the VM Guest. See *Section 13.9, "Enabling Seamless and Synchronized Cursor Movement"* for more information.

Certain key combinations such as `Ctrl`–`Alt`–`Del` are interpreted by the host system and are not passed to the VM Guest. To pass such key combinations to a VM Guest, open the *Send Key* menu from the VNC window and choose the desired key combination entry. The *Send Key* menu is only available when using Virtual Machine Manager and **virt-viewer**. With Virtual Machine Manager you can alternatively use the "sticky key" feature as explained in *Tip: Passing Key Combinations to Virtual Machines*.

 Note: Supported VNC Viewer

Principally all VNC viewers can connect to the console of a VM Guest. However, if you are using SASL authentication and/or TLS/SSL connection to access the guest, the options become limited. Common VNC viewers such as `tigervnc` support neither SASL authentication nor TSL/SSL. The only supported alternative to Virtual Machine Manager and **virt-viewer** is **vinagre**.

10.2.1.1 Opening a Graphical Console with Virtual Machine Manager

1. In the Virtual Machine Manager, right-click a VM Guest entry.

2. Choose *Open* from the pop-up menu.

10.2.1.2 Opening a Graphical Console with **virt-viewer**

virt-viewer is a simple VNC viewer with added functionality for displaying VM Guest consoles. It can, for example, be started in "wait" mode, where it waits for a VM Guest to start before it connects. It also supports automatically reconnecting to a VM Guest that is rebooted.

virt-viewer addresses VM Guests by name, by ID or by UUID. Use **virsh** `list --all` to get this data.

To connect to a guest that is running or paused, use either the ID, UUID, or name. VM Guests that are shut off do not have an ID—you can only connect by UUID or name.

Connect to guest with the ID 8

```
virt-viewer 8
```

Connect to the inactive guest named sles12; **the connection window will open once the guest starts**

```
virt-viewer --wait sles12
```

With the `--wait` option, the connection will be upheld even if the VM Guest is not running at the moment. When the guest starts, the viewer will be launched.

For more information, see **virt-viewer** `--help` or **man 1 virt-viewer**.

 Note: Password Input on Remote connections with SSH

When using **virt-viewer** to open a connection to a remote host via SSH, the SSH password needs to be entered twice. The first time for authenticating with `libvirt`, the second time for authenticating with the VNC server. The second password needs to be provided on the command line where virt-viewer was started.

10.2.2   Opening a Serial Console

As an alternative to the graphical console, which requires a graphical environment on the client accessing the VM Guest, virtual machines managed with libvirt can also be accessed from the shell via the serial console and **virsh**. To open a serial console to a VM Guest named "sles12", run the following command:

```
virsh console sles12
```

virsh console takes two optional flags: `--safe` ensures exclusive access to the console, `--force` disconnects any existing sessions before connecting. Both features need to be supported by the guest operating system.

Being able to connect to a VM Guest via serial console requires that the guest operating system supports serial console access and is properly supported. Refer to the guest operating system manual for more information.

Tip: Enabling Serial Console Access for SUSE Linux Guests

Serial console access in SUSE Linux is disabled by default. To enable it, proceed as follows:

SLES 12 / openSUSE

> Launch the YaST Boot Loader module and switch to the *Kernel Parameters* tab. Add `console=ttyS0` to the field *Optional Kernel Command Line Parameter*.

SLES 11

> Launch the YaST Boot Loader module and select the boot entry for which to activate serial console access. Choose *Edit* and add `console=ttyS0` to the field *Optional Kernel Command Line Parameter*. Additionally, edit `/etc/inittab` and uncomment the line with the following content:

```
#S0:12345:respawn:/sbin/agetty -L 9600 ttyS0 vt102
```

10.3 Changing a VM Guest's State: Start, Stop, Pause

Starting, stopping or pausing a VM Guest can be done with either Virtual Machine Manager or `virsh`. You can also configure a VM Guest to be automatically started when booting the VM Host Server.

When shutting down a VM Guest, you may either shut it down gracefully, or force the shutdown. The latter is equivalent to pulling the power plug on a physical host and is only recommended if there are no alternatives. Forcing a shutdown may cause file system corruption and loss of data on the VM Guest.

Tip: Graceful Shutdown

To be able to perform a graceful shutdown, the VM Guest must be configured to support *ACPI*. If you have created the guest with `vm-install` or with Virtual Machine Manager, *ACPI* should be available in the VM Guest.

Depending on the guest operating system, the avilability *ACPI* may not be sufficient to perform a graceful shutdown. It is strongly recommended to test shutting down and re-booting a guest before releasing it to production. openSUSE or SUSE Linux Enterprise Desktop, for example, may require PolKit authorization for shutdown and reboot. Make sure this policy is turned off on all VM Guests.

If *ACPI* was enabled during a Windows XP/Server 2003 guest installation, turning it on in the VM Guest configuration alone is not sufficient. See the following articles for more information:

http://support.microsoft.com/kb/314088/EN-US/

http://support.microsoft.com/?kbid=309283

A graceful shutdown is of course always possible from within the guest operating system, regardless of the VM Guest's configuration.

10.3.1 Changing a VM Guest's State with Virtual Machine Manager

Changing a VM Guest's state can be done either from Virtual Machine Manager's main window, or from a VNC window.

PROCEDURE 10.1: STATE CHANGE FROM THE VIRTUAL MACHINE MANAGER WINDOW

1. Right-click a VM Guest entry.

2. Choose *Run*, *Pause*, or one of the *Shutdown options* from the pop-up menu.

PROCEDURE 10.2: STATE CHANGE FROM THE VNC WINDOW

1. **Open a VNC Window** as described in *Section 10.2.1.1, "Opening a Graphical Console with Virtual Machine Manager".*

2. Choose *Run*, *Pause*, or one of the *Shut Down* options either from the toolbar or from the *Virtual Machine* menu.

10.3.1.1   Autostarting a VM Guest

Automatically starting a guest when the VM Host Server boots is not enabled by default. This feature needs to be turned on for each VM Guest individually. There is no way to activate it globally.

1. Double-click the VM Guest entry in Virtual Machine Manager to open its console.

2. Choose *View › Details* to open the VM Guest configuration window.

3. Choose *Boot Options* and check *Start virtual machine on host boot up*.

4. Save the new configuration with *Apply*.

10.3.2   Changing a VM Guest's State with `virsh`

In the following examples the state of a VM Guest named "sles12" is changed.

Start

```
virsh start sles12
```

Pause

```
virsh suspend sles12
```

Reboot

```
virsh reboot sles12
```

Graceful shutdown

```
virsh shutdown sles12
```

Force shutdown

```
virsh destroy sles12
```

Turn on autostart

```
virsh autostart sles12
```

Turn off autostart

```
virsh autostart --disable sles12
```

10.4 Saving and Restoring the State of a VM Guest

Saving a VM Guest preserves the exact state of the guest's memory. The operation is slightly similar to *hibernating* a computer. A saved VM Guest can be quickly restored to its previously saved running condition.

When saved, the VM Guest is paused, its current memory state is saved to disk, and then the guest is stopped. The operation does not make a copy of any portion of the VM Guest's virtual disk. The amount of time taken to save the virtual machine depends on the amount of memory allocated. When saved, a VM Guest's memory is returned to the pool of memory available on the VM Host Server.

The restore operation loads a VM Guest's previously saved memory state file and starts it. The guest is not booted but rather resumes at the point where it was previously saved. The operation is slightly similar to coming out of hibernation.

The VM Guest is saved to a state file. Make sure there is enough space on the partition you are going to save to. Issue the following command on the guest to get a rough estimation of the file size in megabytes to be expected:

```
free -mh | awk '/^Mem:/ {print $3}'
```

 Warning: Saved Guests Need to Be Restored, Not Started

After using the save operation, do not boot or start the saved VM Guest. Doing so would cause the machine's virtual disk and the saved memory state to get out of synchronization. This can result in critical errors when restoring the guest.

To be able to work with a saved VM Guest again, always use the restore operation.

10.4.1 Saving/Restoring with Virtual Machine Manager

PROCEDURE 10.3: SAVING A VM GUEST

1. Open a VNC connection window to a VM Guest. Make sure the guest is running.

2. Choose *Virtual Machine › Shutdown › Save*

3. Choose a location and a file name.

4. Click *Save*. Saving the guest's state may take some time. After the operation has finished, the VM Guest will automatically shut down.

PROCEDURE 10.4: RESTORING A VM GUEST

1. Start the Virtual Machine Manager.

2. Type [Alt]–[R] or choose *File › Restore Saved Machine*.

3. Choose the file you want to restore and proceed with *Open*. Once the file has been successfully loaded, the VM Guest is up and running.

10.4.2 Saving and Restoring with `virsh`

Save a running VM Guest with the command **virsh** save and specify the file which it is saved to.

Save the guest named opensuse13

```
virsh save opensuse13 /virtual/saves/opensuse13.vmsav
```

Save the guest with the ID 37

```
virsh save 37 /virtual/saves/opensuse13.vmsave
```

To restore a VM Guest, use **virsh** restore:

```
virsh restore /virtual/saves/opensuse13.vmsave
```

10.5   Creating and Managing Snapshots

VM Guest snapshots are snapshots of the complete virtual machine including the state of CPU, RAM, and the content of all writable disks. To use virtual machine snapshots, you must have at least one non-removable and writable block device using the qcow2 disk image format.

 Note

> Snapshots are supported on KVM VM Host Servers only.

Snapshots let you restore the state of the machine at a particular point in time. This is for example useful to undo a faulty configuration or the installation of a lot of packages. It is also helpful for testing purposes, as it allows you to go back to a defined state at any time.

Snapshots can be taken either from running guests or from a guest currently not running. Taking a screenshot from a guest that is shut down ensures data integrity. In case you want to create a snapshot from a running system, be aware that the snapshot only captures the state of the disk(s), not the state of the memory. Therefore you need to ensure that:

- All running programs have written their data to the disk. If you are unsure, terminate the application and/or stop the respective service.

- Buffers have been written to disk. This can be achieved by running the command **sync** on the VM Guest.

Starting a snapshot reverts the machine back to the state it was in when the snapshot was taken. Any changes written to the disk after that point in time will be lost when starting the snapshot.

Starting a snapshot will restore the machine to the state (shut off or running) it was in when the snapshot was taken. After starting a snapshot that was created while the VM Guest was shut off, you will need to boot it.

10.5.1   Creating and Managing Snapshots with Virtual Machine Manager

To open the snapshot management view in Virtual Machine Manager, open the VNC window as described in *Section 10.2.1.1, "Opening a Graphical Console with Virtual Machine Manager"*. Now either choose *View › Snapshots* or click the snapshot icon in the toolbar.

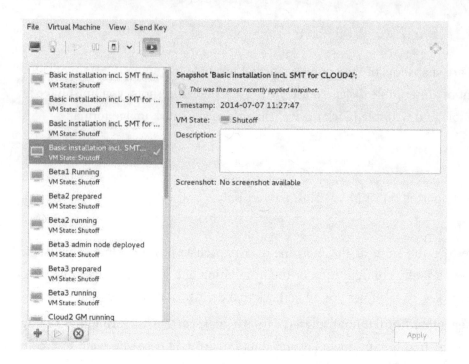

The list of existing snapshots for the chosen VM Guest is displayed in the left-hand part of the window. The snapshot that was last started is marked with a green tick. The right-hand part of the window shows details of the snapshot currently marked in the list. These details include the snapshot's title and time stamp, the state of the VM Guest at the time the snapshot was taken and a description. Snapshots of running guests also include a screenshot. The *Description* can be changed or added directly in this view; the other snapshot data cannot be changed.

10.5.1.1   Creating a Snapshot

To take a new snapshot of a VM Guest, proceed as follows:

1. Shut down the VM Guest in case you want to create a snapshot from a guest that is not running.

2. Click the plus symbol in the bottom left corner of the VNC window to open the *Create Snapshot* window.

3. Provide a *Name* and, optionally, a description. The name cannot be changed after the snapshot has been taken. To be able to identify the snapshot later easily, use a "speaking name".

4. When all data is entered, choose *Finish*.

10.5.1.2 Deleting a Snapshot

To delete a snapshot of a VM Guest, proceed as follows:

1. Click the symbol with the red circle in the bottom left corner of the VNC window.

2. Confirm the deletion with *Yes*.

10.5.1.3 Starting a Snapshot

To start a snapshot, proceed as follows:

1. Click the "play" symbol in the bottom left corner of the VNC window.

2. Confirm the start with *Yes*.

10.5.2 Creating and Managing Snapshots with `virsh`

To list all existing snapshots for a domain (`admin_server` in the following), run the `snapshot-list` command:

```
tux > virsh snapshot-list

 Name                    Creation Time            State
------------------------------------------------------------

 Basic installation incl. SMT finished 2013-09-18 09:45:29 +0200 shutoff

 Basic installation incl. SMT for CLOUD3 2013-12-11 15:11:05 +0100 shutoff

 Basic installation incl. SMT for CLOUD3-HA 2014-03-24 13:44:03 +0100 shutoff

 Basic installation incl. SMT for CLOUD4 2014-07-07 11:27:47 +0200 shutoff

 Beta1 Running          2013-07-12 12:27:28 +0200 shutoff

 Beta2 prepared         2013-07-12 17:00:44 +0200 shutoff

 Beta2 running          2013-07-29 12:14:11 +0200 shutoff

 Beta3 admin node deployed 2013-07-30 16:50:40 +0200 shutoff

 Beta3 prepared         2013-07-30 17:07:35 +0200 shutoff

 Beta3 running          2013-09-02 16:13:25 +0200 shutoff

 Cloud2 GM running      2013-12-10 15:44:58 +0100 shutoff

 CLOUD3 RC prepared     2013-12-20 15:30:19 +0100 shutoff

 CLOUD3-HA Build 680 prepared 2014-03-24 14:20:37 +0100 shutoff
```

```
CLOUD3-HA Build 796 installed (zypper up) 2014-04-14 16:45:18 +0200 shutoff
GMC2 post Cloud install 2013-09-18 10:53:03 +0200 shutoff
GMC2 pre Cloud install 2013-09-18 10:31:17 +0200 shutoff
GMC2 prepared (incl. Add-On Installation) 2013-09-17 16:22:37 +0200 shutoff
GMC_pre prepared      2013-09-03 13:30:38 +0200 shutoff
OS + SMT + eth[01]    2013-06-14 16:17:24 +0200 shutoff
OS + SMT + Mirror + eth[01] 2013-07-30 15:50:16 +0200 shutoff
```

The snapshot that was last started is shown with the snapshot-current command:

```
tux > virsh snapshot-current --name admin_server
Basic installation incl. SMT for CLOUD4
```

Details about a particular snapshot can be obtained by running the snapshot-info command:

```
tux > virsh snapshot-info sles "Basic installation incl. SMT for CLOUD4"
Name:          Basic installation incl. SMT for CLOUD4
Domain:        admin_server
Current:       yes
State:         shutoff
Location:      internal
Parent:        Basic installation incl. SMT for CLOUD3-HA
Children:      0
Descendants:   0
Metadata:      yes
```

10.5.2.1 Creating a Snapshot

To take a new snapshot of a VM Guest currently not running, use the snapshot-create-as command as follows:

```
virsh snapshot-create-as --domain admin_server❶ --name "Snapshot 1"❷ \
--description "First snapshot"❸
```

❶ Domain name. Mandatory.

❷ Name of the snapshot. It is recommended to use a "speaking name", since that makes it easier to identify the snapshot. Mandatory.

③ Description for the snapshot. Optional.

To take a snapshot of a running VM Guest, you need to specify the `--live` parameter:

```
virsh snapshot-create-as --domain admin_server --name "Snapshot 2" \
  --description "First live snapshot" --live
```

Refer to the *SNAPSHOT COMMANDS* section in **man 1 virsh** for more details.

10.5.2.2 Deleting a Snapshot

To delete a snapshot of a VM Guest, use the `snapshot-delete` command:

```
virsh snapshot-delete --domain admin_server --snapshotname "Snapshot 2"
```

10.5.2.3 Starting a Snapshot

To start a snapshot, use the `snapshot-revert` command:

```
virsh snapshot-revert --domain admin_server --snapshotname "Snapshot 1"
```

To start the current snapshot (the one the VM Guest was started off), it is sufficient to use `--current` rather than specifying the snapshot name:

```
virsh snapshot-revert --domain admin_server --current
```

10.6 Deleting a VM Guest

Deleting a VM Guest removes its XML configuration by default. Since the attached storage is not deleted by default, you can use it with another VM Guest. With Virtual Machine Manager, you may also delete a guest's storage files as well—this will completely erase the guest.

To delete a VM Guest, it needs to be shut down first (refer to *Section 10.3, "Changing a VM Guest's State: Start, Stop, Pause"* for instructions). It is not possible to delete a running guest.

10.6.1 Deleting a VM Guest with Virtual Machine Manager

1. In the Virtual Machine Manager, right-click a VM Guest entry.

2. Choose *Delete* from the pop-up menu.

3. A confirmation window opens. Clicking *Delete* will permanently erase the VM Guest. The deletion is not recoverable.

   You may also choose to permanently delete the guest's virtual disk by activating *Delete Associated Storage Files*. The deletion is not recoverable either.

10.6.2   Deleting a VM Guest with `virsh`

To delete a VM Guest with `virsh`, run `virsh` `undefine` *VM_NAME*.

```
virsh undefine sles12
```

There is no option to automatically delete the attached storage files. If they are managed by libvirt, delete them as described in *Section 12.2.4, "Deleting Volumes from a Storage Pool"*.

10.7   Migrating VM Guests

One of the major advantages of virtualization is that VM Guests are portable. When a VM Host Server needs to go down for maintenance, or when the host gets overloaded, the guests can easily be moved to another VM Host Server. KVM and Xen even support "live" migrations during which the VM Guest is constantly available.

10.7.1   Migration Requirements

To successfully migrate a VM Guest to another VM Host Server, the following requirements need to be met:

- It is recommended that the source and destination systems have the same architecture, however it is possible to migrate between hosts with AMD* and Intel* architectures.

- Storage devices must be accessible from both machines (for example, via NFS or iSCSI) and must be configured as a storage pool on both machines (see *Chapter 12, Managing Storage* for more information). This is also true for CD-ROM or floppy images that are connected during the move (however, you may disconnect them prior to the move as described in *Section 13.12, "Ejecting and Changing Floppy or CD/DVD-ROM Media with Virtual Machine Manager"*).

- `libvirtd` needs to run on both VM Host Servers and you must be able to open a remote `libvirt` connection between the target and the source host (or vice versa). Refer to *Section 11.3, "Configuring Remote Connections"* for details.

- If a firewall is running on the target host, ports need to be opened to allow the migration. If you do not specify a port during the migration process, `libvirt` chooses one from the range 49152:49215. Make sure that either this range (recommended) or a dedicated port of your choice is opened in the firewall on the *target host*.

- Host and target machine should be in the same subnet on the network, otherwise networking will not work after the migration.

- No running or paused VM Guest with the same name must exist on the target host. If a shut down machine with the same name exists, its configuration will be overwritten.

- All CPU models except *host cpu* model are supported when migrating VM Guests.

- *SATA* disk device type is not migratable.

- File system pass-through feature is incompatible with migration.

- The VM Host Server and VM Guest need to have proper timekeeping installed. See *Chapter 15, VM Guest Clock Settings*.

- *Section 28.3.1.2, "virtio-blk-data-plane"* is not supported for migration.

- No physical devices can be passed from host to guest. Live migration is currently not supported when using devices with PCI pass-through or *SR-IOV*. In case live migration needs to be supported, you need to use software virtualization (paravirtualization or full virtualization).

- Cache mode setting is an important setting for migration. See: *Section 14.5, "Effect of Cache Modes on Live Migration"*.

- Live migration of VM Guests from a host running one operating system to a host running a different operating system is fully supported for the following scenarios:

  - SLES 12 to SLES 12 SP1

  - SLES 12 SP1 to SLES 12 SP2 (when released)

- SLES 11 SP3 to SLES 12 SP1

- SLES 11 SP4 to SLES 12 SP1

   Backward migration (from SLES 12 to 11 or from SP2 to SP1) is not supported.

- The image directory should be located in the same path on both hosts.

10.7.2   Migrating with `virt-manager`

When using the Virtual Machine Manager to migrate VM Guests, it does not matter on which machine it is started. You can start Virtual Machine Manager on the source or the target host or even on a third host. In the latter case you need to be able to open remote connections to both the target and the source host.

1. Start Virtual Machine Manager and establish a connection to the target or the source host. If the Virtual Machine Manager was started neither on the target nor the source host, connections to both hosts need to be opened.

2. Right-click the VM Guest that is to be migrated and choose *Migrate*. Make sure the guest is running or paused—it is not possible to migrate guests that are shut down.

3. Choose a *New Host* for the VM Guest. If the desired target host does not show up, make sure a connection to this host has been established.
   By default, a "live" migration is performed. If you prefer an "offline" migration where the VM Guest is paused during the migration, tick *Migrate offline*.

4. Click *Migrate* to start a migration with the default port and bandwidth. To change these defaults, make the advanced options available by clicking the triangle at *Advanced Options*. Here you can enter the target host's *Address* (IP address or host name), a *Port* and the *Bandwidth* in megabits per second (Mbps). If you specify a *Port*, you must also specify an *Address*; the *Bandwidth* is optional.

5. When the migration is complete, the *Migrate* window closes and the VM Guest is now listed on the new host in the Virtual Machine Manager window. The original VM Guest will still be available on the target host (in shut down state).

10.7.3 Migrating with `virsh`

To migrate a VM Guest with `virsh migrate`, you need to have direct or remote shell access to the VM Host Server, because the command needs to be run on the host. The migration command looks like this:

```
virsh migrate [OPTIONS] VM_ID_or_NAMECONNECTION URI [--migrateuri
 tcp://REMOTE_HOST:PORT]
```

The most important options are listed below. See `virsh help migrate` for a full list.

`--live`

> Does a live migration. If not specified, an offline migration—where the VM Guest is paused during the migration—will be performed.

`--suspend`

> Does an offline migration and does not restart the VM Guest on the target host.

`--persistent`

> By default a migrated VM Guest will be migrated transient, so its configuration is automatically deleted on the target host if it is shut down. Use this switch to make the migration persistent.

`--undefinesource`

> When specified, the VM Guest definition on the source host will be deleted after a successful migration (however, virtual disks attached to this guest will *not* be deleted).

The following examples use mercury.example.com as the source system and jupiter.example.com as the target system; the VM Guest's name is opensuse131 with Id 37.

Offline migration with default parameters

```
virsh migrate 37 qemu+ssh://tux@jupiter.example.com/system
```

Transient live migration with default parameters

```
virsh migrate --live opensuse131 qemu+ssh://tux@jupiter.example.com/system
```

Persistent live migration; delete VM definition on source

```
virsh migrate --live --persistent --undefinesource 37 \
```

```
qemu+tls://tux@jupiter.example.com/system
```

Offline migration using port 49152

```
virsh migrate opensuse131 qemu+ssh://tux@jupiter.example.com/system \
--migrateuri tcp://@jupiter.example.com:49152
```

 Note: Transient vs. Persistent Migrations

By default `virsh migrate` creates a temporary (transient) copy of the VM Guest on the target host. A shut down version of the original guest description remains on the source host. A transient copy will be deleted from the server after it is shut down.

To create a permanent copy of a guest on the target host, use the switch `--persistent`. A shut down version of the original guest description remains on the source host, too. Use the option `--undefinesource` together with `--persistent` for a "real" move where a permanent copy is created on the target host and the version on the source host is deleted.

It is not recommended to use `--undefinesource` without the `--persistent` option, since this will result in the loss of both VM Guest definitions when the guest is shut down on the target host.

10.7.4 Step-by-Step Example

10.7.4.1 Exporting the Storage

First you need to export the storage, to share the Guest image between host. This can be done by an NFS server. In the following example we want to share the `/volume1/VM` directory for all machines that are on the network 10.0.1.0/24. We will use a SUSE Linux Enterprise NFS server. As root user, edit the `/etc/exports` file and add:

```
/volume1/VM 10.0.1.0/24  (rw,sync,no_root_squash)
```

You need to restart the NFS server:

```
root # systemctl restart nfsserver
root # exportfs
```

```
/volume1/VM        10.0.1.0/24
```

10.7.4.2   Defining the Pool on the Target Hosts

On each host where you want to migrate the VM Guest, the pool must be defined to be able to access the volume (that contains the Guest image). Our NFS server IP address is 10.0.1.99, its share is the /volume1/VM directory, and we want to get it mounted in the /var/lib/libvirt/images/VM directory. The pool name will be *VM*. To define this pool, create a VM.xml file with the following content:

```
<pool type='netfs'>
  <name>VM</name>
  <source>
    <host name='10.0.1.99'/>
    <dir path='/volume1/VM'/>
    <format type='auto'/>
  </source>
  <target>
    <path>/var/lib/libvirt/images/VM</path>
    <permissions>
      <mode>0755</mode>
      <owner>-1</owner>
      <group>-1</group>
    </permissions>
  </target>
</pool>
```

Then load it into libvirt using the **pool-define** command:

```
root # virsh pool-define VM.xml
```

An alternative way to define this pool is to use the **virsh** command:

```
root # virsh pool-define-as VM --type netfs --source-host 10.0.1.99 \
    --source-path /volume1/VM --target /var/lib/libvirt/images/VM
Pool VM created
```

Then the pool can be set to start automatically at host boot (autostart option):

```
virsh # pool-autostart VM
Pool VM marked as autostarted
```

If you want to disable the autostart:

```
virsh # pool-autostart VM --disable
Pool VM unmarked as autostarted
```

Check if the pool is present:

```
virsh # pool-list --all
 Name                State      Autostart
-------------------------------------------
 default             active     yes
 VM                  active     yes


virsh # pool-info VM
Name:           VM
UUID:           42efe1b3-7eaa-4e24-a06a-ba7c9ee29741
State:          running
Persistent:     yes
Autostart:      yes
Capacity:       2,68 TiB
Allocation:     2,38 TiB
Available:      306,05 GiB
```

 Warning: Pool Needs to Exist on All Target Hosts

Remember: this pool must be defined on each host where you want to be able to migrate your VM Guest.

10.7.4.3 Creating the Volume

The pool has been defined—now we need a volume which will contain the disk image:

```
virsh # vol-create-as VM sled12.qcow12 8G --format qcow2
Vol sled12.qcow12 created
```

The volume names shown will be used later to install the guest with virt-install.

10.7.4.4 Creating the VM Guest

Let's create a SUSE Linux Enterprise Desktop VM Guest with the **virt-install** command. The *VM* pool will be specified with the **--disk** option, *cache=none* is recommended if you do not want to use the **--unsafe** option while doing the migration.

```
root # virt-install --connect qemu:///system --virt-type kvm --name \
    sled12 --memory 1024 --disk vol=VM/sled12.qcow2,cache=none --cdrom \
    /mnt/install/ISO/SLE-12-Desktop-DVD-x86_64-Build0327-Media1.iso --graphics \
    vnc --os-variant sled12
Starting install...
Creating domain...
```

10.7.4.5 Migrate the VM Guest

Everything is ready to do the migration now. Run the **migrate** command on the VM Host Server that is currently hosting the VM Guest, and choose the destination.

```
virsh # migrate --live sled12 --verbose qemu+ssh://IP/Hostname/system
Password:
Migration: [ 12 %]
```

10.8 Monitoring

10.8.1   Monitoring with Virtual Machine Manager

After starting Virtual Machine Manager and connecting to the VM Host Server, a CPU usage graph of all the running guests is displayed.

It is also possible to get information about disk and network usage with this tool, however, you must first activate this in *Preferences*:

1. Run `virt-manager`.

2. Select *Edit › Preferences*.

3. Change the tab from *General* to *Polling*.

4. Activate the check boxes for *Disk I/O* and *Network I/O*.

5. If desired, also change the update interval or the number of samples that are kept in the history.

6. Close the *Preferences* dialog.

7. Activate the graphs that should be displayed under *View › Graph*.

Afterwards, the disk and network statistics are also displayed in the main window of the Virtual Machine Manager.

More precise data is available from the VNC window. Open a VNC window as described in *Section 10.2.1, "Opening a Graphical Console"*. Choose *Details* from the toolbar or the *View* menu. The statistics are displayed from the *Performance* entry of the left-hand tree menu.

10.8.2   Monitoring with `virt-top`

`virt-top` is a command line tool similar to the well-known process monitoring tool `top`. `virt-top` uses libvirt and therefore is capable of showing statistics for VM Guests running on different hypervisors. It is recommended to use `virt-top` instead of hypervisor-specific tools like `xentop`.

By default `virt-top` shows statistics for all running VM Guests. Among the data that is displayed is the percentage of memory used (`%MEM`) and CPU (`%CPU`) and the uptime of the guest (`TIME`). The data is updated regularly (every three seconds by default). The following shows the output on a VM Host Server with seven VM Guests, four of them inactive:

```
virt-top 13:40:19 - x86_64 8/8CPU 1283MHz 16067MB 7.6% 0.5%
```

```
7 domains, 3 active, 3 running, 0 sleeping, 0 paused, 4 inactive D:0 0:0 X:0
CPU: 6.1%  Mem: 3072 MB (3072 MB by guests)


  ID S RDRQ WRRQ RXBY TXBY %CPU %MEM    TIME   NAME
   7 R  123    1  18K  196  5.8  6.0  0:24.35 sled12_sp1
   6 R    1    0  18K    0  0.2  6.0  0:42.51 sles12_sp1
   5 R    0    0  18K    0  0.1  6.0 85:45.67 opensuse_leap
   -                                          (Ubuntu_1410)
   -                                          (debian_780)
   -                                          (fedora_21)
   -                                          (sles11sp3)
```

By default the output is sorted by ID. Use the following key combinations to change the sort field:

[Shift]–[P] : CPU usage

[Shift]–[M] : Total memory allocated by the guest

[Shift]–[T] : Time

[Shift]–[I] : ID

To use any other field for sorting, press [Shift]–[F] and select a field from the list. To toggle the sort order, use [Shift]–[R].

virt-top also supports different views on the VM Guests data, which can be changed on-the-fly by pressing the following keys:

[0] : default view

[1] : show physical CPUs

[2] : show network interfaces

[3] : show virtual disks

virt-top supports more hot keys to change the view on the data and also many command line switches that affect the behavior of the program. Refer to **man 1 virt-top** for details.

10.8.3 Monitoring with `kvm_stat`

`kvm_stat` can be used to trace KVM performance events. It monitors `/sys/kernel/de-bug/kvm`, so it needs the debugfs to be mounted. On SUSE Linux Enterprise Server it should be mounted by default. In case it is not mounted, use the following command:

```
mount -t debugfs none /sys/kernel/debug
```

`kvm_stat` can be used in three different modes:

```
kvm_stat                      # update in 1 second intervals
kvm_stat -1                   # 1 second snapshot
kvm_stat -l > kvmstats.log    # update in 1 second intervals in log format
                              # can be imported to a spreadsheet
```

EXAMPLE 10.1: TYPICAL OUTPUT OF kvm_stat

```
kvm statistics

  efer_reload               0         0
  exits              11378946    218130
  fpu_reload            62144       152
  halt_exits           414866       100
  halt_wakeup          260358        50
  host_state_reload    539650       249
  hypercalls                0         0
  insn_emulation      6227331    173067
  insn_emulation_fail       0         0
  invlpg               227281        47
  io_exits             113148        18
  irq_exits            168474       127
  irq_injections       482804       123
  irq_window            51270        18
  largepages                0         0
  mmio_exits             6925         0
  mmu_cache_miss        71820        19
  mmu_flooded           35420         9
  mmu_pde_zapped        64763        20
```

```
mmu_pte_updated         0       0
mmu_pte_write      213782      29
mmu_recycled            0       0
mmu_shadow_zapped  128690      17
mmu_unsync             46      -1
nmi_injections          0       0
nmi_window              0       0
pf_fixed          1553821     857
pf_guest          1018832     562
remote_tlb_flush   174007      37
request_irq             0       0
signal_exits            0       0
tlb_flush          394182     148
```

See http://clalance.blogspot.com/2009/01/kvm-performance-tools.html **for further information on how to interpret these values.**

11 Connecting and Authorizing

Managing several VM Host Servers, each hosting multiple VM Guests, quickly becomes difficult. One benefit of `libvirt` is the ability to connect to several VM Host Servers at once, providing a single interface to manage all VM Guests and to connect to their graphical console.

To ensure only authorized users can connect, `libvirt` offers several connection types (via TLS, SSH, Unix sockets, and TCP) that can be combined with different authorization mechanisms (socket, PolKit, SASL and Kerberos).

11.1 Authentication

The power to manage VM Guests and to access their graphical console is something that should be restricted to a well defined circle of persons. To achieve this goal, you can use the following authentication techniques on the VM Host Server:

- Access control for Unix sockets with permissions and group ownership. This method is available for `libvirtd` connections only.

- Access control for Unix sockets with PolKit. This method is available for local `libvirtd` connections only.

- User name and password authentication with SASL (Simple Authentication and Security Layer). This method is available for both, `libvirtd` and VNC connections. Using SASL does not require real user accounts on the server, since it uses its own database to store user names and passwords. Connections authenticated with SASL are encrypted.

- Kerberos authentication. This method, available for `libvirtd` connections only, is not covered in this manual. Refer to http://libvirt.org/auth.html#ACL_server_kerberos for details.

- Single password authentication. This method is available for VNC connections only.

> **!** **Important: Authentication for `libvirtd` and VNC need to be configured separately**
>
> Access to the VM Guest's management functions (via `libvirtd`) on the one hand, and to its graphical console on the other hand, always needs to be configured separately. When restricting access to the management tools, these restrictions do *not* automatically apply to VNC connections!

When accessing VM Guests from remote via TLS/SSL connections, access can be indirectly controlled on each client by restricting read permissions to the certificate's key file to a certain group. See *Section 11.3.2.5, "Restricting Access (Security Considerations)"* for details.

11.1.1 `libvirtd` Authentication

`libvirtd` authentication is configured in `/etc/libvirt/libvirtd.conf`. The configuration made here applies to all `libvirt` tools such as the Virtual Machine Manager or **`virsh`**.

`libvirt` offers two sockets: a read-only socket for monitoring purposes and a read-write socket to be used for management operations. Access to both sockets can be configured independently. By default, both sockets are owned by `root.root`. Default access permissions on the read-write socket are restricted to the user `root` (`0700`) and fully open on the read-only socket (`0777`).

In the following instructions, you will learn how to configure access permissions for the read-write socket. The same instructions also apply to the read-only socket. All configuration steps need to be carried out on the VM Host Server.

 Note: Default Authentication Settings on SUSE Linux Enterprise Server

The default authentication method on SUSE Linux Enterprise Server is access control for Unix sockets. Only the user `root` may authenticate. When accessing the `libvirt` tools as a non-root user directly on the VM Host Server, you need to provide the `root` password through PolKit once and you are then granted access for the current and for future sessions.

Alternatively, you can configure `libvirt` to allow "system" access to non-privileged users. See *Section 11.2.1, ""system" Access for Non-Privileged Users"* for details.

RECOMMENDED AUTHORIZATION METHODS

Local Connections

Section 11.1.1.2, "Local Access Control for Unix Sockets with PolKit"
Section 11.1.1.1, "Access Control for Unix Sockets with Permissions and Group Ownership"

Remote Tunnel over SSH

Section 11.1.1.1, "Access Control for Unix Sockets with Permissions and Group Ownership"

Section 11.1.1.3, "User name and Password Authentication with SASL"

none (access controlled on the client side by restricting access to the certificates)

11.1.1.1 Access Control for Unix Sockets with Permissions and Group Ownership

To grant access for non-root accounts, configure the sockets to be owned and accessible by a certain group (libvirt in the following example). This authentication method can be used for local and remote SSH connections.

1. In case it does not exist, create the group that should own the socket:

```
groupadd libvirt
```

 Important: Group Needs to Exist

The group must exist prior to restarting libvirtd. If not, the restart will fail.

2. Add the desired users to the group:

```
usermod -A libvirt tux
```

3. Change the configuration in /etc/libvirt/libvirtd.conf as follows:

```
unix_sock_group = "libvirt"❶
unix_sock_rw_perms = "0770"❷
auth_unix_rw = "none"❸
```

❶ Group ownership will be set to group libvirt.

❷ Sets the access permissions for the socket (srwxrwx---).

❸ Disables other authentication methods (PolKit or SASL). Access is solely controlled by the socket permissions.

4. Restart libvirtd:

```
systemctl start libvirtd
```

11.1.1.2   Local Access Control for Unix Sockets with PolKit

Access control for Unix sockets with PolKit is the default authentication method on SUSE Linux Enterprise Server for non-remote connections. Therefore, no `libvirt` configuration changes are needed. With PolKit authorization enabled, permissions on both sockets default to `0777` and each application trying to access a socket needs to authenticate via PolKit.

 Important: PolKit Authentication for Local Connections Only

Authentication with PolKit can only be used for local connections on the VM Host Server itself, since PolKit does not handle remote authentication.

Two policies for accessing `libvirt`'s sockets exist:

- *org.libvirt.unix.monitor*: accessing the read-only socket

- *org.libvirt.unix.manage*: accessing the read-write socket

By default, the policy for accessing the read-write socket is to authenticate with the `root` password once and grant the privilege for the current and for future sessions.

To grant users access to a socket without having to provide the `root` password, you need to create a rule in `/etc/polkit-1/rules.d`. Create the file `/etc/polkit-1/rules.d/10-grant-libvirt` with the following content to grant access to the read-write socket to all members of the group `libvirt`:

```
polkit.addRule(function(action, subject) {
  if (action.id == "org.libvirt.unix.manage" && subject.isInGroup("libvirt")) {
    return polkit.Result.YES;
  }
});
```

11.1.1.3 User name and Password Authentication with SASL

SASL provides user name and password authentication and data encryption (digest-md5, by default). Since SASL maintains its own user database, the users do not need to exist on the VM Host Server. SASL is required by TCP connections and on top of TLS/SSL connections.

> ⊙ **Important: Plain TCP and SASL with digest-md5 Encryption**
>
> Using digest-md5 encryption on an otherwise not encrypted TCP connection does not provide enough security for production environments. It is recommended to only use it in testing environments.

> 💡 **Tip: SASL Authentication on Top of TLS/SSL**
>
> Access from remote TLS/SSL connections can be indirectly controlled on the *client side* by restricting access to the certificate's key file. However, this might prove error-prone when dealing with a large number of clients. Using SASL with TLS adds security by additionally controlling access on the server side.

To configure SASL authentication, proceed as follows:

1. Change the configuration in `/etc/libvirt/libvirtd.conf` as follows:

   a. To enable SASL for TCP connections:

   ```
   auth_tcp = "sasl"
   ```

   b. To enable SASL for TLS/SSL connections:

   ```
   auth_tls = "sasl"
   ```

2. Restart `libvirtd`:

   ```
   systemctl restart libvirtd
   ```

3. The libvirt SASL configuration file is located at `/etc/sasl2/libvirtd.conf`. Normally, there is no need to change the defaults. However, if using SASL on top of TLS, you may turn off session encryption to avoid additional overhead (TLS connections are already encrypted) by commenting the line setting the `mech_list` parameter. Only do this for TSL/SASL, for TCP connections this parameter must be set to digest-md5.

```
#mech_list: digest-md5
```

4. By default, no SASL users are configured, so no logins are possible. Use the following commands to manage users:

Add the user tux

```
saslpasswd2 -a libvirt tux
```

Delete the user tux

```
saslpasswd2 -a libvirt -d tux
```

List existing users

```
sasldblistusers2 -f /etc/libvirt/passwd.db
```

> **Tip: `virsh` and SASL Authentication**
>
> When using SASL authentication, you will be prompted for a user name and password every time you issue a **virsh** command. Avoid this by using **virsh** in shell mode.

11.1.2 VNC Authentication

Since access to the graphical console of a VM Guest is not controlled by `libvirt`, but rather by the specific hypervisor, it is always necessary to additionally configure VNC authentication. The main configuration file is `/etc/libvirt/<hypervisor>.conf`. This section describes the QEMU/KVM hypervisor, so the target configuration file is `/etc/libvirt/qemu.conf`.

Note: VNC Authentication for Xen

In contrast to KVM and LXC, Xen does not yet offer more sophisticated VNC authentication than setting a password on a per VM basis. See the `<graphics type='vnc'...` `libvirt` configuration option below.

Two authentication types are available: SASL and single password authentication. If you are using SASL for `libvirt` authentication, it is strongly recommended to use it for VNC authentication as well—it is possible to share the same database.

A third method to restrict access to the VM Guest is to enable the use of TLS encryption on the VNC server. This requires the VNC clients to have access to x509 client certificates. By restricting access to these certificates, access can indirectly be controlled on the client side. Refer to *Section 11.3.2.4.2, "VNC over TLS/SSL: Client Configuration"* for details.

11.1.2.1　User name and Password Authentication with SASL

SASL provides user name and password authentication and data encryption. Since SASL maintains its own user database, the users do not need to exist on the VM Host Server. As with SASL authentication for `libvirt`, you may use SASL on top of TLS/SSL connections. Refer to *Section 11.3.2.4.2, "VNC over TLS/SSL: Client Configuration"* for details on configuring these connections.

To configure SASL authentication for VNC, proceed as follows:

1. Create a SASL configuration file. It is recommended to use the existing `libvirt` file. If you have already configured SASL for `libvirt` and are planning to use the same settings including the same user name and password database, a simple link is suitable:

```
ln -s /etc/sasl2/libvirt.conf /etc/sasl2/qemu.conf
```

   In case you are setting up SASL for VNC only or you are planning to use a different configuration than for `libvirt`, copy the existing file to use as a template and edit it according to your needs:

```
cp /etc/sasl2/libvirt.conf /etc/sasl2/qemu.conf
```

2. Change the configuration in `/etc/libvirt/qemu.conf` as follows:

```
vnc_listen = "0.0.0.0"
vnc_sasl = 1
sasldb_path: /etc/libvirt/qemu_passwd.db
```

The first parameter enables VNC to listen on all public interfaces (rather than to the local host only), and the second parameter enables SASL authentication.

3. By default, no SASL users are configured, so no logins are possible. Use the following commands to manage users:

Add the user tux

```
saslpasswd2 -f /etc/libvirt/qemu_passwd.db -a qemu tux
```

Delete the user tux

```
saslpasswd2 -f /etc/libvirt/qemu_passwd.db -a qemu -d tux
```

List existing users

```
sasldblistusers2 -f /etc/libvirt/qemu_passwd.db
```

4. Restart `libvirtd`:

```
systemctl restart libvirtd
```

5. Restart all VM Guests that have been running prior to changing the configuration. VM Guests that have not been restarted will not use SASL authentication for VNC connects.

 ## Note: Supported VNC Viewers

SASL authentication is currently supported by Virtual Machine Manager and **virt-viewer**. Both of these viewers also support TLS/SSL connections.

11.1.2.2 Single Password Authentication

Access to the VNC server may also be controlled by setting a VNC password. You can either set a global password for all VM Guests or set individual passwords for each guest. The latter requires to edit the VM Guest's configuration files.

 Note: Always Set a Global Password

> If you are using single password authentication, it is good practice to set a global password even if setting passwords for each VM Guest. This will always leave your virtual machines protected with a "fallback" password if you forget to set a per-machine password. The global password will only be used if no other password is set for the machine.

PROCEDURE 11.1: SETTING A GLOBAL VNC PASSWORD

1. Change the configuration in `/etc/libvirt/qemu.conf` as follows:

```
vnc_listen = "0.0.0.0"
vnc_password = "PASSWORD"
```

   The first parameter enables VNC to listen on all public interfaces (rather than to the local host only), and the second parameter sets the password. The maximum length of the password is eight characters.

2. Restart `libvirtd`:

```
root # systemctl restart libvirtd
```

3. Restart all VM Guests that have been running prior to changing the configuration. VM Guests that have not been restarted will not use password authentication for VNC connects.

PROCEDURE 11.2: SETTING A VM GUEST SPECIFIC VNC PASSWORD

1. Change the configuration in `/etc/libvirt/qemu.conf` as follows to enable VNC to listen on all public interfaces (rather than to the local host only).

```
vnc_listen = "0.0.0.0"
```

2. Open the VM Guest's XML configuration file in an editor. Replace *VM NAME* in the following example with the name of the VM Guest. The editor that is used defaults to `$EDITOR`. If that variable is not set, **vi** is used.

```
virsh edit VM NAME
```

3. Search for the element `<graphics>` with the attribute `type='vnc'`, for example:

```
<graphics type='vnc' port='-1' autoport='yes'/>
```

4. Add the `passwd=PASSWORD` attribute, save the file and exit the editor. The maximum length of the password is eight characters.

```
<graphics type='vnc' port='-1' autoport='yes' passwd='PASSWORD'/>
```

5. Restart `libvirtd`:

```
root # systemctl restart libvirtd
```

6. Restart all VM Guests that have been running prior to changing the configuration. VM Guests that have not been restarted will not use password authentication for VNC connects.

✋ Warning: Security of the VNC Protocol

The VNC protocol is not considered to be safe. Although the password is sent encrypted, it might be vulnerable when an attacker can sniff both the encrypted password and the encryption key. Therefore, it is recommended to use VNC with TLS/SSL or tunneled over SSH. **virt-viewer**, Virtual Machine Manager and **vinagre** from version 2.30 onwards supports both methods.

11.2 Connecting to a VM Host Server

To connect to a hypervisor with `libvirt`, you need to specify a uniform resource identifier (URI). This URI is needed with **virsh** and **virt-viewer** (except when working as `root` on the VM Host Server) and is optional for the Virtual Machine Manager. Although the latter can be called with a connection parameter (for example, **virt-manager -c qemu:///system**), it also offers a graphical interface to create connection URIs. See *Section 11.2.2, "Managing Connections with Virtual Machine Manager"* for details.

```
HYPERVISOR ❶+PROTOCOL ❷://USER@REMOTE ❸/CONNECTION_TYPE ❹
```

1. Specify the hypervisor. SUSE Linux Enterprise Server currently supports the following hypervisors: `test` (dummy for testing), `qemu` (KVM), and `xen` (Xen). This parameter is mandatory.

2. When connecting to a remote host, specify the protocol here. It can be one of: `ssh` (connection via SSH tunnel), `tcp` (TCP connection with SASL/Kerberos authentication), `tls` (TLS/SSL encrypted connection with authentication via x509 certificates).

3. When connecting to a remote host, specify the user name and the remote host name. If no user name is specified, the user name that has called the command (`$USER`) is used. See below for more information. For TLS connections, the host name has to be specified exactly as in the x509 certificate.

4. When connecting to the `QEMU/KVM` hypervisor, two connection types are accepted: `system` for full access rights, or `session` for restricted access. Since `session` access is not supported on SUSE Linux Enterprise Server, this documentation focuses on `system` access.

EXAMPLE HYPERVISOR CONNECTION URIS

`test:///default`
> Connect to the local dummy hypervisor. Useful for testing.

`qemu:///system` or `xen:///system`
> Connect to the QEMU/Xen hypervisor on the local host having full access (type system).

`qemu+ssh://tux@mercury.example.com/system` or `xen+ssh://tux@mercury.example.com/system`
> Connect to the QEMU/Xen hypervisor on the remote host mercury.example.com. The connection is established via an SSH tunnel.

`qemu+tls://saturn.example.com/system` or `xen+tls://saturn.example.com/system`
> Connect to the QEMU/Xen hypervisor on the remote host mercury.example.com. The connection is established using TLS/SSL.

For more details and examples, refer to the `libvirt` documentation at http://libvirt.org/uri.html.

Note: User Names in URIs

A user name needs to be specified when using Unix socket authentication (regardless of whether using the user/password authentication scheme or PolKit). This applies to all SSH and local connections.

There is no need to specify a user name when using SASL authentication (for TCP or TLS connections) or when doing no additional server-side authentication for TLS connections. With SASL the user name will not be evaluated—you will be prompted for an SASL user/password combination in any case.

11.2.1 "system" Access for Non-Privileged Users

As mentioned above, a connection to the QEMU hypervisor can be established using two different protocols: `session` and `system`. A "session" connection is spawned with the same privileges as the client program. Such a connection is intended for desktop virtualization, since it is restricted (for example no USB/PCI device assignments, no virtual network setup, limited remote access to `libvirtd`).

The "system" connection intended for server virtualization has no functional restrictions but is, by default, only accessible by `root`. However, with the addition of the DAC (Discretionary Access Control) driver to `libvirt` it is now possible to grant non-privileged users "system" access. To grant "system" access to the user `tux`, proceed as follows:

PROCEDURE 11.3: GRANTING "SYSTEM" ACCESS TO A REGULAR USER

1. Enable access via Unix sockets as described in *Section 11.1.1.1, "Access Control for Unix Sockets with Permissions and Group Ownership"*. In that example access to libvirt is granted to all members of the group `libvirt` and `tux` is made a member of this group. This ensures that `tux` can connect using **virsh** or Virtual Machine Manager.

2. Edit `/etc/libvirt/qemu.conf` and change the configuration as follows:

```
user = "tux"
group = "libvirt"
dynamic_ownership = 1
```

This ensures that the VM Guests are started by `tux` and that resources bound to the guest (for example virtual disks) can be accessed and modified by `tux`.

3. Make `tux` a member of the group `kvm`:

```
usermod -A kvm tux
```

This step is needed to grant access to `/dev/kvm`, which is required to start VM Guests.

4. Restart `libvirtd`:

```
root # systemctl restart libvirtd
```

11.2.2   Managing Connections with Virtual Machine Manager

The Virtual Machine Manager uses a `Connection` for every VM Host Server it manages. Each connection contains all VM Guests on the respective host. By default, a connection to the local host is already configured and connected.

All configured connections are displayed in the Virtual Machine Manager main window. Active connections are marked with a small triangle, which you can click to fold or unfold the list of VM Guests for this connection.

Inactive connections are listed gray and are marked with `Not Connected`. Either double-click or right-click it and choose *Connect* from the context menu. You can also *Delete* an existing connection from this menu.

 Note: Editing Existing Connections

It is not possible to edit an existing connection. To change a connection, create a new one with the desired parameters and delete the "old" one.

To add a new connection in the Virtual Machine Manager, proceed as follows:

1. Choose *File › Add Connection*

2. Choose the host's *Hypervisor* (*Xen* or *QEMU/KVM*)

3. Choose a *Connection* type—either *Local* for connecting to the host the Virtual Machine Manager was started on, or one of the remote connections (see *Section 11.3, "Configuring Remote Connections"* for more information).

4. In case of a remote connection, enter the *Hostname* of the remote machine as `USERNAME@REMOTE_HOST`. User names must be specified for local connections and for SSH.

> **❗ Important: Specifying a User Name**
>
> There is no need to specify a user name for TCP and TLS connections; it will not be evaluated anyway. A user name must be specified for local connections and for SSH connections—if not, the default user `root` will be used.

5. If you do not want the connection to be automatically activated when starting the Virtual Machine Manager, remove the tick from *Autoconnect*.

6. Finish the configuration by clicking *Connect*.

11.3   Configuring Remote Connections

A major benefit of `libvirt` is the ability to manage VM Guests on different remote hosts from a central location. This section gives detailed instructions on how to configure server and client to allow remote connections.

11.3.1   Remote Tunnel over SSH (qemu+ssh or xen+ssh)

Enabling a remote connection that is tunneled over SSH on the VM Host Server only requires the ability to accept SSH connections. Make sure the SSH daemon is started (`systemctl status sshd`) and that the ports for service `SSH` are opened in the firewall.

User authentication for SSH connections can be done using traditional file user/group ownership and permissions as described in *Section 11.1.1.1, "Access Control for Unix Sockets with Permissions and Group Ownership"*. Connecting as user tux (`qemu+ssh://tuxsIVname;/system` or `xen+ssh://tuxsIVname;/system`) works out of the box and does not require additional configuration on the `libvirt` side.

When connecting via SSH `qemu+ssh://USER@SYSTEM` or `xen+ssh://USER@SYSTEM` you need to provide the password for *USER*. This can be avoided by copying your public key to `~USER/.ssh/authorized_keys` on the VM Host Server as explained in *Book "Security Guide", Chapter 14 "SSH: Secure Network Operations", Section 14.5.2 "Copying an SSH Key"*. Using an ssh-agent on the machine from which you are connecting adds even more convenience—see *Book "Security Guide", Chapter 14 "SSH: Secure Network Operations", Section 14.5.3 "Using the* `ssh-agent`*"* for instructions.

11.3.2 Remote TLS/SSL Connection with x509 Certificate (qemu+tls or xen+tls)

Using TCP connections with TLS/SSL encryption and authentication via x509 certificates is much more complicated to set up than SSH, but it is a lot more scalable. Use this method if you need to manage several VM Host Servers with a varying number of administrators.

11.3.2.1 Basic concept

TLS (Transport Layer Security) encrypts the communication between two computers by using certificates. The computer starting the connection is always considered the "client", using a "client certificate", while the receiving computer is always considered the "server", using a "server certificate". This scenario applies, for example, if you manage your VM Host Servers from a central desktop.

If connections are initiated from both computers, each needs to have a client *and* a server certificate. This is the case, for example, if you migrate a VM Guest from one host to another.

Each x509 certificate has a matching private key file. Only the combination of certificate and private key file can identify itself correctly. To assure that a certificate was issued by the assumed owner, it is signed and issued by a central certificate called certificate authority (CA). Both the client and the server certificates must be issued by the same CA.

> ❗ **Important: User Authentication**
>
> Using a remote TLS/SSL connection only ensures that two computers are allowed to communicate in a certain direction. Restricting access to certain users can indirectly be achieved on the client side by restricting access to the certificates. Refer to *Section 11.3.2.5, "Restricting Access (Security Considerations)"* for details. `libvirt` also supports user authentication on the server with SASL. Read more in *Section 11.3.2.6, "Central User Authentication with SASL for TLS Sockets"*.

11.3.2.2 Configuring the VM Host Server

The VM Host Server is the machine receiving connections. Therefore, the *server* certificates need to be installed. The CA certificate needs to be installed, too. Once the certificates are in place, TLS support can be turned on for `libvirt`.

1. Create the server certificate and export it together with the CA certificate as described in *Section B.2, "Generating x509 Client/Server Certificates".*

2. Create the following directories on the VM Host Server:

   ```
   mkdir -p /etc/pki/CA/ /etc/pki/libvirt/private/
   ```

   Install the certificates as follows:

   ```
   /etc/pki/CA/cacert.pem
   /etc/pki/libvirt/servercert.pem
   /etc/pki/libvirt/private/serverkey.pem
   ```

   > **Important: Restrict Access to Certificates**
   >
   > Make sure to restrict access to certificates as explained in *Section 11.3.2.5, "Restricting Access (Security Considerations)".*

3. Enable TLS support by editing `/etc/libvirt/libvirtd.conf` and setting `listen_tls` = 1. Restart `libvirtd`:

   ```
   root # systemctl restart libvirtd
   ```

4. By default, `libvirt` uses the TCP port 16514 for accepting secure TLS connections. Open this port in the firewall.

> **Important: Restarting** `libvirtd` **with TLS enabled**
>
> If you enable TLS for `libvirt`, the server certificates need to be in place, otherwise restarting `libvirtd` will fail. You also need to restart `libvirtd` in case you change the certificates.

Remote TLS/SSL Connection with x509 Certificate (qemu+tls or xen+tls)

11.3.2.3 Configuring the Client and Testing the Setup

The client is the machine initiating connections. Therefore the *client* certificates need to be installed. The CA certificate needs to be installed, too.

1. Create the client certificate and export it together with the CA certificate as described in *Section B.2, "Generating x509 Client/Server Certificates"*.

2. Create the following directories on the client:

   ```
   mkdir -p /etc/pki/CA/ /etc/pki/libvirt/private/
   ```

   Install the certificates as follows:

   ```
   /etc/pki/CA/cacert.pem
   /etc/pki/libvirt/clientcert.pem
   /etc/pki/libvirt/private/clientkey.pem
   ```

    Important: Restrict Access to Certificates

   Make sure to restrict access to certificates as explained in *Section 11.3.2.5, "Restricting Access (Security Considerations)"*.

3. Test the client/server setup by issuing the following command. Replace *mercury.example.com* with the name of your VM Host Server. Specify the same fully qualified host name as used when creating the server certificate.

   ```
   #QEMU/KVM
   virsh -c qemu+tls://mercury.example.com/system list --all


   #Xen
   virsh -c xen+tls://mercury.example.com/system list --all
   ```

   If your setup is correct, you will see a list of all VM Guests registered with `libvirt` on the VM Host Server.

11.3.2.4 Enabling VNC for TLS/SSL connections

Currently, VNC communication over TLS is only supported by a few tools. The widespread **tightvnc** or **tigervnc** viewer, for example, do not support TLS. Known to work are the Virtual Machine Manager (**virt-manager**), **virt-viewer** and the GNOME VNC viewer **vinagre**.

11.3.2.4.1 VNC over TLS/SSL: VM Host Server Configuration

To access the graphical console via VNC over TLS/SSL, you need to configure the VM Host Server as follows:

1. Open ports for the service VNC in your firewall.

2. Create a directory `/etc/pki/libvirt-vnc` and link the certificates into this directory as follows:

```
mkdir -p /etc/pki/libvirt-vnc && cd /etc/pki/libvirt-vnc
        ln -s /etc/pki/CA/cacert.pem ca-cert.pem
        ln -s /etc/pki/libvirt/servercert.pem server-cert.pem
        ln -s /etc/pki/libvirt/private/serverkey.pem server-key.pem
```

3. Edit `/etc/libvirt/qemu.conf` and set the following parameters:

```
vnc_listen = "0.0.0.0"
        vnc_tls = 1
        vnc_tls_x509_verify = 1
```

4. Restart the `libvirtd`:

```
root # systemctl restart libvirtd
```

 Important: VM Guests Need to be Restarted

The VNC TLS setting is only set when starting a VM Guest. Therefore, you need to restart all machines that have been running prior to making the configuration change.

11.3.2.4.2 VNC over TLS/SSL: Client Configuration

The only action needed on the client side is to place the x509 client certificates in a location recognized by the client of choice. Unfortunately, each supported client—Virtual Machine Manager, `virt-viewer`, and `vinagre`—expects the certificates in a different location. However, Virtual Machine Manager and `vinagre` can either read from a system-wide location applying to all users, or from a per-user location.

Virtual Machine Manager (`virt-manager`)

To connect to the remote host, Virtual Machine Manager requires the setup explained in *Section 11.3.2.3, "Configuring the Client and Testing the Setup"*. To be able to connect via VNC the client certificates also need to be placed in the following locations:

System-wide location

```
/etc/pki/CA/cacert.pem
/etc/pki/libvirt-vnc/clientcert.pem
/etc/pki/libvirt-vnc/private/clientkey.pem
```

Per-user location

```
/etc/pki/CA/cacert.pem
~/.pki/libvirt-vnc/clientcert.pem
~/.pki/libvirt-vnc/private/clientkey.pem
```

`virt-viewer`

`virt-viewer` only accepts certificates from a system-wide location:

```
/etc/pki/CA/cacert.pem
/etc/pki/libvirt-vnc/clientcert.pem
/etc/pki/libvirt-vnc/private/clientkey.pem
```

Important: Restrict Access to Certificates

Make sure to restrict access to certificates as explained in *Section 11.3.2.5, "Restricting Access (Security Considerations)"*.

11.3.2.5 Restricting Access (Security Considerations)

Each x509 certificate consists of two pieces: the public certificate and a private key. A client can only authenticate using both pieces. Therefore, any user that has read access to the client certificate and its private key can access your VM Host Server. On the other hand, an arbitrary machine equipped with the full server certificate can pretend to be the VM Host Server. Since this is probably not desirable, access to at least the private key files needs to be restricted as much as possible. The easiest way to control access to a key file is to use access permissions.

Server Certificates

Server certificates need to be readable for QEMU processes. On SUSE Linux Enterprise Server QEMU processes started from `libvirt` tools are owned by `root`, so it is sufficient if the `root` can read the certificates:

```
chmod 700 /etc/pki/libvirt/private/
chmod 600 /etc/pki/libvirt/private/serverkey.pem
```

If you change the ownership for QEMU processes in `/etc/libvirt/qemu.conf`, you also need to adjust the ownership of the key file.

System Wide Client Certificates

To control access to a key file that is available system-wide, restrict read access to a certain group, so that only members of that group can read the key file. In the following example, a group `libvirt` is created, and group ownership of the `clientkey.pem` file and its parent directory is set to `libvirt`. Afterwards, the access permissions are restricted to owner and group. Finally the user tux is added to the group `libvirt`, and thus can access the key file.

```
CERTPATH="/etc/pki/libvirt/"
# create group libvirt
groupadd libvirt
# change ownership to user root and group libvirt
chown root.libvirt $CERTPATH/private $CERTPATH/clientkey.pem
# restrict permissions
chmod 750 $CERTPATH/private
chmod 640 $CERTPATH/private/clientkey.pem
# add user tux to group libvirt
usermod -A libvirt tux
```

Per-User Certificates

User-specific client certificates for accessing the graphical console of a VM Guest via VNC need to be placed in the user's home directory in `~/.pki`. Contrary to SSH, for example, the VNC viewer using these certificates do not check the access permissions of the private key file. Therefore, it is solely the user's responsibility to make sure the key file is not readable by others.

11.3.2.5.1 Restricting Access from the Server Side

By default, every client that is equipped with appropriate client certificates may connect to a VM Host Server accepting TLS connections. Therefore, it is possible to use additional server-side authentication with SASL as described in *Section 11.1.1.3, "User name and Password Authentication with SASL"*.

It is also possible to restrict access with a whitelist of DNs (distinguished names), so only clients with a certificate matching a DN from the list can connect.

Add a list of allowed DNs to `tls_allowed_dn_list` in `/etc/libvirt/libvirtd.conf`. This list may contain wild cards. Do not specify an empty list, since that would result in refusing all connections.

```
tls_allowed_dn_list = [
   "C=US,L=Provo,O=SUSE Linux Products GmbH,OU=*,CN=venus.example.com,EMAIL=*",
   "C=DE,L=Nuremberg,O=SUSE Linux Products GmbH,OU=Documentation,CN=*"]
```

Get the distinguished name of a certificate with the following command:

```
certtool -i --infile /etc/pki/libvirt/clientcert.pem | grep "Subject:"
```

Restart `libvirtd` after having changed the configuration:

```
root # systemctl restart libvirtd
```

11.3.2.6   Central User Authentication with SASL for TLS Sockets

A direct user authentication via TLS is not possible—this is handled indirectly on each client via the read permissions for the certificates as explained in *Section 11.3.2.5, "Restricting Access (Security Considerations)"*. However, if a central, server-based user authentication is needed, `libvirt` also allows to use SASL (Simple Authentication and Security Layer) on top of TLS for direct user authentication. See *Section 11.1.1.3, "User name and Password Authentication with SASL"* for configuration details.

11.3.2.7 Troubleshooting

11.3.2.7.1 Virtual Machine Manager/`virsh` Cannot Connect to Server

Check the following in the given order:

Is it a firewall issue (TCP port 16514 needs to be open on the server)?

Is the client certificate (certificate and key) readable by the user that has started Virtual Machine Manager/`virsh`?

Has the same full qualified host name as in the server certificate been specified with the connection?

Is TLS enabled on the server (`listen_tls = 1`)?

Has `libvirtd` been restarted on the server?

11.3.2.7.2 VNC Connection fails

Ensure that you can connect to the remote server using Virtual Machine Manager. If so, check whether the virtual machine on the server has been started with TLS support. The virtual machine's name in the following example is "sles".

```
ps ax | grep qemu | grep "\-name sles" | awk -F" -vnc " '{ print FS $2 }'
```

If the output does not begin with a string similar to the following, the machine has not been started with TLS support and must be restarted.

```
 -vnc 0.0.0.0:0,tls,x509verify=/etc/pki/libvirt
```

12 Managing Storage

When managing a VM Guest on the VM Host Server itself, it is possible to access the complete file system of the VM Host Server to attach or create virtual hard disks or to attach existing images to the VM Guest. However, this is not possible when managing VM Guests from a remote host. For this reason, libvirt supports so called "Storage Pools", which can be accessed from remote machines.

 Tip: CD/DVD ISO images

To be able to access CD/DVD ISO images on the VM Host Server from remote, they also need to be placed in a storage pool.

libvirt knows two different types of storage: volumes and pools.

Storage Volume

A storage volume is a storage device that can be assigned to a guest—a virtual disk or a CD/DVD/floppy image. Physically (on the VM Host Server) it can be a block device (a partition, a logical volume, etc.) or a file.

Storage Pool

A storage pool is a storage resource on the VM Host Server that can be used for storing volumes, similar to network storage for a desktop machine. Physically it can be one of the following types:

File System Directory (*dir*)

A directory for hosting image files. The files can be either one of the supported disk formats (raw, qcow2, or qed), or ISO images.

Physical Disk Device (*disk*)

Use a complete physical disk as storage. A partition is created for each volume that is added to the pool.

Pre-Formatted Block Device (*fs*)

Specify a partition to be used in the same way as a file system directory pool (a directory for hosting image files). The only difference to using a file system directory is that libvirt takes care of mounting the device.

iSCSI Target (iscsi)

Set up a pool on an iSCSI target. You need to have been logged into the volume once before, to use it with `libvirt` (use the YaST *iSCSI Initiator* to detect and log in to a volume, see *Book "Storage Administration Guide"* for details). Volume creation on iSCSI pools is not supported, instead each existing Logical Unit Number (LUN) represents a volume. Each volume/LUN also needs a valid (empty) partition table or disk label before you can use it. If missing, use **fdisk** to add it:

```
~ # fdisk -cu /dev/disk/by-path/ip-192.168.2.100:3260-iscsi-
iqn.2010-10.com.example:[...]-lun-2
Device contains neither a valid DOS partition table, nor Sun, SGI
or OSF disklabel
Building a new DOS disklabel with disk identifier 0xc15cdc4e.
Changes will remain in memory only, until you decide to write them.
After that, of course, the previous content won't be recoverable.


Warning: invalid flag 0x0000 of partition table 4 will be corrected by
 w(rite)


Command (m for help): w
The partition table has been altered!


Calling ioctl() to re-read partition table.
Syncing disks.
```

LVM Volume Group (logical)

Use an LVM volume group as a pool. You may either use a predefined volume group, or create a group by specifying the devices to use. Storage volumes are created as partitions on the volume.

 Warning: Deleting the LVM-Based Pool

When the LVM-based pool is deleted in the Storage Manager, the volume group is deleted as well. This results in a non-recoverable loss of all data stored on the pool!

Multipath Devices (*mpath*)

At the moment, multipathing support is limited to assigning existing devices to the guests. Volume creation or configuring multipathing from within `libvirt` is not supported.

Network Exported Directory (*netfs*)

Specify a network directory to be used in the same way as a file system directory pool (a directory for hosting image files). The only difference to using a file system directory is that `libvirt` takes care of mounting the directory. Supported protocols are NFS and glusterfs.

SCSI Host Adapter (*scsi*)

Use an SCSI host adapter in almost the same way as an iSCSI target. It is recommended to use a device name from `/dev/disk/by-*` rather than the simple `/dev/sdX`, since the latter may change (for example when adding or removing hard disks). Volume creation on iSCSI pools is not supported; instead, each existing LUN (Logical Unit Number) represents a volume.

> 🛑 **Warning: Security Considerations**
>
> To avoid data loss or data corruption, do not attempt to use resources such as LVM volume groups, iSCSI targets, etc. that are used to build storage pools on the VM Host Server, as well. There is no need to connect to these resources from the VM Host Server or to mount them on the VM Host Server—`libvirt` takes care of this.
>
> Do not mount partitions on the VM Host Server by label. Under certain circumstances it is possible that a partition is labeled from within a VM Guest with a name already existing on the VM Host Server.

12.1 Managing Storage with Virtual Machine Manager

The Virtual Machine Manager provides a graphical interface—the Storage Manager—to manage storage volumes and pools. To access it, either right-click a connection and choose *Details*, or highlight a connection and choose *Edit > Connection Details*. Select the *Storage* tab.

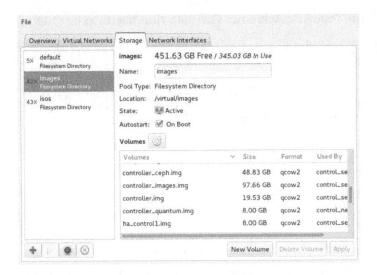

12.1.1   Adding a Storage Pool

To add a storage pool, proceed as follows:

1. Click the plus symbol in the bottom left corner to open the *Add a New Storage Pool Window*.

2. Provide a *Name* for the pool (consisting of alphanumeric characters plus _-.) and select a *Type*. Proceed with *Forward*.

3. Specify the required details in the following window. The data that needs to be entered depends on the type of pool you are creating:

Type*dir:*

- *Target Path*: Specify an existing directory.

Type *disk:*

- *Target Path*: The directory that hosts the devices. The default value `/dev` should usually fit.

- *Format*: Format of the device's partition table. Using *auto* should usually work. If not, get the required format by running the command **parted** `-l` on the VM Host Server.

- *Source Path*: Path to the device. It is recommended to use a device name from `/dev/disk/by-*` rather than the simple `/dev/sdX`, since the latter may change (for example when adding or removing hard disks). You need to specify the path that resembles the whole disk, not a partition on the disk (if existing).

- *Build Pool:* Activating this option formats the device. Use with care—all data on the device will be lost!

Type *fs:*

- *Target Path:* Mount point on the VM Host Server file system.

- *Format:* File system format of the device. The default value `auto` should work.

- *Source Path:* Path to the device file. It is recommended to use a device name from `/dev/disk/by-*` rather than the simple `/dev/sdX`, since the latter may change (for example when adding or removing hard disks).

Type *iscsi:*

Get the necessary data by running the following command on the VM Host Server:

```
iscsiadm --mode node
```

It will return a list of iSCSI volumes with the following format. The elements high-lighted with a bold font are the ones needed:

```
IP_ADDRESS:PORT,TPGT TARGET_NAME_(IQN)
```

- *Target Path:* The directory containing the device file. Use `/dev/disk/by-path` (default) or `/dev/disk/by-id`.

- *Host Name:* Host name or IP address of the iSCSI server.

- *Source Path:* The iSCSI target name (IQN).

Type *logical:*

- *Target Path:* In case you use an existing volume group, specify the existing device path. In case of building a new LVM volume group, specify a device name in the `/dev` directory that does not already exist.

- *Source Path:* Leave empty when using an existing volume group. When creating a new one, specify its devices here.

- *Build Pool:* Only activate when creating a new volume group.

Type *mpath:*

- *Target Path:* Support of multipathing is currently limited to making all multi-path devices available. Therefore you may enter an arbitrary string here (re-quired, otherwise the XML parser will fail); it will be ignored anyway.

Type *netfs:*

- *target Path:* Mount point on the VM Host Server file system.

- *Format:* Network file system protocol.

- *Host Name:* IP address or host name of the server exporting the network file system.

- *Source Path:* Directory on the server that is being exported.

Type *scsi:*

- *Target Path:* The directory containing the device file. Use `/dev/disk/by-path`
  (default) or `/dev/disk/by-id`.

- *Source Path:* Name of the SCSI adapter.

 Note: File Browsing

Using the file browser by clicking *Browse* is not possible when operating from remote.

4. Click *Finish* to add the storage pool.

12.1.2   Managing Storage Pools

Virtual Machine Manager's Storage Manager lets you create or delete volumes in a pool. You
may also temporarily deactivate or permanently delete existing storage pools. Changing the
basic configuration of a pool is currently not supported by SUSE.

12.1.2.1   Starting, Stopping and Deleting Pools

The purpose of storage pools is to provide block devices located on the VM Host Server that can
be added to a VM Guest when managing it from remote. To make a pool temporarily inaccessible
from remote, you may *Stop* it by clicking the stop symbol in the bottom left corner of the Storage
Manager. Stopped pools are marked with *State: Inactive* and are grayed out in the list pane. By
default, a newly created pool will be automatically started *On Boot* of the VM Host Server.

To *Start* an inactive pool and make it available from remote again click the play symbol in the
bottom left corner of the Storage Manager.

 Note: A Pool's State Does not Affect Attached Volumes

Volumes from a pool attached to VM Guests are always available, regardless of the pool's
state (*Active* (stopped) or *Inactive* (started)). The state of the pool solely affects the ability
to attach volumes to a VM Guest via remote management.

To permanently make a pool inaccessible, you can *Delete* it by clicking the shredder symbol in the bottom left corner of the Storage Manager. You may only delete inactive pools. Deleting a pool does not physically erase its contents on VM Host Server—it only deletes the pool configuration. However, you need to be extra careful when deleting pools, especially when deleting LVM volume group-based tools:

 Warning: Deleting Storage Pools

Deleting storage pools based on *local* file system directories, local partitions or disks has no effect on the availability of volumes from these pools currently attached to VM Guests.

Volumes located in pools of type iSCSI, SCSI, LVM group or Network Exported Directory will become inaccessible from the VM Guest if the pool is deleted. Although the volumes themselves will not be deleted, the VM Host Server will no longer have access to the resources.

Volumes on iSCSI/SCSI targets or Network Exported Directory will become accessible again when creating an adequate new pool or when mounting/accessing these resources directly from the host system.

When deleting an LVM group-based storage pool, the LVM group definition will be erased and the LVM group will no longer exist on the host system. The configuration is not recoverable and all volumes from this pool are lost.

12.1.2.2   Adding Volumes to a Storage Pool

Virtual Machine Manager lets you create volumes in all storage pools, except in pools of types Multipath, iSCSI, or SCSI. A volume in these pools is equivalent to a LUN and cannot be changed from within `libvirt`.

1. A new volume can either be created using the Storage Manager or while adding a new storage device to a VM Guest. In both cases, select a *Storage Pool* and then click *New Volume*.

2. Specify a *Name* for the image and choose an image format (note that SUSE currently only supports `raw`, `qcow2`, or `qed` images). The latter option is not available on LVM group-based pools.
   Specify a *Max Capacity* and the amount of space that should initially be allocated. If both values differ, a `sparse` image file, growing on demand, will be created.

3. Start the volume creation by clicking *Finish*.

12.1.2.3 Deleting Volumes From a Storage Pool

Deleting a volume can only be done from the Storage Manager, by selecting a volume and clicking *Delete Volume*. Confirm with *Yes*. Use this function with extreme care!

 Warning: No Checks Upon Volume Deletion

A volume will be deleted in any case, regardless of whether it is currently used in an active or inactive VM Guest. There is no way to recover a deleted volume.

Whether a volume is used by a VM Guest is indicated in the *Used By* column in the Storage Manager.

12.2 Managing Storage with `virsh`

Managing storage from the command line is also possible by using `virsh`. However, creating storage pools is currently not supported by SUSE. Therefore this section is restricted to document functions like starting, stopping and deleting pools and volume management.

A list of all `virsh` subcommands for managing pools and volumes is available by running `virsh help pool` and `virsh help volume`, respectively.

12.2.1 Listing Pools and Volumes

List all pools currently active by executing the following command. To also list inactive pools, add the option `--all`:

```
virsh pool-list --details
```

Details about a specific pool can be obtained with the `pool-info` subcommand:

```
virsh pool-info POOL
```

Volumes can only be listed per pool by default. To list all volumes from a pool, enter the following command.

```
virsh vol-list --details POOL
```

At the moment **virsh** offers no tools to show whether a volume is used by a guest or not. The following procedure describes a way to list volumes from all pools that are currently used by a VM Guest.

PROCEDURE 12.1: LISTING ALL STORAGE VOLUMES CURRENTLY USED ON A VM HOST SERVER

1. Create an XSLT style sheet by saving the following content to a file, for example, ~/libvirt/guest_storage_list.xsl:

```
<?xml version="1.0" encoding="UTF-8"?>
<xsl:stylesheet version="1.0"
  xmlns:xsl="http://www.w3.org/1999/XSL/Transform">
  <xsl:output method="text"/>
  <xsl:template match="text()"/>
  <xsl:strip-space elements="*"/>
  <xsl:template match="disk">
    <xsl:text>  </xsl:text>
    <xsl:value-of select="(source/@file|source/@dev|source/@dir)[1]"/>
    <xsl:text>&#10;</xsl:text>
  </xsl:template>
</xsl:stylesheet>
```

2. Run the following commands in a shell. It is assumed that the guest's XML definitions are all stored in the default location (`/etc/libvirt/qemu`). **xsltproc** is provided by the package `libxslt`.

```
SSHEET="$HOME/libvirt/guest_storage_list.xsl"
cd /etc/libvirt/qemu
for FILE in *.xml; do
  basename $FILE .xml
  xsltproc $SSHEET $FILE
done
```

12.2.2   Starting, Stopping and Deleting Pools

Use the `virsh` pool subcommands to start, stop or delete a pool. Replace *POOL* with the pool's name or its UUID in the following examples:

Stopping a Pool

```
virsh pool-destroy POOL
```

 ### Note: A Pool's State Does not Affect Attached Volumes

Volumes from a pool attached to VM Guests are always available, regardless of the pool's state (*Active* (stopped) or *Inactive* (started)). The state of the pool solely affects the ability to attach volumes to a VM Guest via remote management.

Deleting a Pool

```
virsh pool-delete POOL
```

 ### Warning: Deleting Storage Pools

See *Warning: Deleting Storage Pools*

Starting a Pool

```
virsh pool-start POOL
```

Enable Autostarting a Pool

```
virsh pool-autostart POOL
```

Only pools that are marked to autostart will automatically be started if the VM Host Server reboots.

Disable Autostarting a Pool

```
virsh pool-autostart POOL --disable
```

12.2.3 Adding Volumes to a Storage Pool

`virsh` offers two ways to add volumes to storage pools: either from an XML definition with `vol-create` and `vol-create-from` or via command line arguments with `vol-create-as`. The first two methods are currently not supported by SUSE, therefore this section focuses on the subcommand `vol-create-as`.

To add a volume to an existing pool, enter the following command:

```
virsh vol-create-as POOL❶ NAME❷ 12G --format❸ raw|qcow2|qed❹ --allocation 4G❺
```

❶ Name of the pool to which the volume should be added

❷ Name of the volume

❸ Size of the image, in this example 12 gigabytes. Use the suffixes k, M, G, T for kilobyte, megabyte, gigabyte, and terabyte, respectively.

❹ Format of the volume. SUSE currently supports `raw`, `qcow2`, and `qed`.

❺ Optional parameter. By default `virsh` creates a sparse image file that grows on demand. Specify the amount of space that should be allocated with this parameter (4 gigabytes in this example). Use the suffixes k, M, G, T for kilobyte, megabyte, gigabyte, and terabyte, respectively.

   When not specifying this parameter, a sparse image file with no allocation will be generated. If you want to create a non-sparse volume, specify the whole image size with this parameter (would be `12G` in this example).

12.2.3.1 Cloning Existing Volumes

Another way to add volumes to a pool is to clone an existing volume. The new instance is always created in the same pool as the original.

```
virsh vol-clone NAME_EXISTING_VOLUME❶ NAME_NEW_VOLUME❷ --pool POOL❸
```

❶ Name of the existing volume that should be cloned

❷ Name of the new volume

❸ Optional parameter. `libvirt` tries to locate the existing volume automatically. If that fails, specify this parameter.

12.2.4 Deleting Volumes from a Storage Pool

To permanently delete a volume from a pool, use the subcommand `vol-delete`:

```
virsh vol-delete NAME --pool POOL
```

`--pool` is optional. `libvirt` tries to locate the volume automatically. If that fails, specify this parameter.

 Warning: No Checks Upon Volume Deletion

A volume will be deleted in any case, regardless of whether it is currently used in an active or inactive VM Guest. There is no way to recover a deleted volume.

Whether a volume is used by a VM Guest can only be detected by using by the method described in *Procedure 12.1, "Listing all Storage Volumes Currently Used on a VM Host Server"*.

12.3 Locking Disk Files and Block Devices with `virtlockd`

Locking block devices and disk files prevents concurrent writes to these resources from different VM Guests. It provides protection against starting the same VM Guest twice, or adding the same disk to two different virtual machines. This will reduce the risk of a virtual machine's disk image becoming corrupted because of a wrong configuration.

The locking is controlled by a daemon called `virtlockd`. Since it operates independently from the `libvirtd` daemon, locks will endure a crash or a restart of `libvirtd`. Locks will even persist in the case of an update of the `virtlockd` itself, since it can re-execute itself. This ensures that VM Guests do *not* need to be restarted upon a `virtlockd` update.

 Note: KVM Only

`virtlockd` integration is only supported on a KVM VM Host Server.

12.3.1 Enable Locking

Locking virtual disks is not enabled by default on SUSE Linux Enterprise Server. To enable and automatically start it upon rebooting, perform the following steps:

1. Edit `/etc/libvirt/qemu.conf` and set

   ```
   lock_manager = "lockd"
   ```

2. Start the `virtlockd` daemon with the following command:

   ```
   systemctl start virtlockd
   ```

3. Restart the `libvirtd` daemon with:

   ```
   systemctl restart libvirtd
   ```

4. Make sure `virtlockd` is automatically started when booting the system:

   ```
   systemctl enable virtlockd
   ```

12.3.2 Configure Locking

By default `virtlockd` is configured to automatically lock all disks configured for your VM Guests. The default setting uses a "direct" lockspace, where the locks are acquired against the actual file paths associated with the VM Guest <disk> devices. For example, `flock(2)` will be called directly on `/var/lib/libvirt/images/my-server/disk0.raw` when the VM Guest contains the following <disk> device:

```
<disk type='file' device='disk'>
 <driver name='qemu' type='raw'/>
 <source file='/var/lib/libvirt/images/my-server/disk0.raw'/>
 <target dev='vda' bus='virtio'/>
</disk>
```

The `virtlockd` configuration can be changed by editing the file `/etc/libvirt/qe-mu-lockd.conf`. It also contains detailed comments with further information. Make sure to activate configuration changes by reloading `virtlockd`:

```
systemctl reload virtlockd
```

 Note: Locking Currently Only Available for All Disks

As of SUSE Linux Enterprise Server 12 SP1 locking can only be activated globally, so that all virtual disks are locked. Support for locking selected disks is planned for future releases.

12.3.2.1   Enabling an Indirect Lockspace

`virtlockd`'s default configuration uses a "direct" lockspace, where the locks are acquired against the actual file paths associated with the <disk> devices. If the disk file paths are not accessible to all hosts, `virtlockd` can be configured to allow an "indirect" lockspace, where a hash of the disk file path is used to create a file in the indirect lockspace directory. The locks are then held on these hash files instead of the actual disk file paths. Indirect lockspace is also useful if the file system containing the disk files does not support `fcntl()` locks. An indirect lockspace is specified with the file_lockspace_dir setting:

```
file_lockspace_dir = "/MY_LOCKSPACE_DIRECTORY"
```

12.3.2.2   Enable Locking on LVM or iSCSI Volumes

When wanting to lock virtual disks placed on LVM or iSCSI volumes shared by several hosts, locking needs to be done by UUID rather than by path (which is used by default). Furthermore, the lockspace directory needs to be placed on a shared file system accessible by all hosts sharing the volume. Set the following options for LVM and/or iSCSI:

```
lvm_lockspace_dir = "/MY_LOCKSPACE_DIRECTORY"
iscsi_lockspace_dir = "/MY_LOCKSPACE_DIRECTORY"
```

12.4   Online Resizing of Guest Block Devices

Sometimes you need to change—extend or shrink—the size of the block device used by your guest system. For example, when the disk space originally allocated is no longer enough, it is time to increase its size. If the guest disk resides on a *logical volume*, you can resize it while the guest system is running. This is a big advantage over an offline disk resizing (see the **virt-resize** command from the *Section 16.3, "Guestfs Tools"* package) as the service provided by the guest is not interrupted by the resizing process. To resize a VM Guest disk, follow these steps:

PROCEDURE 12.2: ONLINE RESIZING OF GUEST DISK

1. Inside the guest system, check the current size of the disk (for example /dev/vda).

    ```
    root # fdisk -l /dev/vda
    Disk /dev/sda: 160.0 GB, 160041885696 bytes, 312581808 sectors
    Units = sectors of 1 * 512 = 512 bytes
    Sector size (logical/physical): 512 bytes / 512 bytes
    I/O size (minimum/optimal): 512 bytes / 512 bytes
    ```

2. On the host, resize the logical volume holding the /dev/vda disk of the guest to the required size, for example 200 GB.

    ```
    root # lvresize -L 2048M /dev/mapper/vg00-home
    Extending logical volume home to 2.00 GiB
    Logical volume home successfully resized
    ```

3. On the host, resize the block device related to the disk /dev/mapper/vg00-home of the guest. Note that you can find the *domain_id* with **virsh list**.

    ```
    root # virsh blockresize  --path /dev/vg00/home --size 2048M domain_id
    Block device '/dev/vg00/home' is resized
    ```

4. Check that the new disk size is accepted by the guest.

    ```
    root # fdisk -l /dev/vda
    Disk /dev/sda: 200.0 GB, 200052357120 bytes, 390727260 sectors
    Units = sectors of 1 * 512 = 512 bytes
    Sector size (logical/physical): 512 bytes / 512 bytes
    ```

```
I/O size (minimum/optimal): 512 bytes / 512 bytes
```

12.5 Sharing Directories between Host and Guests (File System Pass-Through)

libvirt allows to share directories between host and guests using QEMU's file system pass-through (also called VirtFS) feature. Such a directory can be also be accessed by several VM Guests at once and therefore be used to exchange files between VM Guests.

 Note: Windows Guests and File System Pass-Through

> Note that sharing directories between VM Host Server and Windows guests via File System Pass-Through does not work, because Windows lacks the drivers required to mount the shared directory.

To make a shared directory available on a VM Guest, proceed as follows:

1. Open the guest's console in Virtual Machine Manager and either choose *View* > *Details* from the menu, or click the bulb icon in the toolbar. Choose *Add Hardware* > *Filesystem* to open the *Filesystem Passthrough* dialog.

2. *Driver* allows you to choose between a *Handle* or *Path* base driver. The default setting is *Path*. *Mode* lets you choose the security model, which influences the way file permissions are set on the host. Three options are available:

   Passthrough (Default)
   > Files on the file system are directly created with the client-user's credentials. This is very similar to what NFSv3 is using.

   Squash
   > Same as *Passthrough*, but failure of privileged operations like `chown` are ignored. This is required when KVM is not run with `root` privileges.

   Mapped
   > Files are created with the file server's credentials (`qemu.qemu`). The user credentials and the client-user's credentials are saved in extended attributes. This model is recommended when host and guest domains should be kept completely isolated.

3. Specify the path to the directory on the VM Host Server with *Source Path*. Enter a string at *Target Path* that will be used as a tag to mount the shared directory. Note that the string of this field is a tag only, not a path on the VM Guest.

4. *Apply* the setting. If the VM Guest is currently running, you need to shut it down to apply the new setting (rebooting the guest is not sufficient).

5. Boot the VM Guest. To mount the shared directory, enter the following command:

```
sudo mount -t 9p -o trans=virtio,version=9p2000.L,rw TAG /MOUNT_POINT
```

To make the shared directory permanently available, add the following line to the `/etc/fstab` file:

```
TAG   /MOUNT_POINT   9p  trans=virtio,version=9p2000.L,rw   0   0
```

13 Configuring Virtual Machines

Virtual Machine Manager's *Details* view offers in-depth information about the VM Guest's complete configuration and hardware equipment. Using this view, you can also change the guest configuration or add and modify virtual hardware. To access this view, open the guest's console in Virtual Machine Manager and either choose *View* › *Details* from the menu, or click the bulb icon in the toolbar.

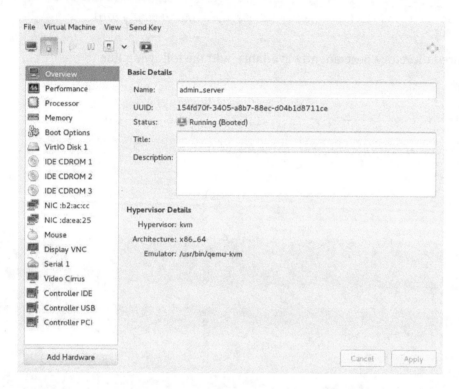

FIGURE 13.1: *DETAILS* VIEW OF A VM GUEST

The left panel of the window lists VM Guest overview and already installed hardware. After clicking an item in the list, you can access its detailed settings in the details view. You can change the hardware parameters to match your needs, then click *Apply* to confirm them. Some changes take effect immediately, while other need reboot of the machine—and `virt-manager` warns you about that fact.

To remove installed hardware form VM Guest, click it in the left panel and then click *Remove* in the bottom right of the window.

To add new hardware, click *Add Hardware* below the left panel, then select the type of the hardware you want to add in the *Add New Virtual Hardware* window. Modify its parameters and confirm with *Finish*.

The following sections describe configuration options for the specific hardware type *being added*. They do not focus on modifying an existing piece of hardware as the options are identical.

13.1 Machine Setup

This section describes hardware components and options that are vital to a VM Guest and you cannot remove them: the processor and memory. It also shows how to view the overview and performance information, and boot options as well.

13.1.1 Overview

Overview shows basic details about VM Guest and the hypervisor.

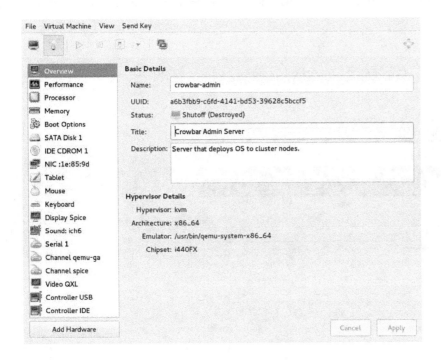

FIGURE 13.2: OVERVIEW DETAILS

Name, Title, and *Description* are editable and help you identify VM Guest in the *Virtual Machine Manager* list of machines.

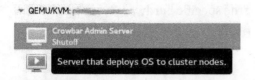

FIGURE 13.3: VM GUEST TITLE AND DESCRIPTION

UUID shows the universally unique identifier of the virtual machine, while *Status* shows its current status—*Running, Paused,* or *Shutoff.*

The *Hypervisor Details* section shows the hypervisor type, CPU architecture, used emulator, and chipset type. None of the hypervisor parameters can be changed.

13.1.2   Performance

Performance shows regularly updated charts of CPU and memory usage, and disk and network I/O.

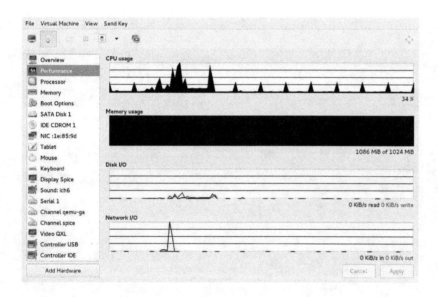

FIGURE 13.4: PERFORMANCE

Tip: Enabling Disabled Charts

Not all the charts in the *Performance* view are enabled by default. To enable disable selected charts, go to *File › View Manager › Polling,* and check the charts that you want to see regularly updated. You can also specify the time interval (in seconds) of the update.

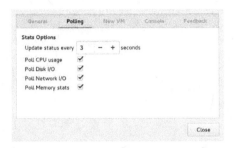

FIGURE 13.5: STATISTICS CHARTS

13.1.3 Processor

Processor includes detailed information about VM Guest processor configuration.

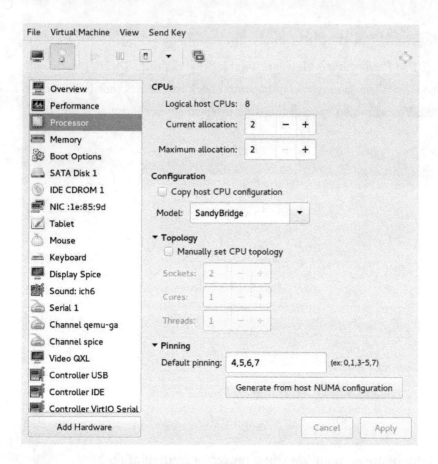

FIGURE 13.6: PROCESSOR VIEW

In the *CPUs* section, you can configure several parameters related to the number of allocated CPUs.

Logical host CPUs

    The real number of CPUs installed on VM Host Server.

Current allocation

    The number of currently allocated CPUs. You can hotplug more CPUs by increasing this value up to the *Maximum allocation* value.

Maximum allocation

    Maximum number of allocable CPUs for the current session. Any change to this value will take effect after next VM Guest reboot.

The *Configuration* section lets you configure the CPU model, topology, and pinning.

When activated, the *Copy host CPU configuration* option uses the host CPU model for VM Guest. Otherwise you need to specify the CPU model from the drop-down list.

After you activate *Manually set CPU topology*, you can specify a custom number of sockets, cores and threads for the CPU.

You can also specify *Default pinning* (see *CPU pinning*) for the CPU, or get the relevant pinning information from the host by clicking *Generate from host NUMA configuration*.

13.1.4 Memory

Memory contains information about the memory that is available to VM Guest.

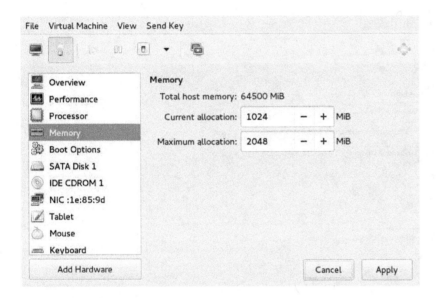

FIGURE 13.7: MEMORY VIEW

Total host memory

   Total amount of memory installed on VM Host Server.

Current allocation

   The amount of memory currently available to VM Guest. You can hotplug more memory by increasing this value up to the value of *Maximum allocation*.

Maximum allocation

   The maximum value to which you can hotplug the currently available memory. Any change to this value will take effect after next VM Guest reboot.

13.1.5 Boot Options

Boot Options introduces options affecting the VM Guest boot process.

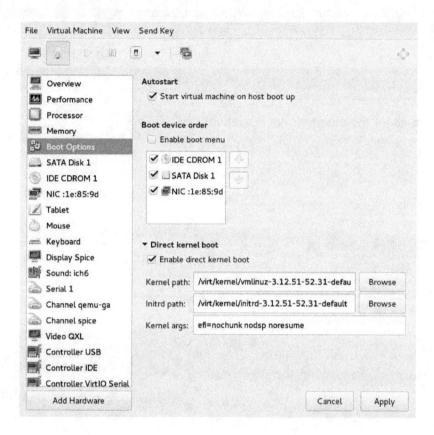

FIGURE 13.8: BOOT OPTIONS

In the *Autostart* section, you can specify whether the virtual machine should automatically start during VM Host Server boot phase.

In the *Boot device order*, activate the devices that will be used for booting VM Guest. You can change their order with the up an down arrows on the right side of the list. If you want to choose from a list of bootable devices on VM Guest startup, activate *Enable boot menu*.

To boot a different kernel than the one on the boot device, activate *Enable direct kernel boot* and specify paths to alternative kernel and initrd placed on the VM Host Server file system. You can also specify kernel arguments that will be passed to the loaded kernel.

13.2 Storage

This section gives you detailed description of configuration options for storage devices. It includes both hard disks and removable media, such as USB or CDROM drives.

PROCEDURE 13.1: ADDING A NEW STORAGE DEVICE

1. Click *Add Hardware* below the left panel, then select *Storage* from the *Add New Virtual Hardware* window.

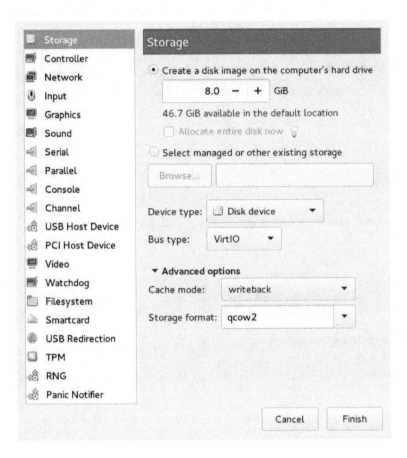

FIGURE 13.9: ADD A NEW STORAGE

2. If you prefer that Virtual Machine Manager creates a disk image for you, activate *Create a disk image on the computer's hard drive* and specify its size in Gigabytes. If you want Virtual Machine Manager to allocate the entire disk space no, activate the relevant option. Note that qcow2 and qed formats do not support full allocation.

If you want to have more control over the disk image creation, activate *Select managed or other existing storage* and click *Browse* to manage storage pools and images. *Choose Storage* window opens, which has almost identical functionality as the *Storage* card described in *Section 12.1, "Managing Storage with Virtual Machine Manager".*

3. After you manage to create and specify the disk image file, specify the *Device type*. It can be either *Disk device, CDROM device, Floppy device*, or *LUN Passthrough*. The latter is required if you want to use an existing SCSI storage directly without adding it into a storage pool.

4. Select the *Bus type* for your device. The list of available options depends on the device type you selected in the previous step. Note that the *Virtio-* based types use paravirtualized drivers.

5. In the *Advanced options* section, select the preferred *Cache mode* and *Storage format*. For more information on cache modes, see *Chapter 14, Disk Cache Modes*.

 Tip: Supported Storage Formats

Only the `raw`, `qcow2`, and `qed` storage formats are supported by SUSE.

6. Confirm your settings with *Finish*. A new storage device appears in the left panel.

13.3 Controllers

This section focuses on adding and configuring new controllers.

PROCEDURE 13.2: ADDING A NEW CONTROLLER

1. Click *Add Hardware* below the left panel, then select *Controller* from the *Add New Virtual Hardware* window.

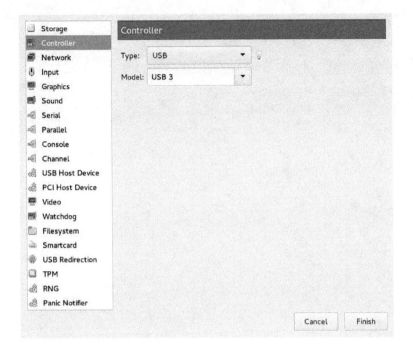

FIGURE 13.10: ADD A NEW CONTROLLER

2. Select the type of the controller. You can choose from *IDE*, *Floppy*, *SCSI*, *SATA*, *VirtIO Serial* (paravirtualized), *USB*, or *CCID* (smart card devices).

3. Optionally, select the model for the controller. It is available for *USB* and *SCSI* types.

4. Confirm your settings with *Finish*. A new controller appears in the left panel.

13.4 Networking

This section describes how to add and configure new network devices.

PROCEDURE 13.3: ADDING A NEW NETWORK DEVICE

1. Click *Add Hardware* below the left panel, then select *Network* from the *Add New Virtual Hardware* window.

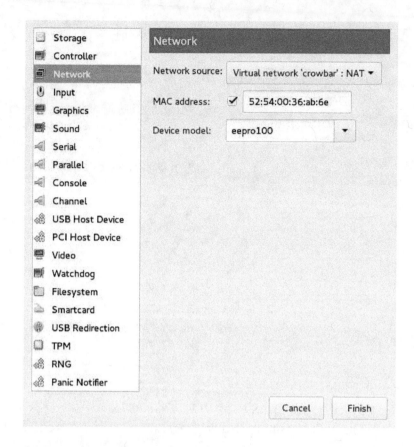

FIGURE 13.11: ADD A NEW CONTROLLER

2. From the *Network source* list, select the source for the network connection. The list includes VM Host Server's available physical network interfaces, network bridges, or network bonds. You can also assign the VM Guest to an already defined virtual network. See *Part II, "Managing Virtual Machines with* libvirt*"* for more information on setting up virtual networks with Virtual Machine Manager.

3. Specify a *MAC address* for the network device. While Virtual Machine Manager pre-fills a random value for your convenience, it is recommended to supply a MAC address appropriate for your network environment to avoid network conflicts.

4. Select a device model from the list. You can either leave the *Hypervisor default,* or specify one of *e1000, eepro100, rtl8139,* or *virtio* models. Note that *virtio* uses paravirtualized drivers.

5. Confirm your settings with *Finish.* A new network device appears in the left panel.

13.5 Input Devices

13.6 Display and Video

13.7 I/O Devices

13.8 Miscellaneouss

13.9 Enabling Seamless and Synchronized Cursor Movement

When you click within a VM Guest's console with the mouse, the cursor is captured by the console window and cannot be used outside the console unless it is explicitly released (by pressing `Alt`–`Ctrl`). To prevent the console from grabbing the key and to enable seamless cursor movement between host and guest instead, add a tablet to the VM Guest.

Adding a tablet has the additional advantage of synchronizing the cursor movement between VM Host Server and VM Guest when using a graphical environment on the guest. With no tablet configured on the guest, you will often see two cursor symbols with one dragging behind the other.

1. Double-click a VM Guest entry in the Virtual Machine Manager to open its console and switch to the *Details* view with *View › Details*.

2. Click *Add Hardware* and choose *Input* and then *EvTouch USB Graphics Tablet* in the pop-up window. Proceed with *Finish*.

3. If you try to add the tablet while the guest is still running, you will be asked whether to enable the tablet after the next reboot. Confirm with *Yes*.

4. When you (re)start the VM Guest, the tablet is available in the VM Guest.

13.10 Adding a CD/DVD-ROM Device with Virtual Machine Manager

KVM supports CD or DVD-ROMs in VM Guest either by directly accessing a physical drive on the VM Host Server or by accessing ISO images. To create an ISO image from an existing CD or DVD, use **dd**:

```
dd if=/dev/cd_dvd_device of=my_distro.iso bs=2048
```

To add a CD/DVD-ROM device to your VM Guest, proceed as follows:

1. Double-click a VM Guest entry in the Virtual Machine Manager to open its console and switch to the *Details* view with *View › Details*.

2. Click *Add Hardware* and choose *Storage* in the pop-up window. Proceed with *Forward*.

3. Change the *Device Type* to *IDE CDROM*.

4. Select *Select Managed or Other Existing Storage*.

   a. To assign the device to a physical medium, enter the path to the VM Host Server's CD/DVD-ROM device (for example, `/dev/cdrom`) next to the *Browse* button. Alternatively you may use the *Browse* button to open a file browser and then click *Browse Local* to select the device. Assigning the device to a physical medium is only possible when the Virtual Machine Manager was started on the VM Host Server.

   b. To assign the device to an existing image, click *Browse* to choose an image from a storage pool. If the Virtual Machine Manager was started on the VM Host Server, you may alternatively choose an image from another location on the file system by clicking *Browse Local*. Select an image and close the file browser with *Choose Volume*.

5. Proceed with *Forward* to review the settings. Apply them with *Finish*, *Yes*, and *Apply*.

6. Reboot the VM Guest to make the new device available. For further information also see *Section 13.12, "Ejecting and Changing Floppy or CD/DVD-ROM Media with Virtual Machine Manager".*

13.11 Adding a Floppy Device with Virtual Machine Manager

Currently KVM only supports the use of floppy disk images—using a physical floppy drive is not supported. Create a floppy disk image from an existing floppy using **dd**:

```
dd if=/dev/fd0 of=/var/lib/libvirt/images/floppy.img
```

To create an empty floppy disk image use one of the following commands:

Raw Image

```
dd if=/dev/zero of=/var/lib/libvirt/images/floppy.img bs=512 count=2880
```

FAT Formatted Image

```
mkfs.msdos -C /var/lib/libvirt/images/floppy.img 1440
```

To add a floppy device to your VM Guest, proceed as follows:

1. Double-click a VM Guest entry in the Virtual Machine Manager to open its console and switch to the *Details* view with *View > Details*.

2. Click *Add Hardware* and choose *Storage* in the pop-up window. Proceed with *Forward*.

3. Change the *Device Type* to *Floppy Disk*.

4. Choose *Select Managed or Other Existing Storage* and click *Browse* to choose an existing image from a storage pool. If Virtual Machine Manager was started on the VM Host Server, you may alternatively choose an image from another location on the file system by clicking *Browse Local*. Select an image and close the file browser with *Choose Volume*.

5. Proceed with *Forward* to review the settings. Apply them with *Finish*, *Yes*, and *Apply*.

6. Reboot the VM Guest to make the new device available. For further information also see *Section 13.12, "Ejecting and Changing Floppy or CD/DVD-ROM Media with Virtual Machine Manager"*.

13.12 Ejecting and Changing Floppy or CD/DVD-ROM Media with Virtual Machine Manager

Regardless of whether you are using the VM Host Server's physical CD/DVD-ROM device or an ISO/floppy image, before you can change the media or image of an existing device in the VM Guest, you first need to `disconnect` the media from the guest.

1. Double-click a VM Guest entry in the Virtual Machine Manager to open its console and switch to the *Details* view with *View > Details*.

2. Choose the Floppy or CD/DVD-ROM device and "eject" the media by clicking *Disconnect*.

3. To "insert" a new media, click *Connect*.

   a. If using the VM Host Server's physical CD/DVD-ROM device, first change the media in the device (this may require unmounting it on the VM Host Server before it can be ejected). Then choose *CD-ROM or DVD* and select the device from the drop-down box.

   b. If using an ISO image, choose *ISO image Location* and select an image by clicking *Browse*. When connecting from a remote host, you may only choose images from existing storage pools.

4. Click *OK* to finish. The new media can now be accessed in the VM Guest.

13.13 Change the Machine Type with `virsh`

By default, when installing with `virt-install` or `vm-install` tools, the machine type for VM Guest is *pc-i440fx*. The machine type is stored in the VM Guest's xml configuration file in `/etc/libvirt/qemu/` in the tag `type` :

```
<type arch='x86_64' machine='pc-i440fx-2.3'>hvm</type>
```

Let's change this value to the new supported q35 machine type. q35 is an Intel* chipset. It includes *PCIe*. q35 supports up to 12 USB ports, and has *SATA* and *IOMMU* support. IRQ routing has also been improved.

1. Check that your VM Guest is inactive:

```
virsh list --inactive
 Id    Name                         State
 --------------------------------------------------
 -     sles11                       shut off
```

2. Edit the configuration for this VM Guest:

```
virsh edit sles11
```

3. Change the value of the `machine` attribute:

```
<type arch='x86_64' machine='pc-q35-2.0'>hvm</type>
```

4. Now you can restart the VM Guest.

```
virsh start sles11
```

5. Now check that the machine type has changed. Log in to the VM Guest as root and run the following command:

```
root # dmidecode | grep Product
Product Name: Standard PC (Q35 + ICH9, 2009)
```

💡 **Tip: Machine Type Update Recommendations**

Whenever the QEMU version on the host system is upgraded (for example when upgrading the VM Host Server to a new service pack), it is also recommended to upgrade the machine type of the VM Guests to the latest available version (check with the command **qemu-system-x86_64 -M help** on the VM Host Server).

The default machine type `pc-i440fx`, for example, is regularly updated. If your VM Guest still runs with a machine type of `pc-i440fx-1.x`, an update to `pc-i440fx-2.x` is strongly recommended. This allows to take advantage of the most recent updates and corrections in the machine definitions, with an eye towards better future-looking compatibility.

13.14 Adding a PCI Device to a VM Guest

You can directly assign host-PCI devices to guests (PCI pass-through). When the PCI device is assigned to one VM Guest, it cannot be used on the host or by another VM Guest unless re-assigned. A prerequisite for this feature is a VM Host Server configuration as described in *Important: Requirements for VFIO and SR-IOV*.

 Note: VFIO vs. KVM PCI Pass-Through

SUSE Linux Enterprise Server currently supports two ways of assigning PCI devices to VM Guests: either via VFIO or via the legacy KVM PCI Pass-Through. Using VFIO is strongly recommended, since it is more stable and secure. Support for the legacy KVM PCI Pass-Through will be removed from future SUSE Linux Enterprise Server releases. See *Section 1.5, "I/O Virtualization"* for more details.

VFIO support is built into libvirt and will automatically be used if the `vfio_pci` driver is loaded (see *Important: Requirements for VFIO and SR-IOV* for setup instructions). In case `vfio_pci` is not loaded, libvirt will automatically fall back to KVM PCI Pass-Through.

13.14.1 Adding a PCI Device with Virtual Machine Manager

The following procedure describes how to add a PCI device to a VM Guest using Virtual Machine Manager:

1. Double-click a VM Guest entry in the Virtual Machine Manager to open its console and switch to the *Details* view with *View > Details*.

2. Click *Add Hardware* and choose the *PCI Host Device* category in the left pane. A list of available PCI devices appears in the right part of the window.

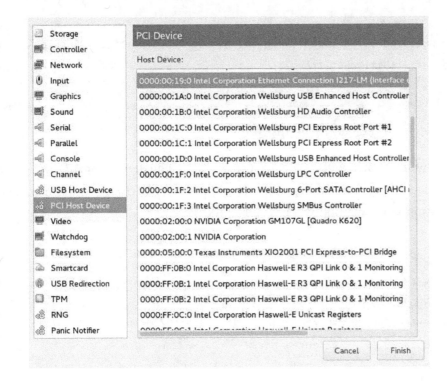

FIGURE 13.12: ADDING A PCI DEVICE

3. From the list of available PCI devices, choose the one you want to pass to the guest. Confirm with *Finish*.

> **💡 Tip: Assigning a PCI Device Requires a VM Guest Shutdown**
>
> Although it is possible to assign a PCI device to a running VM Guest as described above, the device will not become available until you shut down the VM Guest and reboot it afterwards.

13.14.2 Adding a PCI Device with `virsh`

To assign a PCI device to VM Guest with `virsh`, follow these steps:

1. Identify the host PCI device to assign to the guest. In the following example we are assigning a DEC network card to the guest:

```
tux > sudo lspci -nn
```

```
[...]
03:07.0 Ethernet controller [0200]: Digital Equipment Corporation DECchip \
21140 [FasterNet] [1011:0009] (rev 22)
[...]
```

Note down the device ID (03:07.0 in this case).

2. Gather detailed information about the device using **virsh nodedev-dumpxml** *ID* . To get the *ID* , you need to replace colon and period in the device ID (03:07.0) with underscore and prefix the result with "pci_0000_" (pci_0000_03_07_0).

```
tux > virsh nodedev-dumpxml pci_0000_03_07_0
<device>
  <name>pci_0000_03_07_0</name>
  <path>/sys/devices/pci0000:00/0000:00:14.4/0000:03:07.0</path>
  <parent>pci_0000_00_14_4</parent>
  <driver>
    <name>tulip</name>
  </driver>
  <capability type='pci'>
    <domain>0</domain>
    <bus>3</bus>
    <slot>7</slot>
    <function>0</function>
    <product id='0x0009'>DECchip 21140 [FasterNet]</product>
    <vendor id='0x1011'>Digital Equipment Corporation</vendor>
    <numa node='0'/>
  </capability>
</device>
```

Note down the values for domain, bus, and function.

3. Detach the device from the host system prior to attaching it to VM Guest.

```
tux > virsh nodedev-detach pci_0000_03_07_0
  Device pci_0000_03_07_0 detached
```

Tip: Multi-Function PCI Devices

When using a multi-function PCI device that does not support FLR (function level reset) or PM (power management) reset, you need to detach all its functions from the VM Host Server. The whole device must be reset for security reasons. libvirt will refuse to assign the device if one of its functions is still in use by the VM Host Server or another VM Guest.

4. Convert the domain, bus, slot, and function value from decimal to hexadecimal, and prepend 0x to tell the system that the value is hexadecimal. In our example, domain = 0, bus = 3, slot = 7, and function = 0. Their hexadecimal values are:

```
tux > printf %x 0
0
tux > printf %x 3
3
tux > printf %x 7
7
```

This results in domain = 0x0000, bus = 0x03, slot = 0x07 and function = 0x00.

5. Run **virsh edit** on your domain, and add the following device entry in the <devices> section using the values from the previous step:

```
<hostdev mode='subsystem' type='pci' managed='yes'>
  <source>
    <address domain='0x0000' bus='0x03' slot='0x07' function='0x00'/>
  </source>
</hostdev>
```

Tip: managed **vs.** unmanaged

libvirt recognizes two modes for handling PCI devices: they can be either managed or unmanaged. In the managed case, libvirt will handle all the details of unbinding the device from the existing driver if needed, resetting the device, binding it to vfio-pci before starting the domain, etc. When the domain is terminated or the device is removed from the domain, libvirt will unbind from vfio-pci and rebind to the original driver in the case of a managed device. If the device is unmanaged, the user must take care to ensure all of these management aspects of the device are done before assigning it to a domain, and after the device is no longer used by the domain.

In the example above, the managed='yes' option means that the device is managed. To switch the device mode to unmanaged, set managed='no' in the listing above. If you do so, you need to take care of the related driver with the **virsh nodedev-detach** and **virsh nodedev-reattach** commands. That means you need to run **virsh nodedev-detach pci_0000_03_07_0** prior to starting the VM Guest to detach the device from the host. In case the VM Guest is not running, you can make the device available for the host by running **virsh nodedev-reattach pci_0000_03_07_0**.

6. Shut down the VM Guest and restart it to make the assigned PCI device available.

 Tip: SELinux

If you are running SELinux on your VM Host Server, you need to disable it prior to starting the VM Guest with

```
setsebool -P virt_use_sysfs 1
```

13.15 Adding SR-IOV Devices

Single Root I/O Virtualization (*SR-IOV*) capable *PCIe* devices can replicate their resources, so they appear to be multiple devices. Each of these "pseudo-devices" can be assigned to a VM Guest.

SR-IOV is an industry specification that was created by the Peripheral Component Interconnect Special Interest Group (PCI-SIG) consortium. It introduces physical functions (PF) and virtual functions (VF). PFs are full *PCIe* functions used to manage and configure the device. PFs also can move data. VFs lack the configuration and management part—they only can move data and a reduced set of configuration functions. Since VFs do not have all *PCIe* functions, the host operating system or the *Hypervisor* must support *SR-IOV* to be able to access and initialize VFs. The theoretical maximum for VFs is 256 per device (consequently the maximum for a dual-port Ethernet card would be 512). In practice this maximum is much lower, since each VF consumes resources.

13.15.1   Requirements

The following requirements must be met to be able to use *SR-IOV*:

- An *SR-IOV*-capable network card (as of SUSE Linux Enterprise Server 12 SP1, only network cards support *SR-IOV*)

- An AMD64/Intel 64 host supporting hardware virtualization (AMD-V or Intel VT-x), see *Section 7.3, "KVM Hardware Requirements"* for more information

- A chipset that supports device assignment (AMD-Vi or Intel *VT-d*)

- libvirt-0.9.10 or better

- *SR-IOV* drivers must be loaded and configured on the host system

- A host configuration that meets the requirements listed at *Important: Requirements for VFIO and SR-IOV*

- A list of the PCI addresses of the VF(s) that will be assigned to VM Guests

Tip: Checking if a Device is SR-IOV-Capable

The information whether a device is SR-IOV-capable can be obtained from its PCI descriptor by running **lspci**. A device that supports *SR-IOV* reports a capability similar to the following:

```
Capabilities: [160 v1] Single Root I/O Virtualization (SR-IOV)
```

Note: Adding an SR-IOV Device at VM Guest Creation

In case you want to add an SR-IOV device to a VM Guest when initially setting it up, the VM Host Server already needs to be configured as described in *Section 13.15.2, "Loading and Configuring the SR-IOV Host Drivers"*.

13.15.2   Loading and Configuring the SR-IOV Host Drivers

To be able to access and initialize VFs, an SR-IOV-capable driver needs to be loaded on the host system.

1. Before loading the driver, make sure the card is properly detected by running **lspci**. The following example shows the **lspci** output for the dual-port Intel 82576NS network card:

```
tux > sudo /sbin/lspci | grep 82576
01:00.0 Ethernet controller: Intel Corporation 82576NS Gigabit Network
 Connection (rev 01)
01:00.1 Ethernet controller: Intel Corporation 82576NS Gigabit Network
 Connection (rev 01)
04:00.0 Ethernet controller: Intel Corporation 82576NS Gigabit Network
 Connection (rev 01)
04:00.1 Ethernet controller: Intel Corporation 82576NS Gigabit Network
 Connection (rev 01)
```

In case the card is not detected, it is likely that the hardware virtualization support in the BIOS/EFI has not been enabled.

2. Check whether the *SR-IOV* driver is already loaded by running **lsmod**. In the following example a check for the igb driver (for the Intel 82576NS network card) returns a result. That means the driver is already loaded. If the command returns nothing, the driver is not loaded.

```
tux > sudo /sbin/lsmod | egrep "^igb "
igb                   185649  0
```

3. Skip this step if the driver is already loaded.

If the *SR-IOV* driver is not yet loaded, the non-*SR-IOV* driver needs to be removed first, before loading the new driver. Use **rmmod** to unload a driver. The following example unloads the non-*SR-IOV* driver for the Intel 82576NS network card:

```
sudo /sbin/rmmod igbvf
```

Load the *SR-IOV* driver subsequently using the **modprobe** command:

```
sudo /sbin/modprobe igb
```

4. Configure the driver by adding the number of VFs you want to make available and, if necessary, by blacklisting the non-SR-IOV driver:

```
sudo echo -e "options igb max_vfs=8\nblacklist igbvf" >> /etc/modprobe.d/50-
igb/
```

Make sure to replace the example values `igb`, `igbvf` and `50-igb` by values appropriate for your driver.

5. Now make sure the driver is loaded on boot by creating the file `/etc/modules-load.d/igb.conf` with the following content:

```
# Load the igb driver at boot
igb
```

Make sure to replace the example value `igb` by a string appropriate for your driver.

6. Reboot the machine and check if the SR-IOV driver is loaded by re-running the **lspci** command from the first step of this procedure. If the SR-IOV driver was loaded successfully you should see additional lines for the VFs:

```
01:00.0 Ethernet controller: Intel Corporation 82576NS Gigabit Network
 Connection (rev 01)
01:00.1 Ethernet controller: Intel Corporation 82576NS Gigabit Network
 Connection (rev 01)
01:10.0 Ethernet controller: Intel Corporation 82576 Virtual Function (rev 01)
01:10.1 Ethernet controller: Intel Corporation 82576 Virtual Function (rev 01)
01:10.2 Ethernet controller: Intel Corporation 82576 Virtual Function (rev 01)
[...]
```

```
04:00.0 Ethernet controller: Intel Corporation 82576NS Gigabit Network
 Connection (rev 01)
04:00.1 Ethernet controller: Intel Corporation 82576NS Gigabit Network
 Connection (rev 01)
04:10.0 Ethernet controller: Intel Corporation 82576 Virtual Function (rev 01)
04:10.1 Ethernet controller: Intel Corporation 82576 Virtual Function (rev 01)
04:10.2 Ethernet controller: Intel Corporation 82576 Virtual Function (rev 01)
[...]
```

13.15.3   Adding a VF Network Device to an Existing VM Guest

When the *SR-IOV* hardware is properly set up on the VM Host Server, you can add VFs to VM Guests. To do so, you need to collect some data first.

Note: The following procedure is using example data. Make sure to replace it by appropriate data from your setup.

1. Use the **virsh nodedev-list** command to get the PCI address of the VF you want to assign and its corresponding PF. Numerical values from the **lspci** output shown in *Section 13.15.2, "Loading and Configuring the SR-IOV Host Drivers"* (for example `01:00.0` or `04:00.1`) are transformed by adding the prefix "pci_0000_" and by replacing colons and dots with underscores. So a PCI ID listed as "04:00.0" by **lspci** is listed as "pci_0000_04_00_0" by virsh. The following example lists the PCI IDs for the second port of the Intel 82576NS network card:

```
tux > sudo virsh nodedev-list | grep 0000_04_
pci_0000_04_00_0
pci_0000_04_00_1
pci_0000_04_10_0
pci_0000_04_10_1
pci_0000_04_10_2
pci_0000_04_10_3
pci_0000_04_10_4
pci_0000_04_10_5
pci_0000_04_10_6
pci_0000_04_10_7
```

```
pci_0000_04_11_0
pci_0000_04_11_1
pci_0000_04_11_2
pci_0000_04_11_3
pci_0000_04_11_4
pci_0000_04_11_5
```

The first two entries represent the PFs, whereas the other entries represent the VFs.

2. Get more data that will be needed by running the command **virsh nodedev-dumpxml** on the PCI ID of the VF you want to add:

```
tux > sudo virsh nodedev-dumpxml pci_0000_04_10_0
<device>
  <name>pci_0000_04_10_0</name>
  <parent>pci_0000_00_02_0</parent>
  <capability type='pci'>
    <domain>0</domain>
    <bus>4</bus>
    <slot>16</slot>
    <function>0</function>
    <product id='0x10ca'>82576 Virtual Function</product>
    <vendor id='0x8086'>Intel Corporation</vendor>
    <capability type='phys_function'>
      <address domain='0x0000' bus='0x04' slot='0x00' function='0x0'/>
    </capability>
  </capability>
</device>
```

The following data is needed for the next step:

- < domain > 0 < /domain >

- < bus > 4 < /bus >

- < slot > 16 < /slot >

- < function > 0 < /function >

Adding a VF Network Device to an Existing VM Guest

3. Create a temporary XML file (for example `/tmp/vf-interface.xml` containing the data necessary to add a VF network device to an existing VM Guest. The minimal content of the file needs to look like the following:

```
<interface type='hostdev'> ❶
 <source>
  <address type='pci' domain='0' bus='11' slot='16' function='0'2/> ❷
 </source>
</interface>
```

❶ VFs do not get a fixed MAC address; it changes every time the host reboots. When adding network devices the "traditional" way with <hostdev>, it would require to reconfigure the VM Guest's network device after each reboot of the host, because of the MAC address change. To avoid this kind of problem, libvirt introduced the "interface type='hostdev'" directive, which sets up network-specific data *before* assigning the device.

❷ Specify the data you acquired in the previous step here.

4. In case a device is already attached to the host, it cannot be attached to a guest. To make it available for guests, detach it from the host first:

```
virsh nodedev-detach pci_0000_04_10_0
```

5. Last, add the VF interface to an existing VM Guest:

```
virsh attach-device GUEST /tmp/vf-interface.xml --OPTION
```

GUEST needs to be replaced by the domain name, id or uuid of the VM Guest and -- *OPTION* can be one of the following:

`--persistent`

> This option will always add the device to the domain's persistent XML. In addition, if the domain is running, it will be hotplugged.

`--config`

> This option will only affect the persistent XML, even if the domain is running. The device will only show up in the guest on next boot.

--live

> This option will only affect a running domain. If the domain is inactive, the operation will fail. The device is not persisted in the XML and will not be available in the guest on next boot.

--current

> This option affects the current state of the domain. If the domain is inactive, the device is added to the persistent XML and will be available on next boot. If the domain is active, the device is hotplugged but not added to the persistent XML.

> To detach a VF interface, use the **virsh detach-device** command, which also takes the options listed above.

13.15.4 Dynamic Allocation of VFs from a Pool

If you define the PCI address of a VF into a guest's configuration statically as described in *Section 13.15.3, "Adding a VF Network Device to an Existing VM Guest"*, it is hard to migrate such guest to another host. The host must have identical hardware in the same location on the PCI bus, or the guest configuration must be modified prior to each start.

Another approach is to create a `libvirt` network with a device pool that contains all the VFs of an *SR-IOV* device. The guest then references this network, and each time it is started, a single VF is dynamically allocated to it. When the guest is stopped, the VF is returned to the pool, available for another guest.

13.15.4.1 Defining Network with Pool of VFs on VM Host Server

The following example of network definition creates a pool of all VFs for the *SR-IOV* device with its physical function (PF) at the network interface eth0 on the host:

```
<network>
  <name>passthrough</name>
    <forward mode='hostdev' managed='yes'>
      <pf dev='eth0'/>
    </forward>
  </network>
```

To use this network on the host, save the above code to a file, for example `/tmp/passthrough.xml`, and execute the following commands. Remember to replace eth0 with the real network interface name of your *SR-IOV* device's PF:

```
virsh net-define /tmp/passthrough.xml
virsh net-autostart passthrough
virsh net-start passthrough
```

13.15.4.2   Configuring VM Guest to Use VF from the Pool

The following example of guest device interface definition uses a VF of the *SR-IOV* device from the pool created in *Section 13.15.4.1, "Defining Network with Pool of VFs on VM Host Server"*. `libvirt` automatically derives the list of all VFs associated with that PF the first time the guest is started.

```
<interface type='network'>
  <source network='passthrough'>
</interface>
```

To verify the list of associated VFs, run **virsh net-dumpxml passthrough** on the host after the first guest that uses the network with the pool of VFs starts.

```
<network connections='1'>
  <name>passthrough</name>
  <uuid>a6a26429-d483-d4ed-3465-4436ac786437</uuid>
  <forward mode='hostdev' managed='yes'>
    <pf dev='eth0'/>
    <address type='pci' domain='0x0000' bus='0x02' slot='0x10' function='0x1'/>
    <address type='pci' domain='0x0000' bus='0x02' slot='0x10' function='0x3'/>
    <address type='pci' domain='0x0000' bus='0x02' slot='0x10' function='0x5'/>
    <address type='pci' domain='0x0000' bus='0x02' slot='0x10' function='0x7'/>
    <address type='pci' domain='0x0000' bus='0x02' slot='0x11' function='0x1'/>
    <address type='pci' domain='0x0000' bus='0x02' slot='0x11' function='0x3'/>
    <address type='pci' domain='0x0000' bus='0x02' slot='0x11' function='0x5'/>
  </forward>
</network>
```

III Hypervisor-Independent Features

14 Disk Cache Modes

14.1 Disk Interface Cache Modes

Hypervisors allow for various storage caching strategies to be specified when configuring a VM Guest. Each guest disk interface can have one of the following cache modes specified: *writethrough, writeback, none, directsync,* or *unsafe.* If no cache mode is specified, an appropriate default cache mode is used. These cache modes influence how host-based storage is accessed, as follows:

- Read/write data may be cached in the host page cache.

- The guest's storage controller is informed whether a write cache is present, allowing for the use of a flush command.

- Synchronous write mode may be used, in which write requests are reported complete only when committed to the storage device.

- Flush commands (generated by the guest storage controller) may be ignored for performance reasons.

If a disorderly disconnection between the guest and its storage occurs, the cache mode in use will affect whether data loss occurs. The cache mode can also affect disk performance significantly. Additionally, some cache modes are incompatible with live migration, depending on several factors. There are no simple rules about what combination of cache mode, disk image format, image placement, or storage sub-system is best. The user should plan each guest's configuration carefully and experiment with various configurations to determine the optimal performance.

14.2 Description of Cache Modes

cache mode unspecified

In QEMU versions older than v1.2 (for example SLES11 SP2), not specifying a cache mode meant that *writethrough* would be used as the default. Since that version, the various guest storage interfaces have been fixed to handle *writeback* or *writethrough* semantics more correctly, allowing for the default caching mode to be switched to *writeback*. The guest driver for each of `ide`, `scsi`, and `virtio` have within their power to disable the write back cache, causing the caching mode used to revert to *writethrough*. The typical guest's storage drivers will maintain the default caching mode as *writeback*, however.

writethrough

This mode causes the hypervisor to interact with the disk image file or block device with O_DSYNC semantics, where writes are reported as completed only when the data has been committed to the storage device. The host page cache is used in what can be termed a writethrough caching mode. The guest's virtual storage adapter is informed that there is no writeback cache, so the guest would not need to send down flush commands to manage data integrity. The storage behaves as if there is a writethrough cache.

writeback

This mode causes the hypervisor to interact with the disk image file or block device with neither O_DSYNC nor O_DIRECT semantics, so the host page cache is used and writes are reported to the guest as completed when placed in the host page cache, and the normal page cache management will handle commitment to the storage device. Additionally, the guest's virtual storage adapter is informed of the writeback cache, so the guest would be expected to send down flush commands as needed to manage data integrity. Analogous to a raid controller with RAM cache.

none

This mode causes the hypervisor to interact with the disk image file or block device with O_DIRECT semantics, so the host page cache is bypassed and I/O happens directly between the hypervisor userspace buffers and the storage device. Because the actual storage device may report a write as completed when placed in its write queue only, the guest's virtual storage adapter is informed that there is a writeback cache, so the guest would be expected to send down flush commands as needed to manage data integrity. Performance-wise, it is equivalent to direct access to your host's disk.

unsafe

This mode is similar to the `writeback` mode discussed above. The key aspect of this "unsafe" mode, is that all flush commands from the guests are ignored. Using this mode implies that the user has accepted the trade-off of performance over risk of data loss in case of a host failure. Useful, for example, during guest installation, but not for production workloads.

directsync

This mode causes the hypervisor to interact with the disk image file or block device with both O_DSYNC and O_DIRECT semantics, where writes are reported as completed only when the data has been committed to the storage device, and when it is also desirable to bypass the host page cache. Like *writethrough*, it is helpful to guests that do not send flushes when needed. It was the last cache mode added, completing the possible combinations of caching and direct access semantics.

14.3   Data Integrity Implications of Cache Modes

writethrough, none, directsync

These are the safest modes, and considered equally safe, given that the guest operating system is "modern and well behaved", which means that it uses flushes as needed. If you have a suspect guest, use *writethough*, or *directsync*. Note that some file systems are not compatible with `none` or `directsync`, as they do not support O_DIRECT, which these cache modes rely on.

writeback

This mode informs the guest of the presence of a write cache, and relies on the guest to send flush commands as needed to maintain data integrity within its disk image. This is a common storage design which is completely accounted for within modern file systems. But it should be noted that because there is a window of time between the time a write is reported as completed, and that write being committed to the storage device, this mode exposes the guest to data loss in the unlikely case of a host failure.

unsafe

This mode is similar to *writeback* caching except the guest flush commands are ignored, nullifying the data integrity control of these flush commands, and resulting in a higher risk of data loss because of host failure. The name "unsafe" should serve as a warning that there is a much higher potential for data loss because of a host failure than with the other modes. Note that as the guest terminates, the cached data is flushed at that time.

14.4   Performance Implications of Cache Modes

The choice to make full use of the page cache, or to write through it, or to bypass it altogether can have dramatic performance implications. Other factors that influence disk performance include the capabilities of the actual storage system, what disk image format is used, the potential size of the page cache and the IO scheduler used. Additionally, not flushing the write cache increases performance, but with risk, as noted above. As a general rule, high-end systems typically perform best with the cache mode `none`, because of the reduced data copying that occurs. The potential benefit of having multiple guests share the common host page cache, the ratio of reads to writes, and the use of AIO mode `native` (see below) should also be considered.

14.5   Effect of Cache Modes on Live Migration

The caching of storage data and metadata restricts the configurations that support live migration. Currently, only `raw`, `qcow2` and `qed` image formats can be used for live migration. If a clustered file system is used, all cache modes support live migration. Otherwise the only cache mode that supports live migration on read/write shared storage is `none`.

The `libvirt` management layer includes checks for migration compatibility based on several factors. If the guest storage is hosted on a clustered file system, is read-only or is marked sharable, then the cache mode is ignored when determining if migration can be allowed. Otherwise `libvirt` will not allow migration unless the cache mode is set to `none`. However, this restriction can be overridden with the "unsafe" option to the migration APIs, which is also supported by **virsh**, as for example in

```
virsh migrate --live --unsafe
```

 Tip

The cache mode `none` is required for the AIO mode setting `native`. If another cache mode is used, then the AIO mode will silently be switched back to the default `threads`. The guest flush within the host is implemented using `fdatasync()`.

15 VM Guest Clock Settings

Keeping the correct time in a VM Guest is one of the more difficult aspects of virtualization. Keeping the correct time is especially important for network applications and is also a prerequisite to do a live migration of a VM Guest.

 Tip: Timekeeping on the VM Host Server

It is strongly recommended to ensure the VM Host Server keeps the correct time as well, for example, by using NTP (see *Book "Administration Guide", Chapter 21 "Time Synchronization with NTP"* for more information).

15.1 KVM: Using kvm_clock

KVM provides a paravirtualized clock which is currently supported by SUSE Linux Enterprise Server 10 SP3 and newer and RedHat Enterprise Linux 5.4 and newer via the `kvm_clock` driver. It is strongly recommended to use `kvm_clock` when available.

Use the following command inside a VM Guest running Linux to check whether the driver `kvm_clock` has been loaded:

```
tux > sudo dmesg | grep kvm-clock
[    0.000000] kvm-clock: cpu 0, msr 0:7d3a81, boot clock
[    0.000000] kvm-clock: cpu 0, msr 0:1206a81, primary cpu clock
[    0.012000] kvm-clock: cpu 1, msr 0:1306a81, secondary cpu clock
[    0.160082] Switching to clocksource kvm-clock
```

To check which clock source is currently used, run the following command in the VM Guest. It should output `kvm-clock`:

```
cat /sys/devices/system/clocksource/clocksource0/current_clocksource
```

 Important: `kvm-clock` and NTP

When using `kvm-clock`, it is not recommended to use NTP in the VM Guest, as well. Using NTP on the VM Host Server, however, is still recommended.

15.1.1 Other Timekeeping Methods

The paravirtualized `kvm-clock` is currently not for Windows* operating systems. For Windows*, use the `Windows Time Service Tools` for time synchronization (see http://technet.microsoft.com/en-us/library/cc773263%28WS.10%29.aspx for more information).

15.2 Xen Virtual Machine Clock Settings

When booting, virtual machines get their initial clock time from their host. After getting their initial clock time, fully virtual machines manage their time independently from the host. Paravirtual machines manage clock time according to their independent wallclock setting. If the independent wallclock is enabled, the virtual machine manages its time independently and does not synchronize with the host. If the independent wallclock is disabled, the virtual machine periodically synchronizes its time with the host clock.

 Note

> OES 2 NetWare virtual machines manage clock time independently after booting. They do not synchronize with the host clock time.

If a guest operating system is configured for NTP and the virtual machine's independent wallclock setting is disabled, it will still periodically synchronize its time with the host time. This dual type of configuration can result in time drift between virtual machines that need to be synchronized. To effectively use an external time source, such as NTP, for time synchronization on a virtual machine, the virtual machine's independent wallclock setting must be enabled (set to **1**). Otherwise, it will continue to synchronize its time with its host.

PROCEDURE 15.1: VIEWING THE INDEPENDENT WALLCLOCK SETTING

1. Log in to the virtual machine's operating system as `root`.

2. In the virtual machine environment, enter

```
cat /proc/sys/xen/independent_wallclock
```

- **0** means that the virtual machine is getting its time from the host and is not using independent wallclock.

- **1** means that the virtual machine is using independent wallclock and managing its time independently from the host.

1. Log in to the virtual machine environment as `root`.

2. Edit the virtual machine's `/etc/sysctl.conf` file.

3. Add or change the following entry:

```
xen.independent_wallclock=1
```

Enter **1** to enable or **0** to disable the wallclock setting.

4. Save the file and reboot the virtual machine operating system.
   While booting, a virtual machine gets its initial clock time from the host. Then, if the wallclock setting is set to 1 in the `sysctl.conf` file, it manages its clock time independently and does not synchronize with the host clock time.

1. Log in to the virtual machine environment as `root`.

2. Enter the following command:

```
echo "1" > /proc/sys/xen/independent_wallclock
```

Enter **1** to enable or **0** to disable the wallclock setting.

3. Add or change the following entry:

```
xen.independent_wallclock=1
```

Enter **1** to enable or **0** to disable the wallclock setting.

Although the current status of the independent wallclock changes immediately, its clock time might not be immediately synchronized. The setting persists until the virtual machine reboots. Then, it gets its initial clock time from the host and uses the independent wallclock according to the setting specified in the `sysctl.conf` file.

16 libguestfs

*Virtual Machine*s consist of disk images and definition files. Manually accessing and manipulating these guest components (outside of normal hypervisor processes) is possible, but inherently dangerous and risks compromising data integrity. libguestfs is a C library and corresponding set of tools designed for safely accessing and modifying *Virtual Machine* disk images - outside of normal hypervisor processes, but without the risk normally associated with manual editing.

16.1 VM Guest Manipulation Overview

16.1.1 VM Guest Manipulation Risk

As disk images and definition files are simply another type of file in a Linux environment, it is possible to use many different tools to access, edit and write to these files. When used correctly, such tools can be an important part of guest adminitration. However, even correct usage of these tools is not without risk. Risks that should be considered when manually manipulating guest disk images include:

- *Data Corruption*: Concurrently accessing images, by the host machine or another node in a cluster, can cause changes to be lost or data corruption to occur if virtualization protection layers are bypassed.

- *Security*: Mounting disk images as loop devices requires root access. While an image is loop mounted, other users and processes can potentially access the disk contents.

- *Administrator Error*: Bypassing virtualization layers correctly requires advanced understanding of virtual components and tools. Failing to isolate the images or failing to clean up properly after changes have been made can lead to further problems once back in virtualization control.

16.1.2 libguestfs Design

libguestfs C library has been designed to safely and securely create, access and modify virtual machine (VM Guest) disk images. It also provides additional language bindings: for Perl [http:// libguestfs.org/guestfs-perl.3.html], Python [http://libguestfs.org/guestfs-python.3.html], PHP (only for 64-bit machines), and Ruby [http://libguestfs.org/guestfs-ruby.3.html]. libguestfs can access VM Guest disk images without needing root and with multiple layers of defense against rogue disk images.

libguestfs provides many different tools designed for accessing and modifying VM Guest disk images and contents. These tools provide such capabilities as: viewing and editing files inside guests, scripting changes to VM Guests, monitoring disk used/free statistics, creating guests, doing V2V migrations, performing backups, cloning VM Guests, formatting disks, and resizing disks.

 Warning: Best Practices

> You must not use libguestfs tools on live virtual machines. Doing so will probably result in disk corruption in the VM Guest. libguestfs tools try to stop you from doing this, but cannot catch all cases.
>
> However most command have the `--ro` (read-only) option. With this option, you can attach a command to a live virtual machine. The results might be strange or inconsistent at times but you will not risk disk corruption.

16.2 Package Installation

libguestfs is shipped through 3 packages:

- libguestfs0: which provides the main C library

- guestfs-data: which contains the kernel and initrd used when launching images (stored in `/usr/lib64/guestfs`)

- guestfs-tools: the core guestfs tools, man pages, and the `/etc/libguestfs-tools.conf` configuration file.

To install guestfs tools on your system run:

```
zypper in guestfs-tools
```

16.3   Guestfs Tools

16.3.1   Modifying Virtual Machines

The set of tools found within the guestfs-tools package is used for accessing and modifying virtual machine disk images. This functionality is provided through a familiar shell interface with built-in safeguards which ensure image integrity. Guestfs tools shells expose all capabilities of the guestfs API, and use the kernel and initrd found in /usr/lib4/guestfs.

16.3.2   Supported File Systems and Disk Images

Guestfs tools support various file systems including:

- Ext2, Ext3, Ext4

- Xfs

- Brtfs

Multiple disk image formats are also supported:

- raw

- qcow2

 Warning: Unsupported File System

Guestfs may also support Windows* file systems (VFAT, NTFS), BSD* and Apple* file systems, and other disk image formats (VMDK, VHDX...). However, these file systems and disk image formats are unsupported on SUSE Linux Enterprise.

16.3.3 `virt-rescue`

virt-rescue is similar to a rescue CD, but for virtual machines, and without the need for a CD. virt-rescue presents users with a rescue shell and some simple recovery tools which can be used to examine and correct problems within a virtual machine or disk image.

```
tux > virt-rescue -a sles.qcow2
Welcome to virt-rescue, the libguestfs rescue shell.


Note: The contents of / are the rescue appliance.
You need to mount the guest's partitions under /sysroot
before you can examine them. A helper script for that exists:
mount-rootfs-and-do-chroot.sh /dev/sda2


><rescue>
[   67.194384] EXT4-fs (sda1): mounting ext3 file system
using the ext4 subsystem
[   67.199292] EXT4-fs (sda1): mounted filesystem with ordered data
mode. Opts: (null)
mount: /dev/sda1 mounted on /sysroot.
mount: /dev bound on /sysroot/dev.
mount: /dev/pts bound on /sysroot/dev/pts.
mount: /proc bound on /sysroot/proc.
mount: /sys bound on /sysroot/sys.
Directory: /root
Thu Jun  5 13:20:51 UTC 2014
(none):~ #
```

You are now running the VM Guest in rescue mode:

```
(none):~ # cat /etc/fstab
devpts   /dev/pts            devpts  mode=0620,gid=5 0 0
proc     /proc               proc    defaults        0 0
sysfs    /sys                sysfs   noauto          0 0
debugfs /sys/kernel/debug debugfs noauto           0 0
usbfs    /proc/bus/usb       usbfs   noauto          0 0
```

```
tmpfs   /run              tmpfs   noauto          0 0
/dev/disk/by-id/ata-QEMU_HARDDISK_QM00001-part1 / ext3 defaults 1 1
```

16.3.4 `virt-resize`

`virt-resize` is used to resize a virtual machine disk, making it larger or smaller overall, and resizing or deleting any partitions contained within.

PROCEDURE 16.1: EXPANDING A DISK

Full step-by-step example: How to expand a virtual machine disk

1. First, with virtual machine powered off, determine the size of the partitions available on this virtual machine:

```
tux >  virt-filesystems --long --parts --blkdevs -h -a sles.qcow2
Name        Type       MBR  Size  Parent
/dev/sda1   partition  83   16G   /dev/sda
/dev/sda    device     -    16G   -
```

2. `virt-resize` cannot do in-place disk modifications—there must be sufficient space to store the resized output disk. Use the **truncate** command to create a file of suitable size:

```
tux >  truncate -s 32G outdisk.img
```

3. Use **virt-resize** to resize the disk image. **virt-resize** requires two mandatory parameters for the input and output images:

```
tux >  virt-resize --expand /dev/sda1 sles.qcow2 outdisk.img
Examining sles.qcow2 ...
**********

Summary of changes:


/dev/sda1: This partition will be resized from 16,0G to 32,0G.  The
    filesystem ext3 on /dev/sda1 will be expanded using the 'resize2fs'
    method.


**********
```

```
Setting up initial partition table on outdisk.img ...

Copying /dev/sda1 ...

◐ 84%

[▓▓▓▓▓▓▓▓▓▓▓▓▓▓▓▓▓▓▓▓▓▓▓▓▓▓▓▓▓▓▓▓▓▓▓▓▓▓▓▓▓▓▓━━━━━]

 00:03

Expanding /dev/sda1 using the 'resize2fs' method ...


Resize operation completed with no errors.  Before deleting the old

disk, carefully check that the resized disk boots and works correctly.
```

4. Confirm the image was resized properly:

```
tux > virt-filesystems --long --parts --blkdevs -h -a outdisk.img

Name        Type       MBR  Size  Parent

/dev/sda1   partition  83   32G   /dev/sda

/dev/sda    device     -    32G   -
```

5. Bring up the VM Guest using the new disk image and confirm correct operation before deleting the old image.

16.3.5   Other virt-* Tools

Various other guestfs tools exist to simplify administrative tasks—such as viewing and editing files, or obtaining information on the virtual machine.

16.3.5.1 `virt-filesystems`

This tool is used to report information regarding file systems, partitions, and logical volumes in a disk image or virtual machine.

```
tux > virt-filesystems -l -a sles.qcow2

Name        Type        VFS    Label  Size         Parent

/dev/sda1   filesystem  ext3   -      17178820608  -
```

16.3.5.2 `virt-ls`

virt-ls lists file names, file sizes, checksums, extended attributes and more from a virtual machine or disk image. Multiple directory names can be given, in which case the output from each is concatenated. To list directories from a libvirt guest, use the `-d` option to specify the name of the guest. For a disk image, use the `-a` option.

```
tux > virt-ls -h -lR -a sles.qcow2 /var/log/
d 0755       4,0K /var/log/
d 0700       4,0K /var/log//YaST2
- 0644       1,9K /var/log//YaST2/mkinitrd.log
- 0644        496 /var/log//YaST2/perl-BL-standalone-log
- 0600       3,2K /var/log//faillog
d 0700       4,0K /var/log//krb5
- 0644        29K /var/log//lastlog
- 0644        496 /var/log//pbl.log
- 0664          0 /var/log//wtmp
d 0755       4,0K /var/log//zypp
```

16.3.5.3 `virt-cat`

virt-cat is a command line tool to display the contents of a file that exists in the named virtual machine (or disk image). Multiple file names can be given, in which case they are concatenated together. Each file name must be a full path, starting at the root directory (starting with '/').

```
tux > virt-cat -a sles.qcow2 /etc/fstab
devpts /dev/pts devpts mode=0620,gid=5 0 0
proc   /proc    proc    defaults      0 0
```

16.3.5.4 `virt-df`

virt-df is a command line tool to display free space on virtual machine file systems. Unlike other tools, it does not just display the size of disk allocated to a virtual machine, but can look inside disk images to show how much space is actually being used.

```
tux > virt-df -a sles.qcow2
```

```
Filesystem                    1K-blocks      Used   Available  Use%
sles.qcow2:/dev/sda1          16381864     520564    15022492   4%
```

16.3.5.5 `virt-edit`

virt-edit is a command line tool capable of editing files that reside in the named virtual machine (or disk image).

16.3.5.6 `virt-tar-in/out`

virt-tar-in unpacks an uncompressed TAR archive into a virtual machine disk image or named libvirt domain. **virt-tar-out** packs a virtual machine disk image directory into a TAR archive.

```
tux >  virt-tar-out -a sles.qcow2 /home homes.tar
```

16.3.5.7 `virt-copy-in/out`

virt-copy-in copies files and directories from the local disk into a virtual machine disk image or named libvirt domain. **virt-copy-out** copies files and directories out of a virtual machine disk image or named libvirt domain.

```
tux >  virt-copy-in -a sles.qcow2 data.tar /tmp/
virt-ls -a sles.qcow2 /tmp/
.ICE-unix
.X11-unix
data.tar
```

16.3.6 `guestfish`

guestfish is a shell and command line tool for examining and modifying virtual machine file systems. It uses libguestfs and exposes all of the functionality of the guestfs API.

Examples of usage:

```
tux >  guestfish -a disk.img <<EOF
```

```
run
list-filesystems
EOF
```

```
guestfish

Welcome to guestfish, the guest filesystem shell for
editing virtual machine filesystems and disk images.

Type: 'help' for help on commands
      'man' to read the manual
      'quit' to quit the shell

><fs> add sles.qcow2
><fs> run
><fs> list-filesystems
/dev/sda1: ext3
><fs> mount /dev/sda1 /
 cat /etc/fstab
devpts   /dev/pts           devpts   mode=0620,gid=5 0 0
proc     /proc              proc     defaults        0 0
sysfs    /sys               sysfs    noauto          0 0
debugfs  /sys/kernel/debug debugfs noauto          0 0
usbfs    /proc/bus/usb      usbfs    noauto          0 0
tmpfs    /run               tmpfs    noauto          0 0
/dev/disk/by-id/ata-QEMU_HARDDISK_QM00001-part1 / ext3 defaults 1 1
```

16.4 Troubleshooting

16.4.1 Environment

When troubleshooting problems within a libguestfs appliance, the environment variable *LIBGUESTFS_DEBUG = 1* can be used to enable debug messages. To output each command/API call in a format that is similar to guestfish commands, use the environment variable *LIBGUESTFS_TRACE = 1*.

16.4.2 `libguestfs-test-tool`

`libguestfs-test-tool` is a test program that checks if basic libguestfs functionality is working. It will print a large amount of diagnostic messages and details of the guestfs environment, then create a test image and try to start it. If it runs to completion successfully, the following message should be seen near the end:

```
===== TEST FINISHED OK =====
```

16.5 External References

- libguestfs.org [http://libguestfs.org]

- libguestfs FAQ [http://libguestfs.org/guestfs-faq.1.html]

IV Managing Virtual Machines with Xen

17 Setting Up a Virtual Machine Host

This section documents how to set up and use SUSE Linux Enterprise Server 12 SP1 as a virtual machine host.

Usually, the hardware requirements for the Dom0 are the same as those for the SUSE Linux Enterprise Server operating system, but additional CPU, disk, memory, and network resources should be added to accommodate the resource demands of all planned VM Guest systems.

 Tip: Resources

Remember that VM Guest systems, like physical machines, perform better when they run on faster processors and have access to more system memory.

Xen virtualization technology is available in SUSE Linux Enterprise Server products based on code path 10 and later. Code path 10 products include Open Enterprise Server 2 Linux, SUSE Linux Enterprise Server 10, SUSE Linux Enterprise Desktop 10, and openSUSE 10.x.

The virtual machine host requires several software packages and their dependencies to be installed. To install all necessary packages, run YaST *Software Management*, select *View > Patterns* and choose *Xen Virtual Machine Host Server* for installation. The installation can also be performed with YaST using the module *Virtualization > Install Hypervisor and Tools*.

After the Xen software is installed, restart the computer and, on the boot screen, choose the newly added option with the Xen kernel.

Updates are available through your update channel. To be sure to have the latest updates installed, run YaST *Online Update* after the installation has finished.

17.1 Best Practices and Suggestions

When installing and configuring the SUSE Linux Enterprise operating system on the host, be aware of the following best practices and suggestions:

* If the host should always run as Xen host, run YaST *System > Boot Loader* and activate the Xen boot entry as default boot section.

- In YaST, click *System > Boot Loader.*

- Change the default boot to the *Xen* label, then click *Set as Default.*

- Click *Finish.*

- For best performance, only the applications and processes required for virtualization should be installed on the virtual machine host.

- When using both iSCSI and OCFS2 to host Xen images, the latency required for OCFS2 default timeouts in SUSE Linux Enterprise Server 12 may not be met. To reconfigure this timeout, run `systemctl configure o2cb` or edit O2CB_HEARTBEAT_THRESHOLD in the system configuration.

- If you intend to use a watchdog device attached to the Xen host, use only one at a time. It is recommended to use a driver with actual hardware integration over a generic software one.

 Note: Hardware Monitoring

The Dom0 Kernel is running virtualized, so tools like `irqbalance` or `lscpu` will not reflect the real hardware characteristics.

17.2 Managing Dom0 Memory

When the host is set up, a percentage of system memory is reserved for the hypervisor, and all remaining memory is automatically allocated to Dom0.

A better solution is to set a default amount of memory for Dom0, so the memory can be allocated appropriately to the hypervisor. An adequate amount would be 20 percent of the total system memory up to 4 GiB. A recommended minimum amount would be 512 MiB

 Warning: Minimum amount of Memory

The minimum amount of memory heavily depends on how many VM Guest(s) the host should handle. So be sure you have enough memory to support all your VM Guests. If the value is too low, the host system may hang when multiple VM Guests use most of the memory.

17.2.1 Setting a Maximum Amount of Memory

1. Determine the amount of memory to set for Dom0.

2. At Dom0, type `xl info` to view the amount of memory that is available on the machine. The memory that is currently allocated by Dom0 can be determined with the command `xl list`.

3. Run *YaST › Boot Loader*.

4. Select the Xen section.

5. In *Additional Xen Hypervisor Parameters*, add `dom0_mem=` *mem_amount* where *mem_amount* is the maximum amount of memory to allocate to Dom0. Add `K`, `M`, or `G`, to specify the size, for example, `dom0_mem=768M`.

6. Restart the computer to apply the changes.

✋ Warning: Xen Dom0 Memory

When using the XL toolstack and the `dom0_mem=` option for the Xen hypervisor in GRUB 2 you need to disable xl *autoballoon* in `etc/xen/xl.conf`, otherwise launching VMs will fail with errors about not being able to balloon down Dom0. So add *autoballoon=0* to `xl.conf` if you have the `dom0_mem=` option specified for Xen. Also see Xen dom0 memory [http://wiki.xen.org/wiki/Xen_Best_Practices#Xen_dom0_dedicated_memory_and_preventing_dom0_memory_ballooning]

17.3 Network Card in Fully Virtualized Guests

In a fully virtualized guest, the default network card is an emulated Realtek network card. However, it also possible to use the split network driver to run the communication between Dom0 and a VM Guest. By default, both interfaces are presented to the VM Guest, because the drivers of some operating systems require both to be present.

When using SUSE Linux Enterprise, only the paravirtualized network cards are available for the VM Guest by default. The following network options are available:

emulated

> To use an emulated network interface like an emulated Realtek card, specify `type=ioemu` in the `vif` device section of the domain xl configuration. An example configuration would look like:

> ```
> vif = [ 'type=ioemu,mac=00:16:3e:5f:48:e4,bridge=br0' ]
> ```

> Find more details about the xl configuration in the `xl.conf` manual page **man 5 xl.conf**.

paravirtualized

> When you specify `type=vif` and do not specify a model or type, the paravirtualized network interface is used:

> ```
> vif = [ 'type=vif,mac=00:16:3e:5f:48:e4,bridge=br0,backen=0' ]
> ```

emulated and paravirtualized

> If the administrator should be offered both options, simply specify both type and model. The xl configuration would look like:

> ```
> vif = [ 'type=ioemu,mac=00:16:3e:5f:48:e4,model=rtl8139,bridge=br0' ]
> ```

> In this case, one of the network interfaces should be disabled on the VM Guest.

17.4 Starting the Virtual Machine Host

If virtualization software is correctly installed, the computer boots to display the GRUB 2 boot loader with a *Xen* option on the menu. Select this option to start the virtual machine host.

Note: Xen and Kdump

In Xen, the hypervisor manages the memory resource. If you need to reserve system memory for a recovery kernel in Dom0, this memory need to be reserved by the hypervisor. Thus, it is necessary to add the parameter `crashkernel=size` to the `kernel` line instead of using the line with the other boot options.

For more information on the crashkernel parameter, see *Book "System Analysis and Tuning Guide", Chapter 17 "Kexec and Kdump", Section 17.4 "Calculating* `crashkernel` *Allocation Size"*.

If the *Xen* option is not on the GRUB 2 menu, review the steps for installation and verify that the GRUB 2 boot loader has been updated. If the installation has been done without selecting the Xen pattern, run the YaST *Software Management*, select the filter *Patterns* and choose *Xen Virtual Machine Host Server* for installation.

After booting the hypervisor, the Dom0 virtual machine starts and displays its graphical desktop environment. If you did not install a graphical desktop, the command line environment appears.

 Tip: Graphics Problems

Sometimes it may happen that the graphics system does not work properly. In this case, add `vga=ask` to the boot parameters. To activate permanent settings, use `vga=mode-0x???` where `???` is calculated as `0x100` + VESA mode from http://en.wikipedia.org/wiki/VESA_BIOS_Extensions, e.g. `vga=mode-0x361`.

Before starting to install virtual guests, make sure that the system time is correct. To do this, configure NTP (Network Time Protocol) on the controlling domain:

1. In YaST select *Network Services* › *NTP Configuration*.

2. Select the option to automatically start the NTP daemon during boot. Provide the IP address of an existing NTP time server, then click *Finish*.

Note: Time Services on Virtual Guests

Hardware clocks commonly are not very precise. All modern operating systems try to correct the system time compared to the hardware time by means of an additional time source. To get the correct time on all VM Guest systems, also activate the network time services on each respective guest or make sure that the guest uses the system time of the host. For more about `Independent Wallclocks` in SUSE Linux Enterprise Server see *Section 15.2, "Xen Virtual Machine Clock Settings"*.

For more information about managing virtual machines, see *Chapter 19, Managing a Virtualization Environment*.

17.5 PCI Pass-Through

To take full advantage of VM Guest systems, it is sometimes necessary to assign specific PCI devices to a dedicated domain. When using fully virtualized guests, this functionality is only available if the chipset of the system supports this feature, and if it is activated from the BIOS.

This feature is available from both AMD* and Intel*. For AMD machines, the feature is called *IOMMU*; in Intel speak, this is *VT-d*. Note that Intel-VT technology is not sufficient to use this feature for fully virtualized guests. To make sure that your computer supports this feature, ask your supplier specifically to deliver a system that supports PCI Pass-Through.

LIMITATIONS

- Some graphics drivers use highly optimized ways to access DMA. This is not supported, and thus using graphics cards may be difficult.

- When accessing PCI devices behind a *PCIe* bridge, all of the PCI devices must be assigned to a single guest. This limitation does not apply to *PCIe* devices.

- Guests with dedicated PCI devices cannot be migrated live to a different host.

The configuration of PCI Pass-Through is twofold. First, the hypervisor must be informed at boot time that a PCI device should be available for reassigning. Second, the PCI device must be assigned to the VM Guest.

17.5.1 Configuring the Hypervisor for PCI Pass-Through

1. Select a device to reassign to a VM Guest. To do this, run **lspci** and read the device number. For example, if **lspci** contains the following line:

```
06:01.0 Ethernet controller: Digital Equipment Corporation DECchip 21142/43
 (rev 41)
```

In this case, the PCI number is (06:01.0).

2. Run *YaST › System › Boot Loader.*

3. Select the Xen section and press *Edit.*

4. Add the PCI number to the *Optional Kernel Command Line Parameter* line:

```
pciback.hide=(06:01.0)
```

5. Press *OK* and exit YaST.

6. Reboot the system.

7. Check if the device is in the list of assignable devices with the command

```
xl pci-assignable-list
```

17.5.1.1   Dynamic Assignment with xl

If you want to avoid restarting the host system, you can use dynamic assignment with xl to use PCI Pass-Through.

Begin by making sure that dom0 has the pciback module loaded:

```
modprobe pciback
```

Then make a device assignable by using **xl pci-assignable-add**. For example, if you wanted to make the device *06:01.0* available for guests, you should type the following:

```
xl pci-assignable-add 06:01.0
```

17.5.2   Assigning PCI Devices to VM Guest Systems

There are several possibilities to dedicate a PCI device to a VM Guest:

Adding the device while installing:

During installation, add the `pci` line to the configuration file:

```
pci=['06:01.0']
```

Hotplugging PCI devices to VM Guest systems

The command `xl` can be used to add or remove PCI devices on the fly. To add the device with number `06:01.0` to a guest with name `sles12` use:

```
xl pci-attach sles12 06:01.0
```

Adding the PCI device to Xend

To add the device to the guest permanently, add the following snippet to the guest configuration file:

```
pci = [ '06:01.0,power_mgmt=1,permissive=1' ]
```

After assigning the PCI device to the VM Guest, the guest system must care for the configuration and device drivers for this device.

17.5.3   VGA Pass-Through

Xen 4.0 and newer supports VGA graphics adapter pass-through on fully virtualized VM Guests. The guest can take full control of the graphics adapter with high-performance full 3D and video acceleration.

LIMITATIONS

- VGA Pass-Through functionality is similar to PCI Pass-Through and as such also requires *IOMMU* (or Intel VT-d) support from the mainboard chipset and BIOS.

- Only the primary graphics adapter (the one that is used when you power on the computer) can be used with VGA Pass-Through.

- VGA Pass-Through is supported only for fully virtualized guests. Paravirtual guests (PV) are not supported.

- The graphics card cannot be shared between multiple VM Guests using VGA Pass-Through — you can dedicate it to one guest only.

To enable VGA Pass-Through, add the following settings to your fully virtualized guest configuration file:

```
gfx_passthru=1
pci=['yy:zz.n']
```

where `yy:zz.n` is the PCI controller ID of the VGA graphics adapter as found with **lspci -v** on Dom0.

17.5.4   Troubleshooting

In some circumstances, problems may occur during the installation of the VM Guest. This section describes some known problems and their solutions.

During boot, the system hangs

The software I/O translation buffer allocates a large chunk of low memory early in the bootstrap process. If the requests for memory exceed the size of the buffer it usually results in a hung boot process. To check if this is the case, switch to console 10 and check the output there for a message similar to

```
kernel: PCI-DMA: Out of SW-IOMMU space for 32768 bytes at device 000:01:02.0
```

In this case you need to increase the size of the `swiotlb`. Add `swiotlb=128` on the cmdline of Dom0. Note that the number can be adjusted up or down to find the optimal size for the machine.

 Note: swiotlb a PV guest

The `swiotlb=force` kernel parameter is required for DMA access to work for PCI devices on a PV guest. For more information about IOMMU and the `swiotlb` option see the file `boot-options.txt` from the package `kernel-source`.

17.5.5   For More Information

There are several resources on the Internet that provide interesting information about PCI Pass-Through:

- http://wiki.xensource.com/xenwiki/VTdHowTo

- http://software.intel.com/en-us/articles/intel-virtualization-technology-for-directed-io-vt-d-enhancing-intel-platforms-for-efficient-virtualization-of-io-devices/

- http://support.amd.com/TechDocs/48882_IOMMU.pdf

18 Virtual Networking

A VM Guest system needs some means to communicate either with other VM Guest systems or with a local network. The network interface to the VM Guest system is made of a split device driver, which means that any virtual Ethernet device has a corresponding network interface in Dom0. This interface is set up to access a virtual network that is run in Dom0. The bridged virtual network is fully integrated into the system configuration of SUSE Linux Enterprise Server and can be configured with YaST.

When installing a Xen VM Host Server, a bridged network configuration will be proposed during normal network configuration. The user can choose to change the configuration during the installation and customize it to the local needs.

If desired, Xen VM Host Server can be installed after performing a default Physical Server installation using the `Install Hypervisor and Tools` module in YaST. This module will prepare the system for hosting virtual machines, including invocation of the default bridge networking proposal.

In case the necessary packages for a Xen VM Host Server are installed manually with `rpm` or `zypper`, the remaining system configuration has to be done by the administrator manually or with the help of YaST.

The network scripts that are provided by Xen are not used by default in SUSE Linux Enterprise Server. They are only delivered for reference but disabled. The network configuration that is used in SUSE Linux Enterprise Server is done by means of the YaST system configuration similar to the configuration of network interfaces in SUSE Linux Enterprise Server.

18.1 Virtual Bridges

When using SUSE Linux Enterprise Server, the system configures one bridge for each physical network device by default. For each virtual bridge, a physical Ethernet device is enslaved, and the IP address assigned to the bridge.

To add a new bridge, for example after installing an additional Ethernet device, or to create a bridge that is not connected to a real network, proceed as follows:

1. Start *yast2* › *System* › *Network Settings*.

2. Click the tab *Overview* and press *Add*.

3. Select *Device Type Bridge*. The parameter *Configuration Name* will be set to the next free number. Click *Next*.

4. Either use *Dynamic Address (DHCP)* as selected by default, or assign a static IP address to the bridge. Using *Dynamic Address* is only useful when also assigning a device to the bridge that is connected to some DHCP server.

   If you intend to create a virtual bridge that has no connection to a real Ethernet device, use *Statically assigned IP Address*. In this case, it is a good idea to use addresses from the private IP address ranges, for example, `192.168.x.x` or `10.x.x.x`.

   To create a bridge that should only serve as a connection between the different guests without connection to the host system, set the IP address to `0.0.0.0` and the netmask to `255.255.255.255`. The network scripts handle this special address as an unset IP address.

After the bridge is created, it may be used by any of the Xen VM Guest systems. A purely virtual bridge without connection to a real network device is good to provide fast network connections between different VM Guest systems. If you provide a `DHCP` server on Dom0 that also defines routing information to the respective guest for the bridge, the network setup of the respective VM Guest is simplified.

18.2   Network Devices for Guest Systems

The Xen hypervisor can provide different types of network interfaces to the VM Guest systems. The preferred network device should be a paravirtualized network interface. This yields the highest transfer rates with the lowest system requirements. Up to eight network interfaces may be provided for each VM Guest.

Systems that are not aware of paravirtualized hardware may not have this option. To connect systems to a network that can only run fully virtualized, several emulated network interfaces are available. The following emulations are at your disposal:

- Realtek 8139 (PCI). This is the default emulated network card.

- AMD PCnet32 (PCI)

- NE2000 (PCI)

- NE2000 (ISA)

- Intel e100 (PCI)

- Intel e1000 and its variants e1000-82540em, e1000-82544gc, e1000-82545em (PCI)

All these network interfaces are software interfaces. Because every network interface must have a unique MAC address, an address range has been assigned to Xensource that can be used by these interfaces.

 Tip: Virtual Network Interfaces and MAC Addresses

The default configuration of MAC addresses in virtualized environments creates a random MAC address that looks like 00:16:3E:xx:xx:xx. Normally, the amount of available MAC addresses should be big enough to get only unique addresses. However, if you have a very big installation, or if you want to make sure that no problems arise from random MAC address assignment, you can also manually assign these addresses.

For debugging or system management purposes, it may be useful to know which virtual interface in Dom0 is connected to which Ethernet device in a running guest. This information may be read from the device naming in Dom0. All virtual devices follow the rule `vif<domain number>.<interface_number>`.

For example, if you want to know the device name for the third interface (eth2) of the VM Guest with id 5, the device in Dom0 would be `vif5.2`. To obtain a list of all available interfaces, run the command `ip a`.

The device naming does not contain any information about which bridge this interface is connected to. However, this information is available in Dom0. To get an overview about which interface is connected to which bridge, run the command `brctl show`. The output may look like the following:

```
# brctl show
bridge name     bridge id               STP enabled     interfaces
br0             8000.001cc0309083       no              eth0
                                                        vif2.1
br1             8000.000476f060cc       no              eth1
                                                        vif2.0
br2             8000.000000000000       no
```

In this example, there are three configured bridges: br0, br1 and br2. Currently, br0 and br1 each have a real Ethernet device added: eth0 and eth1, respectively. There is one VM Guest running with the id 2 that has two Ethernet devices available. eth0 on the VM Guest is bridged with eth1 on the VM Host Server and eth1 on the VM Guest is connected to eth0 on the VM Host Server. The third bridge with the name br2 is not connected to any VM Guest nor any real Ethernet device.

18.3 Host-Based Routing in Xen

Xen can be set up to use host-based routing in the controlling Dom0. Unfortunately, this is not yet well supported from YaST and requires quite an amount of manual editing of configuration files. Thus, this is a task that requires an advanced administrator.

The following configuration will only work when using fixed IP addresses. Using DHCP is not practicable with this procedure, because the IP address must be known to both, the VM Guest and the VM Host Server system.

The easiest way to create a routed guest is to change the networking from a bridged to a routed network. As a requirement to the following procedures, a VM Guest with a bridged network setup must be installed. For example, the VM Host Server is named earth with the IP 192.168.1.20, and the VM Guest has the name alice with the IP 192.168.1.21.

PROCEDURE 18.1: CONFIGURING A ROUTED IPV4 VM GUEST

1. Make sure that alice is shut down. Use `xl` commands to shut down and check.

2. Prepare the network configuration on the VM Host Server earth:

   a. Create a hotplug interface that will be used to route the traffic. To accomplish this, create a file named `/etc/sysconfig/network/ifcfg-alice.0` with the following content:

   ```
   NAME="Xen guest alice"
   BOOTPROTO="static"
   STARTMODE="hotplug"
   ```

   b. Edit the file `/etc/sysconfig/SuSEfirewall2` and add the following configurations:

      • Add alice.0 to the devices in FW_DEV_EXT:

```
FW_DEV_EXT="br0 alice.0"
```

- Switch on the routing in the firewall:

```
FW_ROUTE="yes"
```

- Tell the firewall which address should be forwarded:

```
FW_FORWARD="192.168.1.21/32,0/0"
```

- Finally, restart the firewall with the command:

```
sudo systemctl restart SuSEfirewall2
```

c. Add a static route to the interface of alice. To accomplish this, add the following line to the end of /etc/sysconfig/network/routes:

```
192.168.1.21  -  -  alice.0
```

d. To make sure that the switches and routers that the VM Host Server is connected to know about the routed interface, activate proxy_arp on earth. Add the following lines to /etc/sysctl.conf:

```
net.ipv4.conf.default.proxy_arp = 1
net.ipv4.conf.all.proxy_arp = 1
```

e. Activate all changes with the commands:

```
sudo systemctl restart systemd-sysctl wicked
```

3. Proceed with configuring the Xen configuration of the VM Guest by changing the vif interface configuration for alice as described in *Section 19.1, "XL—Xen Management Tool"*. Make the following changes to the text file you generate during the process:

a. Remove the snippet

```
bridge=br0
```

b. And add the following one:

```
vifname=vifalice.0
```

or

```
vifname=vifalice.0=emu
```

for a fully virtualized domain.

   c. Change the script that is used to set up the interface to the following:

```
script=/etc/xen/scripts/vif-route-ifup
```

   d. Activate the new configuration and start the VM Guest.

4. The remaining configuration tasks must be accomplished from inside the VM Guest.

   a. Open a console to the VM Guest with **xl console** *domain* and log in.

   b. Check that the guest IP is set to 192.168.1.21.

   c. Provide VM Guest with a host route and a default gateway to the VM Host Server. Do this by adding the following lines to /etc/sysconfig/network/routes:

```
192.168.1.20 - - eth0
default 192.168.1.20 - -
```

5. Finally, test the network connection from the VM Guest to the world outside and from the network to your VM Guest.

18.4 Creating a Masqueraded Network Setup

Creating a masqueraded network setup is quite similar to the routed setup. However, there is no proxy_arp needed, and some firewall rules are different. To create a masqueraded network to a guest dolly with the IP address 192.168.100.1 where the host has its external interface on br0, proceed as follows. For easier configuration, only the already installed guest is modified to use a masqueraded network:

PROCEDURE 18.2: CONFIGURING A MASQUERADED IPV4 VM GUEST

1. Shut down the VM Guest system with **xl shutdown** *domain*.

2. Prepare the network configuration on the VM Host Server:

   a. Create a hotplug interface that will be used to route the traffic. To accomplish this, create a file named /etc/sysconfig/network/ifcfg-dolly.0 with the following content:

   ```
   NAME="Xen guest dolly"
   BOOTPROTO="static"
   STARTMODE="hotplug"
   ```

   b. Edit the file /etc/sysconfig/SuSEfirewall2 and add the following configurations:

   - Add dolly.0 to the devices in FW_DEV_DMZ:

   ```
   FW_DEV_DMZ="dolly.0"
   ```

   - Switch on the routing in the firewall:

   ```
   FW_ROUTE="yes"
   ```

   - Switch on masquerading in the firewall:

   ```
   FW_MASQUERADE="yes"
   ```

   - Tell the firewall which network should be masqueraded:

   ```
   FW_MASQ_NETS="192.168.100.1/32"
   ```

   - Remove the networks from the masquerading exceptions:

   ```
   FW_NOMASQ_NETS=""
   ```

   - Finally, restart the firewall with the command:

   ```
   sudo systemctl restart SuSEfirewall2
   ```

c. Add a static route to the interface of dolly. To accomplish this, add the following line to the end of `/etc/sysconfig/network/routes`:

```
192.168.100.1 - - dolly.0
```

d. Activate all changes with the command:

```
sudo systemctl restart wicked
```

3. Proceed with configuring the Xen configuration of the VM Guest.

a. Change the vif interface configuration for dolly as described in *Section 19.1, "XL—Xen Management Tool"*.

b. Remove the entry:

```
bridge=br0
```

c. And add the following one:

```
vifname=vifdolly.0
```

d. Change the script that is used to set up the interface to the following:

```
script=/etc/xen/scripts/vif-route-ifup
```

e. Activate the new configuration and start the VM Guest.

4. The remaining configuration tasks need to be accomplished from inside the VM Guest.

a. Open a console to the VM Guest with **xl console** *domain* and log in.

b. Check whether the guest IP is set to 192.168.100.1.

c. Provide VM Guest with a host route and a default gateway to the VM Host Server. Do this by adding the following lines to `/etc/sysconfig/network/routes`:

```
192.168.1.20 - - eth0
default 192.168.1.20 - -
```

5. Finally, test the network connection from the VM Guest to the outside world.

18.5 Special Configurations

There are many network configuration possibilities available to Xen. The following configurations are not activated by default:

18.5.1 Bandwidth Throttling in Virtual Networks

With Xen, you may limit the network transfer rate a virtual guest may use to access a bridge. To configure this, you need to modify the VM Guest configuration as described in *Section 19.1, "XL—Xen Management Tool"*.

In the configuration file, first search for the device that is connected to the virtual bridge. The configuration looks like the following:

```
vif = [ 'mac=00:16:3e:4f:94:a9,bridge=br0' ]
```

To add a maximum transfer rate, add a parameter `rate` to this configuration as in:

```
vif = [ 'mac=00:16:3e:4f:94:a9,bridge=br0,rate=100Mb/s' ]
```

Note that the rate is either `Mb/s` (megabits per second) or `MB/s` (megabytes per second). In the above example, the maximum transfer rate of the virtual interface is 100 megabits. By default, there is no limitation to the bandwidth of a guest to the virtual bridge.

It is even possible to fine-tune the behavior by specifying the time window that is used to define the granularity of the credit replenishment:

```
vif = [ 'mac=00:16:3e:4f:94:a9,bridge=br0,rate=100Mb/s@20ms' ]
```

18.5.2 Monitoring the Network Traffic

To monitor the traffic on a specific interface, the little application `iftop` is a nice program that displays the current network traffic in a terminal.

When running a Xen VM Host Server, you need to define the interface that is monitored. The interface that Dom0 uses to get access to the physical network is the bridge device, for example br0. This, however, may vary on your system. To monitor all traffic to the physical interface, run a terminal as root and use the command:

```
iftop -i br0
```

To monitor the network traffic of a special network interface of a specific VM Guest, supply the correct virtual interface. For example, to monitor the first Ethernet device of the domain with id 5, use the command:

```
ftop -i vif5.0
```

To quit **iftop**, press the key ⌨Q. More options and possibilities are available in the manual page **man 8 iftop**.

18.5.3   Using VLAN Interfaces

Sometimes, it is necessary to create a private connection either between two Xen hosts or between VM Guest systems. For example, if you want to migrate VM Guest to hosts in a different network segment, or if you want to create a private bridge that only VM Guest systems may connect to, even when running on different VM Host Server systems. An easy way to build such connections is to set up VLAN networks.

VLAN interfaces are commonly set up on the VM Host Server and either interconnect the different VM Host Server systems, or they may be set up as a physical interface to an otherwise virtual-only bridge. It is even possible to create a bridge with a VLAN as a physical interface that has no IP address in the VM Host Server. That way, the guest systems have no possibility to access Dom0 over this network.

Run the YaST module *System › Network Settings*. Follow this procedure to actually set up the VLAN device:

PROCEDURE 18.3: SETTING UP VLAN INTERFACES WITH YAST

1. Press *Add* to create a new network interface.

2. In the *Hardware Dialog*, select *Device Type VLAN*.

3. Change the value of *Configuration Name* to the ID of your VLAN. Note that VLAN ID 1 is commonly used for management purposes.

4. Press *Next*.

5. Select the interface that the VLAN device should connect to below *Real Interface for VLAN*. If the desired interface does not appear in the list, first set up this interface without an IP Address.

6. Select the desired method for assigning an IP address to the VLAN device.

7. Press *Next* to finish the configuration.

It is also possible to use the VLAN interface as a physical interface of a bridge. This makes it possible to connect several VM Host Server-only networks and allows to live-migrate VM Guest systems that are connected to such a network.

YaST does not always allow to set no IP address. However, this may be a desired feature especially if VM Host Server-only networks should be connected. In this case, use the special address `0.0.0.0` with netmask `255.255.255.255`. The system scripts handle this address as no IP address set.

Using VLAN Interfaces

19 Managing a Virtualization Environment

Apart from using the recommended `libvirt` library (*Part II, "Managing Virtual Machines with libvirt"*), you can manage Xen guest domains with the **xl** tool from the command line.

19.1 XL—Xen Management Tool

The **xl** program is a tool for managing Xen guest domains. It is based on the LibXenlight library, and can be used for general domain management, such as domain creation, listing, pausing, or shutting down. Usually you need to be root to execute **xl** commands.

 Note

xl can only manage running guest domains specified by their configuration file. If a guest domain is not running, you cannot manage it with **xl**.

 Tip

To allow users to continue to have managed guest domains in the way the obsolete **xm** command allowed, we now recommend using `libvirt`'s **virsh** and **virt-manager** tools. For more information, see *Part II, "Managing Virtual Machines with libvirt"*.

xl operations rely upon `xenstored` and `xenconsoled` services. Make sure you start

```
systemctl start xencommons
```

at boot time to initialize all the daemons required by **xl**.

 Tip: Set up a `xenbr0` **Network Bridge in the Host Domain**

In the most common network configuration, you need to set up a bridge in the host domain named `xenbr0` to have a working network for the guest domains.

The basic structure of every **xl** command is:

```
xl <subcommand> [options] domain_id
```

where <subcommand> is the xl command to run, domain_id is the ID number assigned to a domain or the name of the virtual machine, and **OPTIONS** indicates subcommand-specific options.

For a complete list of the available **xl** subcommands, run **xl help**. For each command, there is a more detailed help available that is obtained with the extra parameter --help. More information about the respective subcommands is available in the manual page of **xl**.

For example, the **xl list --help** displays all options that are available to the list command. As an example, the **xl list** command displays the status of all virtual machines.

```
# xl list
Name                        ID    Mem VCPUs      State   Time(s)
Domain-0                     0    457   2        r-----   2712.9
sles12                       7    512   1        -b----     16.3
opensuse                          512   1                   12.9
```

The *State* information indicates if a machine is running, and in which state it is. The most common flags are r (running) and b (blocked) where blocked means it is either waiting for IO, or sleeping because there is nothing to do. For more details about the state flags, see **man 1 xl**.

Other useful **xl** commands include:

- **xl create** creates a virtual machine from a given configuration file.

- **xl reboot** reboots a virtual machine.

- **xl destroy** immediately terminates a virtual machine.

- **xl block-list** displays all virtual block devices attached to a virtual machine.

19.1.1   Guest Domain Configuration File

When operating domains, **xl** requires a domain configuration file for each domain. The typical directory to store such configuration files is /etc/xen/.

A domain configuration file is a plain text file. It consists of several key=value pairs. Some keys are mandatory, some are general and apply to any guest, and some apply only to a specific guest type (para or fully virtualized). A value can either be a `"string"` surrounded by single or double quotes, a number, a boolean value, or a list of several values enclosed in brackets `[ value1, value2, ... ]`.

EXAMPLE 19.1: GUEST DOMAIN CONFIGURATION FILE

```
# less /etc/xen/sled12.cfg
name= "sled12"
builder = "hvm"
vncviewer = 1
memory = 512
disk = [ '/var/lib/xen/images/sled12.raw,,hda', '/dev/cdrom,,hdc,cdrom' ]
vif = [ 'mac=00:16:3e:5f:48:e4,model=rtl8139,bridge=br0' ]
boot = "n"
```

To start such domain, run **xl create /etc/xen/sled12.cfg**.

19.2 Automatic Start of Guest Domains

To make a guest domain start automatically after the host system boots, follow these steps:

1. Create the domain configuration file if it does not exist, and save it in the `/etc/xen/` directory, for example `/etc/xen/domain_name.cfg`.

2. Make a symbolic link of the guest domain configuration file in the `auto/` subdirectory.

   ```
   ln -s /etc/xen/domain_name.cfg /etc/xen/auto/domain_name.cfg
   ```

3. On the next system boot, the guest domain defined in `domain_name.cfg` will be started.

19.3 Event Actions

In the guest domain configuration file, you can define actions to be performed on a predefined set of events. For example, to tell the domain to restart itself after it is powered off, include the following line in its configuration file:

```
on_poweroff="restart"
```

A list of predefined events for a guest domain follows:

LIST OF EVENTS

on_poweroff

> Specifies what should be done with the domain if it shuts itself down.

on_reboot

> Action to take if the domain shuts down with a reason code requesting a reboot.

on_watchdog

> Action to take if the domain shuts down because of a Xen watchdog timeout.

on_crash

> Action to take if the domain crashes.

For these events, you can define one of the following actions:

LIST OF RELATED ACTIONS

destroy

> Destroy the domain.

restart

> Destroy the domain and immediately create a new domain with the same configuration.

rename-restart

> Rename the domain that terminated, and then immediately create a new domain with the same configuration as the original.

preserve

> Keep the domain. It can be examined, and later destroyed with **xl destroy**.

coredump-destroy

> Write a core dump of the domain to `/var/xen/dump/NAME` and then destroy the domain.

coredump-restart

Write a core dump of the domain to `/var/xen/dump/NAME` and then restart the domain.

19.4 Saving Virtual Machines

PROCEDURE 19.1: SAVE A VIRTUAL MACHINE'S CURRENT STATE

1. Make sure the virtual machine to be saved is running.

2. In the host environment, enter

```
xl save ID state-file
```

where `ID` is the virtual machine ID you want to save, and `state-file` is the name you specify for the memory state file. By default, the domain will no longer be running after you create its snapshot. Use `-c` to keep it running even after you create the snapshot.

19.5 Restoring Virtual Machines

PROCEDURE 19.2: RESTORE A VIRTUAL MACHINE'S CURRENT STATE

1. Make sure the virtual machine to be restored has not been started since you ran the save operation.

2. In the host environment, enter

```
xl restore state-file
```

where `state-file` is the previously saved memory state file. By default, the domain will be running after it is restored. To pause it after the restore, use `-p`.

19.6 Virtual Machine States

A virtual machine's state can be displayed by viewing the results of the **xl list** command, which abbreviates the state using a single character.

- **r** - running - The virtual machine is currently running and consuming allocated resources.

- **b** - blocked - The virtual machine's processor is not running and not able to run. It is either waiting for I/O or has stopped working.

- **p** - paused - The virtual machine is paused. It does not interact with the hypervisor but still maintains its allocated resources, such as memory.

- **s** - shutdown - The guest operating system is in the process of being shut down, rebooted, or suspended, and the virtual machine is being stopped.

- **c** - crashed - The virtual machine has crashed and is not running.

- **d** - dying - The virtual machine is in the process of shutting down or crashing.

20 Block Devices in Xen

20.1 Mapping Physical Storage to Virtual Disks

The disk(s) specification for a Xen domain in the domain configuration file is as straightforward as the following example:

```
disk = [ 'format=raw,vdev=hdc,access=ro,devtype=cdrom,target=/root/image.iso' ]
```

It defines a disk block device based on the /root/image.iso disk image file. The disk will be seen as hdc by the guest, with read-only (ro) access. The type of the device is cdrom with raw format.

The following example defines an identical device, but using simplified positional syntax:

```
disk = [ '/root/image.iso,raw,hdc,ro,cdrom' ]
```

You can include more disk definitions in the same line, each one separated by a comma. If a parameter is not specified, then its default value is taken:

```
disk = [ '/root/image.iso,raw,hdc,ro,cdrom','/dev/vg/guest-volume,,hda','...' ]
```

LIST OF PARAMETERS

target

> Source block device or disk image file path.

format

> The format of the image file. Default is raw.

vdev

> Virtual device as seen by the guest. Supported values are hd[x], xvd[x], sd[x] etc. See /usr/share/doc/packages/xen/html/misc/vbd-interface.txt for more details. This parameter is mandatory.

access

> Whether the block device is provided to the guest in read-only or read-write mode. Supported values are ro or r for read-only, and rw or w for read/write access. Default is ro for devtype=cdrom, and rw for other device types.

devtype

Qualifies virtual device type. Supported value is `cdrom`.

backendtype

The back-end implementation to use. Supported values are `phy`, `tap`, and `qdisk`. Normally this option should not be specified as the back-end type is automatically determined.

script

Specifies that `target` is not a normal host path, but rather information to be interpreted by the executable program. The specified script file is looked for in `/etc/xen/scripts` if it does not point to an absolute path. These scripts are normally called `block-<script_name>`.

For more information on virtual disk specification see `/usr/share/doc/packages/xen/html/misc/xl-disk-configuration.txt`.

20.2 File-Backed Virtual Disks and Loopback Devices

When a virtual machine is running, each of its file-backed virtual disks consumes a loopback device on the host. By default, the host allows up to 64 loopback devices to be consumed.

To simultaneously run more file-backed virtual disks on a host, you can increase the number of available loopback devices by adding the following option to the host's `/etc/modprobe.conf.local` file.

```
options loop max_loop=x
```

where **x** is the maximum number of loopback devices to create.

Changes take effect after the module is reloaded.

 Tip

Enter **rmmod loop** and **modprobe loop** to unload and reload the module. In case **rmmod** does not work, unmount all existing loop devices or reboot the computer.

20.3 Resizing Block Devices

While it is always possible to add new block devices to a VM Guest system, it is sometimes more desirable to increase the size of an existing block device. In case such a system modification is already planned during deployment of the VM Guest, some basic considerations should be done:

- Use a block device that may be increased in size. LVM devices and file system images are commonly used.

- Do not partition the device inside the VM Guest, but use the main device directly to apply the file system. For example, use `/dev/xvdb` directly instead of adding partitions to `/dev/xvdb`.

- Make sure that the file system to be used can be resized. Sometimes, for example with ext3, some features must be switched off to be able to resize the file system. A file system that can be resized online and mounted is `XFS`. Use the command **`xfs_growfs`** to resize that file system after the underlying block device has been increased in size. For more information about `XFS`, see **`man 8 xfs_growfs`**.

When resizing an LVM device that is assigned to a VM Guest, the new size is automatically known to the VM Guest. No further action is needed to inform the VM Guest about the new size of the block device.

When using file system images, a loop device is used to attach the image file to the guest. For more information about resizing that image and refreshing the size information for the VM Guest, see *Section 22.2, "Sparse Image Files and Disk Space"*.

21 Virtualization: Configuration Options and Settings

The documentation in this section, describes advanced management tasks and configuration options that might help technology innovators implement leading-edge virtualization solutions. It is provided as a courtesy and does not imply that all documented options and tasks are supported by Novell, Inc.

21.1 Virtual CD Readers

Virtual CD readers can be set up when a virtual machine is created or added to an existing virtual machine. A virtual CD reader can be based on a physical CD/DVD, or based on an ISO image. Virtual CD readers work differently depending on whether they are paravirtual or fully virtual.

21.1.1 Virtual CD Readers on Paravirtual Machines

A paravirtual machine can have up to 100 block devices composed of virtual CD readers and virtual disks. On paravirtual machines, virtual CD readers present the CD as a virtual disk with read-only access. Virtual CD readers cannot be used to write data to a CD.

After you have finished accessing a CD on a paravirtual machine, it is recommended that you remove the virtual CD reader from the virtual machine.

Paravirtualized guests can use the device type `devtype=cdrom`. This partly emulates the behavior of a real CD reader, and allows CDs to be changed. It is even possible to use the eject command to open the tray of the CD reader.

21.1.2 Virtual CD Readers on Fully Virtual Machines

A fully virtual machine can have up to four block devices composed of virtual CD readers and virtual disks. A virtual CD reader on a fully virtual machine interacts with an inserted CD in the way you would expect a physical CD reader to interact. For example, in a Windows* XP* virtual machine, the inserted CD appears in the `Devices with Removable Storage` section of `My Computer`.

When a CD is inserted in the physical CD reader on the host computer, all virtual machines with virtual CD readers based on the physical CD reader, such as /dev/cdrom/ , can read the inserted CD. Assuming the operating system has automount functionality, the CD should automatically appear in the file system. Virtual CD readers cannot be used to write data to a CD. They are configured as read-only devices.

21.1.3   Adding Virtual CD Readers

Virtual CD readers can be based on a CD inserted into the CD reader or on an ISO image file.

1. Make sure that the virtual machine is running and the operating system has finished booting.

2. Insert the desired CD into the physical CD reader or copy the desired ISO image to a location available to Dom0.

3. Select a new, unused block device in your VM Guest, such as /dev/xvdb .

4. Choose the CD reader or ISO image that you want to assign to the guest.

5. When using a real CD reader, use the following command to assign the CD reader to your VM Guest. In this example, the name of the guest is alice:

```
xl block-attach alice target=/dev/sr0,vdev=xvdb,access=ro
```

6. When assigning an image file, use the following command:

```
xl block-attach alice target=/path/to/file.iso,vdev=xvdb,access=ro
```

7. A new block device, such as /dev/xvdb , is added to the virtual machine.

8. If the virtual machine is running Linux, complete the following:

    a. Open a terminal in the virtual machine and enter **fdisk -l** to verify that the device was properly added. You can also enter **ls /sys/block** to see all disks available to the virtual machine.
    The CD is recognized by the virtual machine as a virtual disk with a drive designation, for example:

    ```
    /dev/xvdb
    ```

b. Enter the command to mount the CD or ISO image using its drive designation. For example,

```
mount -o ro /dev/xvdb /mnt
```

mounts the CD to a mount point named **/mnt**.

The CD or ISO image file should be available to the virtual machine at the specified mount point.

9. If the virtual machine is running Windows, reboot the virtual machine.
Verify that the virtual CD reader appears in its My Computer section.

21.1.4   Removing Virtual CD Readers

1. Make sure that the virtual machine is running and the operating system has finished booting.

2. If the virtual CD reader is mounted, unmount it from within the virtual machine.

3. Enter **xl block-list alice** on the host view of the guest block devices.

4. Enter **xl block-detach alice** *block_dev_id* to remove the virtual device from the guest. If that fails, try to add -f to force the removal.

5. Press the hardware eject button to eject the CD.

21.2   Remote Access Methods

Some configurations, such as those that include rack-mounted servers, require a computer to run without a video monitor, keyboard, or mouse. This type of configuration is often called headless and requires the use of remote administration technologies.

Typical configuration scenarios and technologies include:

Graphical Desktop with X Window Server

If a graphical desktop, such as GNOME, is installed on the virtual machine host, you can use a remote viewer, such as a VNC viewer. On a remote computer, log in and manage the remote guest environment by using graphical tools, such as **tigervnc** or **virt-viewer**.

Text Only

You can use the `ssh` command from a remote computer to log in to a virtual machine host and access its text-based console. You can then use the `xl` command to manage virtual machines and the `virt-install` or `vm-install` commands to create new virtual machines.

21.3 VNC Viewer

VNC viewer is used to view the environment of the running guest system in a graphical way. You can use it from Dom0 (known as local access or on-box access), or from a remote computer.

You can use the IP address of a VM Host Server and a VNC viewer to view the display of this VM Guest. When a virtual machine is running, the VNC server on the host assigns the virtual machine a port number to be used for VNC viewer connections. The assigned port number is the lowest port number available when the virtual machine starts. The number is only available for the virtual machine while it is running. After shutting down, the port number might be assigned to other virtual machines.

For example, if ports 1 and 2 and 4 and 5 are assigned to the running virtual machines, the VNC viewer assigns the lowest available port number, 3. If port number 3 is still in use the next time the virtual machine starts, the VNC server assigns a different port number to the virtual machine.

To use the VNC viewer from a remote computer, the firewall must permit access to as many ports as VM Guest systems run from. This means from port 5900 and up. For example, if you want to run 10 VM Guest systems, you need to open the TCP ports 5900:5910.

To access the virtual machine from the local console running a VNC viewer client, enter one of the following commands:

- `vncviewer ::590#`

- `vncviewer :#`

`#` is the VNC viewer port number assigned to the virtual machine.

When accessing the VM Guest from a machine other than Dom0, use the following syntax:

```
vncviewer 192.168.1.20::590#
```

In this case, the IP address of Dom0 is 192.168.1.20.

21.3.1 Assigning VNC Viewer Port Numbers to Virtual Machines

Although the default behavior of VNC viewer is to assign the first available port number, you might want to assign a specific VNC viewer port number to a specific virtual machine.

To assign a specific port number on a VM Guest, edit the xl setting of the virtual machine and change the `vnclisten` to the desired value. Note that for example for port number 5902, specify 2 only, as 5900 is added automatically:

```
vfb = [ 'vnc=1,vnclisten="localhost:2"' ]
```

For more information regarding editing the xl settings of a guest domain, see *Section 19.1, "XL —Xen Management Tool"*.

 Tip

Assign higher port numbers to avoid conflict with port numbers assigned by the VNC viewer, which uses the lowest available port number.

21.3.2 Using SDL instead of a VNC Viewer

If you access a virtual machine's display from the virtual machine host console (known as local or on-box access), you might want to use SDL instead of VNC viewer. VNC viewer is faster for viewing desktops over a network, but SDL is faster for viewing desktops from the same computer.

To set the default to use SDL instead of VNC, change the virtual machine's configuration information to the following. For instructions, see *Section 19.1, "XL—Xen Management Tool"*.

```
vfb = [ 'sdl=1' ]
```

Remember that, unlike a VNC viewer window, closing an SDL window terminates the virtual machine.

21.4 Virtual Keyboards

When a virtual machine is started, the host creates a virtual keyboard that matches the **keymap** entry according to the virtual machine's settings. If there is no **keymap** entry specified, the virtual machine's keyboard defaults to English (US).

To view a virtual machine's current **keymap** entry, enter the following command on the Dom0:

```
xl list -l vm_name | grep keymap
```

To configure a virtual keyboard for a guest, use the following snippet:

```
vfb = [ 'keymap="de"' ]
```

For a complete list of supported keyboard layouts, see the Keymaps section of the **xl.cfg** manual page **man 5 xl.cfg**.

21.5 Dedicating CPU Resources

In Xen it is possible to specify how many and which CPU cores the Dom0 or VM Guest should use to retain its performance. The performance of Dom0 is important for the overall system, as the disk and network drivers are running on it. Also I/O intensive guests' workloads may consume lots of Dom0s' CPU cycles. On the other hand, the performance of VM Guests is also important, to be able to accomplish the task they were set up for.

21.5.1 Dom0

Dedicating CPU resources to Dom0 results in a better overall performance of the virtualized environment because Dom0 has free CPU time to process I/O requests from VM Guests. Failing to dedicate exclusive CPU resources to Dom0 usually results in a poor performance and can cause the VM Guests to function incorrectly.

Dedicating CPU resources involves three basic steps: modifying Xen boot line, binding Dom0's VCPUs to a physical processor, and configuring CPU-related options on VM Guests:

1. First you need to append the dom0_max_vcpus=X to the Xen boot line. Do so by adding the following line to /etc/default/grub:

```
GRUB_CMDLINE_XEN="dom0_max_vcpus=X"
```

If /etc/default/grub already contains a line setting GRUB_CMDLINE_XEN, rather append dom0_max_vcpus=X to this line.

X needs to be replaced by the number of VCPUs dedicated to Dom0.

2. Update the GRUB 2 configuration file by running the following command:

```
grub2-mkconfig -o /boot/grub2/grub.cfg
```

3. Reboot for the change to take effect.

4. The next step is to bind (or "pin") each Dom0's VCPU to a physical processor.

```
xl vcpu-pin Domain-0 0 0
xl vcpu-pin Domain-0 1 1
```

The first line binds Dom0's VCPU number 0 to the physical processor number 0, while the second line binds Dom0's VCPU number 1 to the physical processor number 1.

5. Lastly, you need to make sure no VM Guest uses the physical processors dedicated to VCPUs of Dom0. Assuming you are running an 8-CPU system, you need to add

```
cpus="2-8"
```

to the configuration file of the relevant VM Guest.

21.5.2 VM Guests

It is often necessary to dedicate specific CPU resources to a virtual machine. By default, a virtual machine uses any available CPU core. Its performance can be improved by assigning a reasonable number of physical processors to it as other VM Guests are not allowed to use them after that. Assuming a machine with 8 CPU cores while a virtual machine needs to use 2 of them, change its configuration file as follows:

```
vcpus=2
cpus="2,3"
```

The above example dedicates 2 processors to the VM Guest, and these being the 3rd and 4th one, (2 and 3 counted from zero). If you need to assign more physical processors, use the cpus="2-8" syntax.

If you need to change the CPU assignment for a guest named "alice" in a hotplug manner, do the following on the related Dom0:

```
xl vcpu-set alice 2
xl vcpu-pin alice 0 2
xl vcpu-pin alice 1 3
```

The example will dedicate 2 physical processors to the guest, and bind its VCPU 0 to physical processor 2 and VCPU 1 to physical processor 3. Now check the assignment:

```
xl vcpu-list alice
Name                    ID VCPUs   CPU State   Time(s) CPU Affinity
alice                   4    0      2   -b-       1.9 2-3
alice                   4    1      3   -b-       2.8 2-3
```

21.6   HVM Features

In Xen some features are only available for fully virtualized domains. They are not very often used, but still may be interesting in some environments.

21.6.1   Specify Boot Device on Boot

Just as with physical hardware, it is sometimes desirable to boot a VM Guest from a different device than its own boot device. For fully virtual machines, it is possible to select a boot device with the boot parameter in a domain xl configuration file:

```
boot = boot_device
```

boot_device can be one of c for hard disk, d for CD-ROM, or n for Network/PXE. You can specify multiple options, and they will be attempted in the given order. For example,

```
boot = dc
```

boots from CD-ROM, and falls back to the hard disk if CD-ROM is not bootable.

21.6.2   Changing CPUIDs for Guests

To be able to migrate a VM Guest from one VM Host Server to a different VM Host Server, it is mandatory, that the VM Guest system only uses CPU features that are available on both VM Host Server systems. If the actual CPUs are different on both hosts, it may be necessary to hide some features before the VM Guest is started to maintain the possibility to migrate the VM Guest between both hosts. For fully virtualized guests, this can be achieved by configuring the `cpuid` that is available to the guest.

To gain an overview of the current CPU, have a look at `/proc/cpuinfo`. This contains all the important information that defines the current CPU.

To redefine a CPU, first have a look at the respective cpuid definitions of the CPU vendor. These are available from:

Intel

http://www.intel.com/Assets/PDF/appnote/241618.pdf

```
cpuid = "host,tm=0,sse3=0"
```

The syntax is a comma-separated list of key = value pairs, preceded by the word "host". A few keys take a numerical value, while all others take a single character which describes what to do with the feature bit. See **man 5 xl.cfg** for a complete list of cpuid keys. The respective bits may be changed by using the following values:

1

Force the corresponding bit to 1

0

Force the corresponding bit to 0

x

Use the values of the default policy

k

Use the values defined by the host

s

Like k, but preserve the value over migrations

Note that counting bits is done from right to left, starting with bit `0`.

21.6.3 Increasing the Number of PCI-IRQs

In case you need to increase the default number of PCI-IRQs available to Dom0 and/or VM Guest, you can do so by modifying the Xen kernel command line. Use the command **extra_guest_irqs=** *domu_irgs,dom0_irgs*. The optional first number *domu_irgs* is common for all VM Guests, while the optional second number *dom0_irgs* (preceded by a comma) is for Dom0. Changing the setting for VM Guest has no impact on Dom0 and vice versa. For example to change Dom0 without changing VM Guest, use

```
extra_guest_irqs=,512
```

22 Administrative Tasks

22.1 The Boot Loader Program

The boot loader controls how the virtualization software boots and runs. You can modify the boot loader properties by using YaST, or by directly editing the boot loader configuration file.

The YaST boot loader program is located at *YaST › System › Boot Loader*. Click the *Bootloader Options* tab and select the line containing the Xen kernel as the *Default Boot Section*.

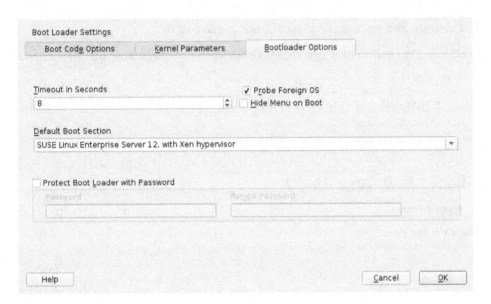

FIGURE 22.1: BOOT LOADER SETTINGS

Confirm with *OK*. Next time you boot the host, it will be ready to provide the Xen virtualization environment.

You can use the Boot Loader program to specify functionality, such as:

- Pass kernel command line parameters.

- Specify the kernel image and initial RAM disk.

- Select a specific hypervisor.

- Pass additional parameters to the hypervisor. See http://xenbits.xen.org/docs/unstable/misc/xen-command-line.html for their complete list.

You can customize your virtualization environment by editing the /etc/default/grub file. Add the following line to this file: GRUB_CMDLINE_XEN="<boot_parameters>". Do not forget to run **grub2-mkconfig -o /boot/grub2/grub.cfg** after editing the file.

22.2 Sparse Image Files and Disk Space

If the host's physical disk reaches a state where it has no available space, a virtual machine using a virtual disk based on a sparse image file cannot write to its disk. Consequently, it reports I/O errors.

If this situation occurs, you should free up available space on the physical disk, remount the virtual machine's file system, and set the file system back to read-write.

To check the actual disk requirements of a sparse image file, use the command **du -h <image file>**.

To increase the available space of a sparse image file, first increase the file size and then the file system.

 Warning: Back Up Before Resizing

Touching the sizes of partitions or sparse files always bears the risk of data failure. Do not work without a backup.

The resizing of the image file can be done online, while the VM Guest is running. Increase the size of a sparse image file with:

```
dd if=/dev/zero of=<image file> count=0 bs=1M seek=<new size in MB>
```

For example, to increase the file /var/lib/xen/images/sles/disk0 to a size of 16GB, use the command:

```
dd if=/dev/zero of=/var/lib/xen/images/sles/disk0 count=0 bs=1M seek=16000
```

Note: Increasing Non-Sparse Images

It is also possible to increase the image files of devices that are not sparse files. However, you must know exactly where the previous image ends. Use the seek parameter to point to the end of the image file and use a command similar to the following:

```
dd if=/dev/zero of=/var/lib/xen/images/sles/disk0 seek=8000 bs=1M count=2000
```

Be sure to use the right seek, else data loss may happen.

If the VM Guest is running during the resize operation, also resize the loop device that provides the image file to the VM Guest. First detect the correct loop device with the command:

```
losetup -j /var/lib/xen/images/sles/disk0
```

Then resize the loop device, for example /dev/loop0, with the following command:

```
losetup -c /dev/loop0
```

Finally check the size of the block device inside the guest system with the command **fdisk - l /dev/xvdb**. The device name depends on the actually increased device.

The resizing of the file system inside the sparse file involves tools that are depending on the actual file system. This is described in detail in the *Book* "Storage Administration Guide".

22.3 Migrating Xen VM Guest Systems

With Xen it is possible to migrate a VM Guest system from one VM Host Server to another with almost no service interruption. This could be used for example to move a busy VM Guest to a VM Host Server that has stronger hardware or is not yet loaded. Or, if a service of a VM Host Server is required, all VM Guest systems running on this machine can be migrated to other machines to avoid interruption of service. These are only two examples—many more reasons may apply to your personal situation.

Before starting, some preliminary considerations regarding the VM Host Server should be taken into account:

- All VM Host Server systems should use a similar CPU. The frequency is not so important, but they should be using the same CPU family. To get more information about the used CPU, see `cat /proc/cpuinfo`.

- All resources that are used by a specific guest system must be available on all involved VM Host Server systems—for example all used block devices must exist on both VM Host Server systems.

- If the hosts included in the migration process run in different subnets, make sure that either DHCP relay is available to the guests, or for guests with static network configuration, set up the network manually.

- Using special features like `PCI Pass-Through` may be problematic. Do not implement these when deploying for an environment that should migrate VM Guest systems between different VM Host Server systems.

- For fast migrations, a fast network is mandatory. If possible, use GB Ethernet and fast switches. Deploying VLAN might also help avoid collisions.

22.3.1 Preparing Block Devices for Migrations

The block devices needed by the VM Guest system must be available on all involved VM Host Server systems. This is done by implementing some kind of shared storage that serves as container for the root file system of the migrated VM Guest system. Common possibilities include:

- `iSCSI` can be set up to give access to the same block devices from different systems at the same time. For more information about iSCSI, see *Book "Storage Administration Guide", Chapter 13 "Mass Storage over IP Networks: iSCSI".*

- `NFS` is a widely used root file system that can easily be accessed from different locations. For more information, see *Book "Administration Guide", Chapter 26 "Sharing File Systems with NFS".*

- `DRBD` can be used if only two VM Host Server systems are involved. This gives some extra data security, because the used data is mirrored over the network. For more information, see the *SUSE Linux Enterprise High Availability Extension 12 SP1* documentation at http://www.suse.com/doc/.

- **SCSI** can also be used if the available hardware permits shared access to the same disks.

- **NPIV** is a special mode to use Fibre channel disks. However, in this case all migration hosts must be attached to the same Fibre channel switch. For more information about NPIV, see *Section 20.1, "Mapping Physical Storage to Virtual Disks"*. Commonly, this works if the Fibre channel environment supports 4 Gbit or faster connections.

22.3.2   Migrating VM Guest Systems

The actual migration of the VM Guest system is done with the command:

```
xl migrate <domain_name> <host>
```

The speed of the migration depends on how fast the memory print can be saved to disk, sent to the new VM Host Server and loaded there. This means that small VM Guest systems can be migrated faster than big systems with a lot of memory.

22.4   Monitoring Xen

For a regular operation of many virtual guests, having a possibility to check the sanity of all the different VM Guest systems is indispensable. Xen offers several tools besides the system tools to gather information about the system.

 Tip: Monitoring the VM Host Server

> Basic monitoring of the VM Host Server (I/O and CPU) is available via the Virtual Machine Manager. Refer to *Section 10.8.1, "Monitoring with Virtual Machine Manager"* for details.

22.4.1   Monitor Xen with **xentop**

The preferred terminal application to gather information about Xen virtual environment is **xentop**. Unfortunately, this tool needs a rather broad terminal, else it inserts line breaks into the display.

`xentop` has several command keys that can give you more information about the system that is monitored. Some of the more important are:

D

Change the delay between the refreshes of the screen.

N

Also display network statistics. Note, that only standard configurations will be displayed. If you use a special configuration like a routed network, no network will be displayed.

B

Display the respective block devices and their cumulated usage count.

For more information about **xentop** see the manual page **man 1 xentop**.

 Tip: `virt-top`

libvirt offers the hypervisor-agnostic tool **virt-top**, which is recommended for monitoring VM Guests. See *Section 10.8.2, "Monitoring with `virt-top`"* for details.

22.4.2   More Helpful Tools

There are many different system tools that also help monitoring or debugging a running SUSE Linux Enterprise system. Many of these are covered in the official SUSE Linux Enterprise documentation. Especially useful for monitoring a virtualization environment are the following tools:

ip

The command line utility **ip** may be used to monitor arbitrary network interfaces. This is especially useful if you have set up a network that is routed or applied a masqueraded network. To monitor a network interface with the name `alice.0`, run the following command:

```
watch ip -s link show alice.0
```

brctl

In a standard setup, all the Xen VM Guest systems are attached to a virtual network bridge. `brctl` allows you to determine the connection between the bridge and the virtual network adapter in the VM Guest system. For example, the output of `brctl show` may look like the following:

```
bridge name    bridge id          STP enabled    interfaces
br0            8000.000476f060cc   no             eth0
                                                  vif1.0
br1            8000.00001cb5a9e7   no             vlan22
```

This shows that there are two virtual bridges defined on the system. One is connected to the physical Ethernet device `eth0`, the other one is connected to a VLAN interface `vlan22`. There is only one guest interface active in this setup, `vif1.0`. This means that the guest with ID 1 has an Ethernet interface `eth0` assigned, that is connected to `br0` in the VM Host Server.

iptables-save

Especially when using masquerade networks, or if several Ethernet interfaces are set up together with a firewall setup, it may be helpful to check the current firewall rules.

The command `iptables` may be used to check all the different firewall settings. To list all the rules of a chain, or even of the complete setup, you may use the commands `iptables-save` or `iptables -S`.

22.5   Providing Host Information for VM Guest Systems

In a standard Xen environment, the VM Guest systems have only very limited information about the VM Host Server system they are running on. If a guest should know more about the VM Host Server it runs on, `vhostmd` can provide more information to selected guests. To set up your system to run `vhostmd`, proceed as follows:

1. Install the package vhostmd on the VM Host Server.

2. Edit the file `/etc/vhostmd/vhostmd.conf` if you want to add or remove `metric` sections from the configuration. However, the default works well.

3. Check the validity of the `vhostmd.conf` configuration file with the command:

```
cd /etc/vhostmd
xmllint --postvalid --noout vhostmd.conf
```

4. Start the vhostmd daemon with the command **sudo systemctl start vhostmd**. If vhostmd should be started automatically during start-up of the system, run the command:

```
sudo systemctl enable vhostmd
```

5. Attach the image file `/dev/shm/vhostmd0` to the VM Guest system named alice with the command:

```
xl block-attach opensuse /dev/shm/vhostmd0,,xvdb,ro
```

6. Log on the VM Guest system.

7. Install the client package `vm-dump-metrics`.

8. Run the command **vm-dump-metrics**. If you want to have the result in a file, use the option `-d <filename>`.

The result of the `vm-dump-metrics` is an XML output. The respective metric entries follow the DTD `/etc/vhostmd/metric.dtd`.

For more information, see the manual pages **man 8 vhostmd** and `/usr/share/doc/vhost-md/README` on the VM Host Server system. On the guest, see the manual page **man 1 vm-dump-metrics**.

23 XenStore: Configuration Database Shared between Domains

This section introduces basic information about XenStore, its role in the Xen environment, the directory structure of files used by XenStore, and the description of XenStore's commands.

23.1 Introduction

XenStore is a database of configuration and status information shared between VM Guests and the management tools running in Dom0. VM Guests and the management tools read and write to XenStore to convey configuration information, status updates, and state changes. The XenStore database is managed by Dom0 and supports simple operations such as reading and writing a key. VM Guests and management tools can be notified of any changes in XenStore by watching entries of interest. Note that the `xenstored` daemon is managed by the `xencommons` service.

XenStore is located on Dom0 in a single database file `/var/lib/xenstored/tdb` (`tdb` represents *tree database*).

23.2 File System Interface

XenStore database content is represented by a virtual file system similar to `/proc` (for more information on `/proc`, see *Book* "System Analysis and Tuning Guide", *Chapter 2* "*System Monitoring Utilities*", *Section 2.6* "*The* `/proc` *File System*"). The tree has three main paths: `/vm`, `/local/domain`, and `/tool`.

- `/vm` - stores information about the VM Guest configuration.

- `/local/domain` - stores information about VM Guest on the local node.

- `/tool` - stores general information about various tools.

Tip

Each VM Guest has two different ID numbers. The *universal unique identifier* (UUID) remains the same even if the VM Guest is migrated to another machine. The *domain identifier* (DOMID) is an identification number that represents a particular running instance. It typically changes when the VM Guest is migrated to another machine.

23.2.1   XenStore Commands

The file system structure of the XenStore database can be operated with the following commands:

xenstore-ls

Displays the full dump of the XenStore database.

xenstore-read path_to_xenstore_entry

Displays the value of the specified XenStore entry.

xenstore-exists xenstore_path

Reports whether the specified XenStore path exists.

xenstore-list xenstore_path

Displays all the children entries of the specified XenStore path.

xenstore-write path_to_xenstore_entry

Updates the value of the specified XenStore entry.

xenstore-rm xenstore_path

Removes the specified XenStore entry or directory.

xenstore-chmod xenstore_path mode

Updates the read/write permission on the specified XenStore path.

xenstore-control

Sends a command to the xenstored back-end, such as triggering an integrity check.

23.2.2　/vm

The `/vm` path is indexed by the UUID of each VM Guest, and stores configuration information such as the number of virtual CPUs and the amount of allocated memory. There is a `/vm/<uuid>` directory for each VM Guest. To list the directory content, use **xenstore-list**.

```
# xenstore-list /vm
00000000-0000-0000-0000-000000000000
9b30841b-43bc-2af9-2ed3-5a649f466d79-1
```

The first line of the output belongs to Dom0, and the second one to a running VM Guest. The following command lists all the entries related to the VM Guest:

```
# xenstore-list /vm/9b30841b-43bc-2af9-2ed3-5a649f466d79-1
image
rtc
device
pool_name
shadow_memory
uuid
on_reboot
start_time
on_poweroff
bootloader_args
on_crash
vcpus
vcpu_avail
bootloader
name
```

To read a value of an entry, for example the number of virtual CPUs dedicated to the VM Guest, use **xenstore-read**:

```
# xenstore-read /vm/9b30841b-43bc-2af9-2ed3-5a649f466d79-1/vcpus
1
```

A list of some `/vm/<uuid>` entries follows:

`uuid`

> UUID of the VM Guest. It does not change during the migration process.

`on_reboot`

> Specifies whether to destroy or restart the VM Guest in response to a reboot request.

`on_poweroff`

> Specifies whether to destroy or restart the VM Guest in response to a halt request.

`on_crash`

> Specifies whether to destroy or restart the VM Guest in response to a crash.

`vcpus`

> Number of virtual CPUs allocated to the VM Guest.

`vcpu_avail`

> Bitmask of active virtual CPUs for the VM Guest. The bitmask has several bits equal to the value of `vcpus`, with a bit set for each online virtual CPU.

`name`

> The name of the VM Guest.

Regular VM Guests (not Dom0) use the `/vm/<uuid>/image` path:

```
# xenstore-list /vm/9b30841b-43bc-2af9-2ed3-5a649f466d79-1/image
ostype
kernel
cmdline
ramdisk
dmargs
device-model
display
```

An explanation of the used entries follows:

`ostype`

> The OS type of the VM Guest.

`kernel`

> The path on Dom0 to the kernel for the VM Guest.

cmdline

> The kernel command line for the VM Guest used when booting.

ramdisk

> The path on Dom0 to the RAM disk for the VM Guest.

dmargs

> Shows arguments passed to the QEMU process. If you look at the QEMU process with **ps**, you should see the same arguments as in `/vm/<uuid>/image/dmargs`.

23.2.3 `/local/domain/<domid>`

This path is indexed by the running domain (VM Guest) ID, and contains information about the running VM Guest. Remember that the domain ID changes during VM Guest migration. The following entries are available:

vm

> The path of the `/vm` directory for this VM Guest.

on_reboot, on_poweroff, on_crash, name

> See identical options in *Section 23.2.2, "`/vm`"*

domid

> Domain identifier for the VM Guest.

cpu

> The current CPU to which the VM Guest is pinned.

cpu_weight

> The weight assigned to the VM Guest for scheduling purposes. Higher weights use the physical CPUs more often.

Apart from the individual entries described above, there are also several subdirectories under `/local/domain/<domid>`, containing specific entries. To see all entries available, refer to XenStore Reference [http://wiki.xen.org/wiki/XenStore_Reference].

/local/domain/<domid>/memory

> Contains memory information. `/local/domain/<domid>/memory/target` contains target memory size for the VM Guest (in kilobytes).

`/local/domain/<domid>/console`

Contains information about a console used by the VM Guest.

`/local/domain/<domid>/backend`

Contains information about all back-end devices used by the VM Guest. The path has subdirectories of its own.

`/local/domain/<domid>/device`

Contains information about the front-end devices for the VM Guest.

`/local/domain/<domid>/device-misc`

Contains miscellaneous information about devices.

`/local/domain/<domid>/store`

Contains information about the VM Guest's store.

24 Xen as a High-Availability Virtualization Host

Setting up two Xen hosts as a failover system has several advantages compared to a setup where every server runs on dedicated hardware.

- Failure of a single server does not cause major interruption of the service.

- A single big machine is normally way cheaper than multiple smaller machines.

- Adding new servers as needed is a trivial task.

- The utilization of the server is improved, which has positive effects on the power consumption of the system.

The setup of migration for Xen hosts is described in *Section 22.3, "Migrating Xen VM Guest Systems"*. In the following, several typical scenarios are described.

24.1 Xen HA with Remote Storage

Xen can directly provide several remote block devices to the respective Xen guest systems. These include iSCSI, NPIV, and NBD. All of these may be used to do live migrations. When a storage system is already in place, first try to use the same device type you already used in the network.

If the storage system cannot be used directly but provides a possibility to offer the needed space over NFS, it is also possible to create image files on NFS. If the NFS file system is available on all Xen host systems, this method also allows live migrations of Xen guests.

When setting up a new system, one of the main considerations is whether a dedicated storage area network should be implemented. The following possibilities are available:

TABLE 24.1: XEN REMOTE STORAGE

Method	Complexity	Comments
Ethernet	low	Note that all block device traffic goes over the same Ethernet interface as the network traffic. This may be limiting the performance of the guest.

Method	Complexity	Comments
Ethernet dedicated to storage.	medium	Running the storage traffic over a dedicated Ethernet interface may eliminate a bottleneck on the server side. However, planning your own network with your own IP address range and possibly a VLAN dedicated to storage requires numerous considerations.
NPIV	high	NPIV is a method to virtualize Fibre channel connections. This is available with adapters that support a data rate of at least 4 Gbit/s and allows the setup of complex storage systems.

Typically, a 1 Gbit/s Ethernet device can fully use a typical hard disk or storage system. When using very fast storage systems, such an Ethernet device will probably limit the speed of the system.

24.2   Xen HA with Local Storage

For space or budget reasons, it may be necessary to rely on storage that is local to the Xen host systems. To still maintain the possibility of live migrations, it is necessary to build block devices that are mirrored to both Xen hosts. The software that allows this is called Distributed Replicated Block Device (DRBD).

If a system that uses DRBD to mirror the block devices or files between two Xen hosts should be set up, both hosts should use the identical hardware. If one of the hosts has slower hard disks, both hosts will suffer from this limitation.

During the setup, each of the required block devices should use its own DRBD device. The setup of such a system is quite a complex task.

24.3 Xen HA and Private Bridges

When using several guest systems that need to communicate between each other, it is possible to do this over the regular interface. However, for security reasons it may be advisable to create a bridge that is only connected to guest systems.

In an HA environment that also should support live migrations, such a private bridge must be connected to the other Xen hosts. This is possible by using dedicated physical Ethernet devices and a dedicated network.

A different implementation method is using VLAN interfaces. In that case, all the traffic goes over the regular Ethernet interface. However, the VLAN interface does not get the regular traffic, because only the VLAN packets that are tagged for the correct VLAN are forwarded.

For more information about the setup of a VLAN interface see *Section 18.5.3, "Using VLAN Interfaces"*.

V Managing Virtual Machines with QEMU

25 QEMU Overview

QEMU is a fast, cross-platform open source machine emulator which can emulate a huge number of hardware architectures for you. QEMU lets you run a complete unmodified operating system (VM Guest) on top of your existing system (VM Host Server).

You can also use QEMU for debugging purposes—you can easily stop your running virtual machine, inspect its state and save and restore it later.

QEMU consists of the following parts:

- processor emulator (x86, s390x, PowerPC, Sparc)

- emulated devices (graphic card, network card, hard disks, mice)

- generic devices used to connect the emulated devices to the related host devices

- descriptions of the emulated machines (PC, Power Mac)

- debugger

- user interface used to interact with the emulator

QEMU is central to KVM and Xen Virtualization, where it provides the general machine emulation. Xen's usage of QEMU is somewhat hidden from the user, while KVM's usage exposes most QEMU features transparently. If the VM Guest hardware architecture is the same as the VM Host Server's architecture, QEMU can take advantage of the KVM acceleration (SUSE only supports QEMU with the KVM acceleration loaded).

Apart from providing a core virtualization infrastructure and processor-specific drivers, QEMU also provides an architecture-specific userspace program for managing VM Guests. Depending on the architecture this program is one of:

- `qemu-system-i386`

- `qemu-system-s390x`

- `qemu-system-x86_64`

In the following this command is called `qemu-system-ARCH`; in examples the `qemu-system-x86_64` command is used.

26 Setting Up a KVM VM Host Server

This section documents how to set up and use SUSE Linux Enterprise Server 12 SP1 as a QEMU-KVM based virtual machine host.

 Tip: Resources

In general, the virtual guest system needs the same hardware resources as SUSE Linux Enterprise Server installed on a physical machine. The more guests you plan to run on the host system, the more hardware resources—CPU, disk, memory, and network—you need to add.

26.1 CPU Support for Virtualization

In order to run KVM, your CPU must support virtualization, and virtualization needs to be enabled in BIOS. The file `/proc/cpuinfo` includes information about your CPU features.

To find out whether your system supports virtualization, see *Section 7.3, "KVM Hardware Requirements"*.

26.2 Required Software

The KVM host requires several packages to be installed. To install all necessary packages, do the following:

1. Run *YaST* › *Virtualization* › *Install Hypervisor and Tools*.

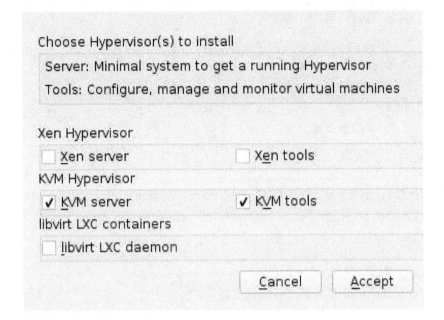

FIGURE 26.1: INSTALLING THE KVM HYPERVISOR AND TOOLS

2. Select *KVM server* and preferably also *KVM tools*, and confirm with *Accept*.

3. During the installation process, you can optionally let YaST create a *Network Bridge* for you automatically. If you do not plan to dedicate an additional physical network card to your virtual guests, network bridge is a standard way to connect the guest machines to the network.

FIGURE 26.2: NETWORK BRIDGE

4. After all the required packages are installed (and new network setup activated), try to load the KVM kernel module relevant for your CPU type—`kvm-intel` or `kvm-amd`:

Required Software

```
root # modprobe kvm-intel
```

Check if the module is loaded into memory:

```
tux > lsmod | grep kvm
kvm_intel              64835  6
kvm                   411041  1 kvm_intel
```

Now the KVM host is ready for serving KVM VM Guests. For more information, see *Chapter 28, Running Virtual Machines with qemu-system-ARCH*.

26.3   KVM Host-Specific Features

You can improve the performance of KVM-based VM Guests by letting them fully utilize specific features of the VM Host Server's hardware (*paravirtualization*). This section introduces techniques to make the guests access the physical host's hardware directly—without the emulation layer—to make the most use of it.

 Tip

> Examples included in this section assume basic knowledge of the **qemu-system-***ARCH* command line options. For more information, see *Chapter 28, Running Virtual Machines with qemu-system-ARCH*.

26.3.1   Using the Host Storage with `virtio-scsi`

`virtio-scsi` is an advanced storage stack for KVM. It replaces the former `virtio-blk` stack for SCSI devices pass-through. It has several advantages over `virtio-blk`:

Improved scalability

> KVM guests have a limited number of PCI controllers which results in a limited number of possibly attached devices. `virtio-scsi` solves this limitation by grouping multiple storage devices on a single controller. Each device on a `virtio-scsi` controller is represented as a logical unit, or *LUN*.

Standard command set

> While `virtio-blk` uses a small set of commands which has to be known to both the `virtio-blk` driver and the virtual machine monitor. To introduce a new command means to update both the driver and the monitor.
>
> However, `virtio-scsi` does not define commands, but a transport protocol for these commands following the industry-standard SCSI specification. This approach is shared with a number of other technologies, such as Fibre Channel, ATAPI, or USB devices.

Device naming

> `virtio-blk` devices are presented inside the guest as `/dev/vdX` which is different from device names in physical systems and may cause migration problems.
>
> `virtio-scsi` keeps the device names identical to those on physical systems, making the virtual machines easily relocatable.

SCSI device pass-through

> For virtual disks backed by a whole LUN on the host, it is preferable for the guest to send SCSI commands directly to the LUN (pass-through). This is limited in `virtio-blk`, as guests need to use the virtio-blk protocol instead of SCSI command pass-through, and, moreover, it is not available for Windows guests. `virtio-scsi` natively removes these limitations.

26.3.1.1 virtio-scsi Usage

KVM supports SCSI pass-through feature with the `virtio-scsi-pci` device:

```
qemu-system-x86_64 [...] \
-device virtio-scsi-pci,id=scsi
```

26.3.2 Accelerated Networking with vhost-net

The `vhost-net` module is used to accelerate KVM's paravirtualized network drivers. It provides better latency and greater throughput for network. Use the `vhost-net` driver by starting the guest with the following example command line:

```
qemu-system-x86_64 [...] \
-netdev tap,id=guest0,vhost=on,script=no \
```

```
-net nic,model=virtio,netdev=guest0,macaddr=00:16:35:AF:94:4B
```

Note that `guest0` is an identification string of the vhost-driven device.

26.3.3 Scaling Network Performance with Multiqueue virtio-net

As the number of virtual CPUs increases in VM Guests, QEMU offers a way of improving the network performance using *multiqueue*. Multiqueue virtio-net scales the network performance by allowing VM Guest virtual CPUs to transfer packets in parallel. Multiqueue support is required on both VM Host Server and VM Guest side.

 Tip: Performance Benefit

The Multiqueue virtio-net solution is most beneficial in the following cases:

- Network traffic packets are large.

- VM Guest has more connections active at the same time, mainly between the guest systems, or between the guest and the host, or between the guest and an external system.

- The number of active queues is equal to the number of virtual CPUs in the VM Guest.

 Note

While multiqueue virtio-net increases the total network throughput, it increases CPU consumption as it uses of the virtual CPU's power.

PROCEDURE 26.1: HOW TO ENABLE MULTIQUEUE VIRTIO-NET

The following procedure lists important steps to enable the multiqueue feature with **qemu-system-ARCH**. It assumes that a tap network device with multiqueue capability (supported since kernel version 3.8) is set up on the VM Host Server.

1. In **qemu-system-ARCH**, enable multiqueue for the tap device:

```
-netdev tap,vhost=on,queues=N
```

where N stands for the number of queue pairs.

2. In **qemu-system-ARCH**, enable multiqueue and specify MSI-X (Message Signaled Interrupt) vectors for the virtio-net-pci device:

```
-device virtio-net-pci,mq=on,vectors=2*N+2
```

where the formula for the number of MSI-X vectors results from: N vectors for TX (transmit) queues, N for RX (receive) queues, one for configuration purposes, and one for possible VQ (vector quantization) control.

3. In VM Guest, enable multiqueue on the relevant network interface (eth0 in this example):

```
ethtool -L eth0 combined 2*N
```

The resulting **qemu-system-ARCH** command line will look similar to the following example:

```
qemu-system-x86_64 [...] -netdev tap,id=guest0,queues=4,vhost=on \
-device virtio-net-pci,netdev=guest0,mq=on,vectors=10
```

Note that the id of the network device (guest0) needs to be identical for both options. Inside the running VM Guest, specify the following command as root :

```
ethtool -L eth0 combined 8
```

Now the guest system networking uses the multiqueue support from the **qemu-system-ARCH** hypervisor.

26.3.4 VFIO: Secure Direct Access to Devices

Directly assigning a PCI device to a VM Guest (PCI pass-through) avoids performance issues caused by avoiding any emulation in performance critical paths. VFIO replaces the traditional KVM PCI Pass-Through device assignment. Prerequisite for this feature is a VM Host Server configuration described in *Important: Requirements for VFIO and SR-IOV*.

To be able to assign a PCI device via VFIO to a VM Guest, you need to find out which IOMMU Group it belongs to. The *IOMMU* (input/output memory management unit that connects a direct memory access-capable I/O bus to the main memory) API supports the notion of groups. A group is a set of devices that can be isolated from all other devices in the system. Groups are therefore the unit of ownership used by *VFIO*.

PROCEDURE 26.2: ASSIGNING A PCI DEVICE TO A VM GUEST VIA VFIO

1. Identify the host PCI device to assign to the guest.

```
tux > sudo lspci -nn
[...]
00:10.0 Ethernet controller [0200]: Intel Corporation 82576 \
Virtual Function [8086:10ca] (rev 01)
[...]
```

   Note down the device ID (00:10.0 in this case) and the vendor ID (8086:10ca).

2. Find the IOMMU group of this device:

```
tux > sudo readlink /sys/bus/pci/devices/0000\:00\:10.0/iommu_group
../../../kernel/iommu_groups/20
```

   The IOMMU group for this device is 20 .Now you can check the devices belonging to the same IOMMU group:

```
ls -l /sys/bus/pci/devices/0000:01:10.0/iommu_group/devices/0000:01:10.0
[...] 0000:00:1e.0 -> ../../../../devices/pci0000:00/0000:00:1e.0
[...] 0000:01:10.0 -> ../../../../devices/pci0000:00/0000:00:1e.0/0000:01:10.0
[...] 0000:01:10.1 -> ../../../../devices/pci0000:00/0000:00:1e.0/0000:01:10.1
```

3. Unbind the device from the device driver:

```
sudo echo "0000:01:10.0" > /sys/bus/pci/devices/0000\:01\:10.0/driver/unbind
```

4. Bind the device to the vfio-pci driver using the vendor ID from step 1:

```
sudo echo "8086 153a" > /sys/bus/pci/drivers/vfio-pci/new_id
```

A new device `/dev/vfio/IOMMU_GROUP` will be created as a result, `/dev/vfio/20` in this case.

5. Change the ownership of the newly created device:

```
chown qemu.qemu /dev/vfio/DEVICE
```

6. Now run the VM Guest with the PCI device assigned.

```
qemu-system-ARCH [...] -device
      vfio-pci,host=00:10.0,id=ID
```

> **❗ Important: No Hot-plugging**
>
> As of SUSE Linux Enterprise Server 12 SP1 hot-plugging of PCI devices passed to a VM Guest via VFIO is not supported.

You can find more detailed information on the *VFIO* driver in the `/usr/src/linux/Documentation/vfio.txt` file (package `kernel-source` has to be installed).

26.3.5   USB Pass-Through

To assign an existing host USB device to a VM Guest, you need to find out its host bus and device ID.

```
tux@vmhost:~> lsusb
[...]
Bus 002 Device 005: ID 12d1:1406 Huawei Technologies Co., Ltd. E1750
[...]
```

In the above example, we want to assign a USB stick connected to the host's USB bus number 2 with device number 5. Now run the VM Guest with the following additional options:

```
qemu-system-x86_64 [...] -usb -device usb-host,hostbus=2,hostaddr=5
```

After the guest is booted, check that the assigned USB device is present on it.

```
tux@vmguest:~> lsusb
[...]
Bus 001 Device 002: ID 12d1:1406 Huawei Technologies Co., Ltd. E1750
[...]
```

 Note

The guest operating system must take care of mounting the assigned USB device so that it is accessible for the user.

26.3.6 PCI Pass-Through (Deprecated)

PCI Pass-Through is a technique to give your VM Guest exclusive access to a VM Host Server PCI device. Prerequisite for this feature is a VM Host Server configuration described in *Important: Requirements for VFIO and SR-IOV*. Assigning graphics cards is not supported by SUSE.

 Important: PCI Pass-Through is deprecated

KVM PCI Pass-Through has been replaced by VFIO (see *VFIO* for more information). Although it is still supported by SUSE, it is recommended to use VFIO for assigning PCI devices as described in *Section 26.3.4, "VFIO: Secure Direct Access to Devices"*. **vt.io.vfio**

PROCEDURE 26.3: CONFIGURING PCI PASS-THROUGH (DEPRECATED)

1. Identify the host PCI device to assign to the guest.

```
tux > sudo lspci -nn
[...] 00:1b.0 Audio device [0403]: Intel Corporation 82801H (ICH8 Family) \
HD Audio Controller [8086:284b] (rev 02) [...]
```

Note down the device (00:1b.0) and vendor (8086:284b) ID.

2. Unbind the device from host Kernel driver and bind it to the PCI stub driver.

```
sudo modprobe pci_stub
sudo echo "8086 284b" > /sys/bus/pci/drivers/pci-stub/new_id
```

```
sudo echo "0000:00:1b.0" > /sys/bus/pci/devices/0000:00:1b.0/driver/unbind
sudo echo "0000:00:1b.0" > /sys/bus/pci/drivers/pci-stub/bind
```

3. Now run the VM Guest with the PCI device assigned.

```
qemu-system-x86_64 [...] -device pci-assign,host=00:1b.0
```

 Note: IRQ Sharing

If the PCI device shares IRQ with other devices, it cannot be assigned to a VM Guest.

KVM also supports PCI device hot-plugging to a VM Guest. To achieve this, you need to switch to a QEMU monitor (see *Chapter 29, Virtual Machine Administration Using QEMU Monitor* for more information) and issue the following commands:

- hot-add:

```
device_add pci-assign,host=00:1b.0,id=new_pci_device
```

- hot-remove:

```
device_del new_pci_device
```

26.3.7   VirtFS: Sharing Directories between Host and Guests

VM Guests usually run in a separate computing space—they are provided their own memory range, dedicated CPUs, and file system space. The ability to share parts of the VM Host Server's file system makes the virtualization environment more flexible by simplifying mutual data exchange. Network file systems, such as CIFS and NFS, have been the traditional way of sharing directories. But as they are not specifically designed for virtualization purposes, they suffer from major performance and feature issues.

KVM introduces a new optimized method called *VirtFS* (sometimes called "file system passthrough"). VirtFS uses a paravirtual file system driver, which avoids converting the guest application file system operations into block device operations, and then again into host file system operations.

You typically use VirtFS for the following situations:

- To access a shared directory from several guests, or to provide guest-to-guest file system access.

- To replace the virtual disk as the root file system to which the guest's RAM disk connects during the guest boot process.

- To provide storage services to different customers from a single host file system in a cloud environment.

26.3.7.1 Implementation

In QEMU, the implementation of VirtFS is facilitated by defining two types of devices:

- `virtio-9p-pci` device which transports protocol messages and data between the host and the guest.

- `fsdev` device which defines the export file system properties, such as file system type and security model.

EXAMPLE 26.1: EXPORTING HOST'S FILE SYSTEM WITH VIRTFS

```
qemu-system-x86_64 [...] \
-fsdev local,id=exp1❶,path=/tmp/❷,security_model=mapped❸ \
-device virtio-9p-pci,fsdev=exp1❹,mount_tag=v_tmp❺
```

❶ Identification of the file system to be exported.

❷ File system path on the host to be exported.

❸ Security model to be used—`mapped` keeps the guest file system modes and permissions isolated from the host, while `none` invokes a "pass-through" security model in which permission changes on the guest's files are reflected on the host as well.

❹ The exported file system ID defined before with `-fsdev id=`.

❺ Mount tag used later on the guest to mount the exported file system.

Such an exported file system can be mounted on the guest like this

```
sudo mount -t 9p -o trans=virtio v_tmp /mnt
```

where `v_tmp` is the mount tag defined earlier with `-device mount_tag=` and `/mnt` is the mount point where you want to mount the exported file system.

26.3.8   KSM: Sharing Memory Pages between Guests

Kernel SamePage Merging (*KSM*) is a Linux Kernel feature that merges identical memory pages from multiple running processes into one memory region. Because KVM guests run as processes under Linux, *KSM* provides the memory overcommit feature to hypervisors for more efficient use of memory. Therefore, if you need to run multiple virtual machines on a host with limited memory, *KSM* may be helpful to you.

KSM stores its status information in the files under the `/sys/kernel/mm/ksm` directory:

```
tux > ls -1 /sys/kernel/mm/ksm
full_scans
merge_across_nodes
pages_shared
pages_sharing
pages_to_scan
pages_unshared
pages_volatile
run
sleep_millisecs
```

For more information on the meaning of the `/sys/kernel/mm/ksm/*` files, see `/usr/src/linux/Documentation/vm/ksm.txt` (package `kernel-source`).

To use *KSM*, do the following.

1. Although SLES 12 SP1 includes *KSM* support in the kernel, it is disabled by default. To enable it, run the following command: SLES.

```
root # echo 1 > /sys/kernel/mm/ksm/run
```

2. Now run several VM Guests under KVM and inspect the content of files `pages_sharing` and `pages_shared`, for example:

```
while [ 1 ]; do cat /sys/kernel/mm/ksm/pages_shared; sleep 1; done
```

```
13522
13523
13519
13518
13520
13520
13528
```

KSM: Sharing Memory Pages between Guests

27   Guest Installation

The `libvirt`-based tools such as **virt-manager**, **virt-install**, or **vm-install** offer convenient interfaces to set up and manage virtual machines. They act as a kind of wrapper for the **qemu-system-ARCH** command. However, it is also possible to use **qemu-system-ARCH** directly without using `libvirt`-based tools.

 Warning: qemu-system-ARCH and libvirt

*Virtual Machine*s created with **qemu-system-ARCH** are not "visible" for the `libvirt`-based tools.

27.1   Basic Installation with **qemu-system-ARCH**

In the following example, a virtual machine for a SUSE Linux Enterprise Server 11 installation is created. For detailed information on the commands, refer to the respective man pages.

If you do not already have an image of a system that you want to run in a virtualized environment, you need to create one from the installation media. In such case, you need to prepare a hard disk image, and obtain an image of the installation media or the media itself.

Create a hard disk with **qemu-img**.

```
qemu-img create❶ -f raw❷ /images/sles/hda❸ 8G❹
```

❶ The subcommand `create` tells **qemu-img** to create a new image.

❷ Specify the disk's format with the `-f` parameter.

❸ The full path to the image file.

❹ The size of the image—8 GB in this case. The image is created as a *Sparse image file* file that grows when the disk is filled with data. The specified size defines the maximum size to which the image file can grow.

After at least one hard disk image is created, you can set up a virtual machine with **qemu-system-ARCH** that will boot into the installation system:

```
qemu-system-x86_64 -name "sles"❶ -machine accel=kvm -M.pc❷ -m 768❸ \
-smp 2❹ -boot d❺ \
```

```
-drive file=/images/sles/hda,if=virtio,index=0,media=disk,format=raw❻ \
-drive file=/isos/SLES-11-SP3-DVD-x86_64-GM-DVD1.iso,index=1,media=cdrom❼ \
-net nic,model=virtio,macaddr=52:54:00:05:11:11❽ -net user\
-vga cirrus❾ -balloon virtio❿
```

❶ Name of the virtual machine that will be displayed in the window caption and be used for the VNC server. This name must be unique.

❷ Specifies the machine type. Use `qemu-system-ARCH` `-M ?` to display a list of valid parameters. `pc` is the default *Standard PC*.

❸ Maximum amount of memory for the virtual machine.

❹ Defines an SMP system with two processors.

❺ Specifies the boot order. Valid values are `a`, `b` (floppy 1 and 2), `c` (first hard disk), `d` (first CD-ROM), or `n` to `p` (Ether-boot from network adapter 1-3). Defaults to `c`.

❻ Defines the first (`index=0`) hard disk. It will be accessed as a paravirtualized (`if=virtio`) drive in `raw` format.

❼ The second (`index=1`) image drive will act as a CD-ROM.

❽ Defines a paravirtualized (`model=virtio`) network adapter with the MAC address `52:54:00:05:11:11`. Be sure to specify a unique MAC address, otherwise a network conflict may occur.

❾ Specifies the graphic card. If you specify `none`, the graphic card will be disabled.

❿ Defines the paravirtualized balloon device that allows to dynamically change the amount of memory (up to the maximum value specified with the parameter `-m`).

After the installation of the guest operating system finishes, you can easily start the related virtual machine without the need to specify the CD-ROM device:

```
qemu-system-x86_64 -name "sles" -machine type=pc,accel=kvm -m 768 \
-smp 2 -boot c \
-drive file=/images/sles/hda,if=virtio,index=0,media=disk,format=raw \
-net nic,model=virtio,macaddr=52:54:00:05:11:11 \
-vga cirrus -balloon virtio
```

27.2 Managing Disk Images with `qemu-img`

In the previous section (see *Section 27.1, "Basic Installation with* `qemu-system-ARCH`*"*), we used the `qemu-img` command to create an image of a hard disk. You can, however, use `qemu-img` for general disk image manipulation. This section introduces useful `qemu-img` subcommands to help manage the disk images flexibly.

27.2.1 General Information on qemu-img Invocation

`qemu-img` uses subcommands (like `zypper` does) to do specific tasks. Each subcommand understands a different set of options. Some options are general and used by more of these subcommands, while some are unique to the related subcommand. See the qemu-img manual page (`man 1 qemu-img`) for a list of all supported options. `qemu-img` uses the following general syntax:

```
qemu-img subcommand [options]
```

and supports the following subcommands:

create
: Creates a new disk image on the file system.

check
: Checks an existing disk image for errors.

compare
: Check if two images have the same content.

map
: Dumps the metadata of the image file name and its backing file chain.

amend
: Amends the image format specific options for the image file name.

convert
: Converts an existing disk image to a new one in a different format.

info
: Displays information about the relevant disk image.

snapshot
: Manages snapshots of existing disk images.

`commit`

> Applies changes made to an existing disk image.

`rebase`

> Creates a new base image based on an existing image.

`resize`

> Increases or decreases the size of an existing image.

27.2.2 Creating, Converting and Checking Disk Images

This section describes how to create disk images, check their condition, convert a disk image from one format to another, and get detailed information about a particular disk image.

27.2.2.1 qemu-img create

Use **qemu-img create** to create a new disk image for your VM Guest operating system. The command uses the following syntax:

```
qemu-img create -f fmt❶ -o options❷ fname❸ size❹
```

❶ The format of the target image. Supported formats are `qed`, `qcow2`, and `raw`.

❷ Some image formats support additional options to be passed on the command line. You can specify them here with the `-o` option. The `raw` image format supports only the `size` option, so it is possible to insert `-o size=8G` instead of adding the size option at the end of the command.

❸ Path to the target disk image to be created.

❹ Size of the target disk image (if not already specified with the `-o size=<image_size>` option. Optional suffixes for the image size are `K` (kilobyte), `M` (megabyte), `G` (gigabyte), or `T` (terabyte).

To create a new disk image `sles.raw` in the directory `/images` growing up to a maximum size of 4 GB, run the following command:

```
tux > qemu-img create -f raw -o size=4G /images/sles.raw
Formatting '/images/sles.raw', fmt=raw size=4294967296
```

```
tux > ls -l /images/sles.raw
-rw-r--r-- 1 tux users 4294967296 Nov 15 15:56 /images/sles.raw


tux > qemu-img info /images/sles.raw
image: /images/sles11.raw
file format: raw
virtual size: 4.0G (4294967296 bytes)
disk size: 0
```

As you can see, the *virtual* size of the newly created image is 4 GB, but the actual reported disk size is 0 as no data has been written to the image yet.

 Tip: VM Guest Images on the Btrfs File System

If you need to create a disk image on the Btrfs file system, you can use `nocow=on` to reduce the performance overhead created by the copy-on-write feature of Btrfs:

```
qemu-img create -o nocow=on test.img 8G
```

If you, however, want to use copy-on-write (for example for creating snapshots or sharing them across virtual machines), then leave the command line without the `nocow` option.

27.2.2.2 qemu-img convert

Use **qemu-img convert** to convert disk images to another format. To get a complete list of image formats supported by QEMU, run **qemu-img** `-h` and look at the last line of the output. The command uses the following syntax:

```
qemu-img convert -c❶ -f fmt❷ -O out_fmt❸ -o options❹ fname❺ out_fname❻
```

❶ Applies compression on the target disk image. Only qcow and qcow2 formats support compression.

❷ The format of the source disk image. It is usually autodetected and can therefore be omitted.

❸ The format of the target disk image.

❹ Specify additional options relevant for the target image format. Use `-o ?` to view the list of options supported by the target image format.

Creating, Converting and Checking Disk Images

⑤   Path to the source disk image to be converted.

⑥   Path to the converted target disk image.

```
tux > qemu-img convert -O vmdk /images/sles.raw \
/images/sles.vmdk


tux > ls -l /images/
-rw-r--r-- 1 tux users 4294967296 16. lis 10.50 sles.raw
-rw-r--r-- 1 tux users 2574450688 16. lis 14.18 sles.vmdk
```

To see a list of options relevant for the selected target image format, run the following command
(replace vmdk with your image format):

```
tux > qemu-img convert -O vmdk /images/sles.raw \
/images/sles.vmdk -o ?
Supported options:
size               Virtual disk size
backing_file       File name of a base image
compat6            VMDK version 6 image
subformat          VMDK flat extent format, can be one of {monolithicSparse \
    (default) | monolithicFlat | twoGbMaxExtentSparse | twoGbMaxExtentFlat}
scsi               SCSI image
```

27.2.2.3   qemu-img check

Use **qemu-img check** to check the existing disk image for errors. Not all disk image formats
support this feature. The command uses the following syntax:

```
qemu-img check -f fmt① fname②
```

①   The format of the source disk image. It is usually autodetected and can therefore be omitted.

②   Path to the source disk image to be checked.

If no error is found, the command returns no output. Otherwise, the type and number of errors
found is shown.

```
tux > qemu-img check -f qcow2 /images/sles.qcow2
```

```
ERROR: invalid cluster offset=0x2af0000
[...]
ERROR: invalid cluster offset=0x34ab0000
378 errors were found on the image.
```

27.2.2.4   Increasing the Size of an Existing Disk Image

When creating a new image, you must specify its maximum size before the image is created (see *Section 27.2.2.1, "qemu-img create"*). After you have installed the VM Guest and have been using it for some time, the initial size of the image may no longer be sufficient and you may need to add more space to it.

To increase the size of an existing disk image by 2 Gigabytes, use:

```
qemu-img resize /images/sles.raw +2GB
```

 Note

> You can resize the disk image using the formats raw, qcow2 and qed . To resize an image in another format, convert it to a supported format with **qemu-img convert** first.

The image now contains an empty space of 2 GB after the final partition. You can resize the existing partitions or add new ones.

Creating, Converting and Checking Disk Images

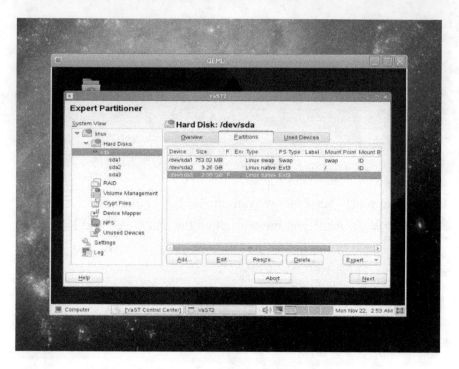

FIGURE 27.1: NEW 2GB PARTITION IN GUEST YAST PARTITIONER

27.2.3 Managing Snapshots of Virtual Machines with qemu-img

Virtual Machine snapshots are snapshots of the complete environment in which a VM Guest is running. The snapshot includes the state of the processor (CPU), memory (RAM), devices, and all writable disks.

Snapshots are helpful when you need to save your virtual machine in a particular state. For example, after you configured network services on a virtualized server and want to quickly start the virtual machine in the same state you last saved it. Or you can create a snapshot after the virtual machine has been powered off to create a backup state before you try something experimental and possibly make VM Guest unstable. This section introduces the latter case, while the former is described in *Chapter 29, Virtual Machine Administration Using QEMU Monitor*.

To use snapshots, your VM Guest must contain at least one writable hard disk image in `qcow2` format. This device is usually the first virtual hard disk.

Virtual Machine snapshots are created with the `savevm` command in the interactive QEMU monitor. To make identifying a particular snapshot easier, you can assign it a *tag*. For more information on QEMU monitor, see *Chapter 29, Virtual Machine Administration Using QEMU Monitor*.

Once your qcow2 disk image contains saved snapshots, you can inspect them with the **qemu-img snapshot** command.

 Warning: Shut Down the VM Guest

Do not create or delete virtual machine snapshots with the **qemu-img snapshot** command while the virtual machine is running. Otherwise, you may damage the disk image with the state of the virtual machine saved.

27.2.3.1   Listing Existing Snapshots

Use **qemu-img snapshot -l** *disk_image* to view a list of all existing snapshots saved in the disk_image image. You can get the list even while the VM Guest is running.

```
tux > qemu-img snapshot -l /images/sles.qcow2
Snapshot list:
ID❶        TAG❷               VM SIZE❸         DATE❹             VM CLOCK❺
1          booting            4.4M 2013-11-22 10:51:10   00:00:20.476
2          booted             184M 2013-11-22 10:53:03   00:02:05.394
3          logged_in          273M 2013-11-22 11:00:25   00:04:34.843
4          ff_and_term_running 372M 2013-11-22 11:12:27  00:08:44.965
```

❶   Unique identification number of the snapshot. Usually auto-incremented.

❷   Unique description string of the snapshot. It is meant as a human-readable version of the ID.

❸   The disk space occupied by the snapshot. Note that the more memory is consumed by running applications, the bigger the snapshot is.

❹   Time and date the snapshot was created.

❺   The current state of the virtual machine's clock.

27.2.3.2   Creating Snapshots of a Powered-Off Virtual Machine

Use **qemu-img snapshot -c** *snapshot_title* *disk_image* to create a snapshot of the current state of a virtual machine that was previously powered off.

```
tux > qemu-img snapshot -c backup_snapshot /images/sles.qcow2
```

```
tux > qemu-img snapshot -l /images/sles.qcow2
Snapshot list:
ID      TAG                 VM SIZE               DATE        VM CLOCK
1       booting             4.4M  2013-11-22 10:51:10   00:00:20.476
2       booted              184M  2013-11-22 10:53:03   00:02:05.394
3       logged_in           273M  2013-11-22 11:00:25   00:04:34.843
4       ff_and_term_running 372M  2013-11-22 11:12:27   00:08:44.965
5       backup_snapshot       0  2013-11-22 14:14:00   00:00:00.000
```

If something breaks in your VM Guest and you need to restore the state of the saved snapshot (ID 5 in our example), power off your VM Guest and execute the following command:

```
tux > qemu-img snapshot -a 5 /images/sles.qcow2
```

The next time you run the virtual machine with **qemu-system-ARCH**, it will be in the state of snapshot number 5.

 Note

> The **qemu-img snapshot -c** command is not related to the savevm command of QEMU monitor (see *Chapter 29, Virtual Machine Administration Using QEMU Monitor*). For example, you cannot apply a snapshot with **qemu-img snapshot -a** on a snapshot created with savevm in QEMU's monitor.

27.2.3.3   Deleting Snapshots

Use **qemu-img snapshot -d** *snapshot_id disk_image* to delete old or unneeded snapshots of a virtual machine. This saves some disk space inside the qcow2 disk image as the space occupied by the snapshot data is restored:

```
tux > qemu-img snapshot -d 2 /images/sles.qcow2
```

27.2.4 Manipulate Disk Images Effectively

Imagine the following real-life situation: you are a server administrator who runs and manages several virtualized operating systems. One group of these systems is based on one specific distribution, while another group (or groups) is based on different versions of the distribution or even on a different (and maybe non-Unix) platform. And to make the case even more complex, individual virtual guest systems based on the same distribution usually differ according to the department and deployment: a file server typically uses a different setup and services than a Web server does, while both may still be based on SUSE® Linux Enterprise Server.

With QEMU it is possible to create "base" disk images. You can use them as template virtual machines. These base images will save you plenty of time because you will never need to install the same operating system more than once.

27.2.4.1 Base and Derived Images

First, build a disk image as usual and install the target system on it. For more information, see *Section 27.1, "Basic Installation with* `qemu-system-ARCH`*"* and *Section 27.2.2, "Creating, Converting and Checking Disk Images"*. Then build a new image while using the first one as a base image. The base image is also called a *backing* file. After your new *derived* image is built, never boot the base image again, but boot the derived image instead. Several derived images may depend on one base image at the same time. Therefore, changing the base image can damage the dependencies. While using your derived image, QEMU writes changes to it and uses the base image only for reading.

It is a good practice to create a base image from a freshly installed (and, if needed, registered) operating system with no patches applied and no additional applications installed or removed. Later on, you can create another base image with the latest patches applied and based on the original base image.

27.2.4.2 Creating Derived Images

 Note

While you can use the `raw` format for base images, you cannot use it for derived images because the `raw` format does not support the `backing_file` option. Use for example the `qcow2` format for the derived images.

For example, `/images/sles_base.raw` is the base image holding a freshly installed system.

```
tux > qemu-img info /images/sles_base.raw
image: /images/sles_base.raw
file format: raw
virtual size: 4.0G (4294967296 bytes)
disk size: 2.4G
```

The image's reserved size is 4 GB, the actual size is 2.4 GB, and its format is `raw`. Create an image derived from the `/images/sles_base.raw` base image with:

```
tux > qemu-img create -f qcow2 /images/sles_derived.qcow2 \
-o backing_file=/images/sles_base.raw
Formatting '/images/sles_derived.qcow2', fmt=qcow2 size=4294967296 \
backing_file='/images/sles_base.raw' encryption=off cluster_size=0
```

Look at the derived image details:

```
tux > qemu-img info /images/sles_derived.qcow2
image: /images/sles_derived.qcow2
file format: qcow2
virtual size: 4.0G (4294967296 bytes)
disk size: 140K
cluster_size: 65536
backing file: /images/sles_base.raw \
(actual path: /images/sles_base.raw)
```

Although the reserved size of the derived image is the same as the size of the base image (4 GB), the actual size is 140 KB only. The reason is that only changes made to the system inside the derived image are saved. Run the derived virtual machine, register it, if needed, and apply the latest patches. Do any other changes in the system such as removing unneeded or installing new software packages. Then shut the VM Guest down and examine its details once more:

```
tux > qemu-img info /images/sles_derived.qcow2
image: /images/sles_derived.qcow2
file format: qcow2
virtual size: 4.0G (4294967296 bytes)
```

```
disk size: 1.1G
cluster_size: 65536
backing file: /images/sles_base.raw \
(actual path: /images/sles_base.raw)
```

The `disk size` value has grown to 1.1 GB, which is the disk space occupied by the changes on the file system compared to the base image.

27.2.4.3   Rebasing Derived Images

After you have modified the derived image (applied patches, installed specific applications, changed environment settings, etc.), it reaches the desired state. At that point, you may want to merge the original base image and the derived image to create a new base image.

Your original base image (`/images/sles_base.raw`) holds a freshly installed system and can be a template for new modified base images, while the new one can contain the same system as the first one plus all security and update patches applied, for example. After you have created this new base image, you can use it as a template for more specialized derived images as well. The new base image becomes independent of the original one. The process of creating base images from derived ones is called *rebasing*:

```
tux > qemu-img convert /images/sles_derived.qcow2 \
-O raw /images/sles_base2.raw
```

This command created the new base image `/images/sles_base2.raw` using the `raw` format.

```
tux > qemu-img info /images/sles_base2.raw
image: /images/sles11_base2.raw
file format: raw
virtual size: 4.0G (4294967296 bytes)
disk size: 2.8G
```

The new image is 0.4 gigabytes bigger than the original base image. It uses no backing file, and you can easily create new derived images based upon it. This lets you create a sophisticated hierarchy of virtual disk images for your organization, saving a lot of time and work.

27.2.4.4 Mounting an Image on a VM Host Server

Sometimes it is useful to mount a virtual disk image under the host system. It is strongly recommended to read *Chapter 16, libguestfs* and use dedicated tools to access a virtual machine image. But if for some reason you need to do it manually, just follow this guide.

Linux systems can mount an internal partition of a <u>raw</u> disk image using a loopback device. The first example procedure is more complex but more illustrative, while the second one is straightforward:

PROCEDURE 27.1: MOUNTING DISK IMAGE BY CALCULATING PARTITION OFFSET

1. Set a *loop* device on the disk image whose partition you want to mount.

   ```
   tux > losetup /dev/loop0 /images/sles_base.raw
   ```

2. Find the *sector size* and the starting *sector number* of the partition you want to mount.

   ```
   tux > fdisk -lu /dev/loop0

   Disk /dev/loop0: 4294 MB, 4294967296 bytes
   255 heads, 63 sectors/track, 522 cylinders, total 8388608 sectors
   Units = sectors of 1 * 512 = 512❶ bytes
   Disk identifier: 0x000ceca8


        Device Boot      Start         End      Blocks   Id  System
   /dev/loop0p1             63     1542239      771088+  82  Linux swap
   /dev/loop0p2   *     1542240❷    8385929     3421845  83  Linux
   ```

   ❶ The disk sector size.

   ❷ The starting sector of the partition.

3. Calculate the partition start offset:

   sector_size * sector_start = 512 * 1542240 = 789626880

4. Delete the loop and mount the partition inside the disk image with the calculated offset on a prepared directory.

   ```
   tux > losetup -d /dev/loop0
   tux > mount -o loop,offset=789626880 \
   ```

```
/images/sles_base.raw /mnt/sles/
tux > ls -l /mnt/sles/
total 112
drwxr-xr-x   2 root root   4096 Nov 16 10:02 bin
drwxr-xr-x   3 root root   4096 Nov 16 10:27 boot
drwxr-xr-x   5 root root   4096 Nov 16 09:11 dev
[...]
drwxrwxrwt  14 root root   4096 Nov 24 09:50 tmp
drwxr-xr-x  12 root root   4096 Nov 16 09:16 usr
drwxr-xr-x  15 root root   4096 Nov 16 09:22 var
```

5. Copy one or more files onto the mounted partition and unmount it when finished.

```
tux > cp /etc/X11/xorg.conf /mnt/sles/root/tmp
tux > ls -l /mnt/sles/root/tmp
tux > umount /mnt/sles/
```

Warning: Do not Write to Images Currently in Use

Never mount a partition of an image of a running virtual machine in a read-write mode. This could corrupt the partition and break the whole VM Guest.

Manipulate Disk Images Effectively

28 Running Virtual Machines with qemu-system-ARCH

Once you have a virtual disk image ready (for more information on disk images, see *Section 27.2, "Managing Disk Images with* `qemu-img`*"*), it is time to start the related virtual machine. *Section 27.1, "Basic Installation with* `qemu-system-ARCH`*"* introduced simple commands to install and run a VM Guest. This chapter focuses on a more detailed explanation of `qemu-system-ARCH` usage, and shows solutions for more specific tasks. For a complete list of `qemu-system-ARCH`'s options, see its manual page (`man 1 qemu`).

28.1 Basic `qemu-system-ARCH` Invocation

The `qemu-system-ARCH` command uses the following syntax:

```
qemu-system-ARCH options❶ disk_img❷
```

❶ `qemu-system-ARCH` understands many options. Most of them define parameters of the emulated hardware, while others affect more general emulator behavior. If you do not supply any options, default values are used, and you need to supply the path to a disk image to be run.

❷ Path to the disk image holding the guest system you want to virtualize. `qemu-system-ARCH` supports many image formats. Use `qemu-img` `--help` to list them. If you do not supply the path to a disk image as a separate argument, you need to use the `-drive file=` option.

28.2 General `qemu-system-ARCH` Options

This section introduces general `qemu-system-ARCH` options and options related to the basic emulated hardware, such as the virtual machine's processor, memory, model type, or time processing methods.

`-name `*`name_of_guest`*
    Specifies the name of the running guest system. The name is displayed in the window caption and used for the VNC server.

`-boot` *options*

> Specifies the order in which the defined drives will be booted. Drives are represented by letters, where a and b stand for the floppy drives 1 and 2, c stands for the first hard disk, d stands for the first CD-ROM drive, and n to p stand for Ether-boot network adapters. For example, `qemu-system-ARCH [...] -boot order=ndc` first tries to boot from network, then from the first CD-ROM drive, and finally from the first hard disk.

`-pidfile` *fname*

> Stores the QEMU's process identification number (PID) in a file. This is useful if you run QEMU from a script.

`-nodefaults`

> By default QEMU creates basic virtual devices even if you do not specify them on the command line. This option turns this feature off, and you must specify every single device manually, including graphical and network cards, parallel or serial ports, or virtual consoles. Even QEMU monitor is not attached by default.

`-daemonize`

> "Daemonizes" the QEMU process after it is started. QEMU will detach from the standard input and standard output after it is ready to receive connections on any of its devices.

 Note: SeaBIOS BIOS Implementation

> SeaBIOS is the default BIOS used. You can boot USB devices, any drive (CD-ROM, Floppy, or a hard disk). It has USB mouse and keyboard support and supports multiple VGA cards. For more information about SeaBIOS, refer to the SeaBIOS Website [http://www.seabios.org/SeaBIOS].

28.2.1 Basic Virtual Hardware

28.2.1.1 Machine Type

You can specifies the type of the emulated machine. Run **qemu-system-ARCH -M help** to view a list of supported machine types.

```
tux > qemu-system-x86_64 -M help
```

```
Supported machines are:
pc                 Standard PC (i440FX + PIIX, 1996) (alias of pc-i440fx-2.3)
pc-i440fx-2.3      Standard PC (i440FX + PIIX, 1996) (default)
pc-i440fx-2.2      Standard PC (i440FX + PIIX, 1996)
pc-i440fx-2.1      Standard PC (i440FX + PIIX, 1996)
pc-i440fx-2.0      Standard PC (i440FX + PIIX, 1996)
pc-i440fx-1.7      Standard PC (i440FX + PIIX, 1996)
pc-i440fx-1.6      Standard PC (i440FX + PIIX, 1996)
pc-i440fx-1.5      Standard PC (i440FX + PIIX, 1996)
pc-i440fx-1.4      Standard PC (i440FX + PIIX, 1996)
pc-1.3             Standard PC (i440FX + PIIX, 1996)
pc-1.2             Standard PC (i440FX + PIIX, 1996)
pc-1.1             Standard PC (i440FX + PIIX, 1996)
pc-1.0             Standard PC (i440FX + PIIX, 1996)
pc-0.15            Standard PC (i440FX + PIIX, 1996)
pc-0.14            Standard PC (i440FX + PIIX, 1996)
pc-0.13            Standard PC (i440FX + PIIX, 1996)
pc-0.12            Standard PC (i440FX + PIIX, 1996)
pc-0.11            Standard PC (i440FX + PIIX, 1996)
pc-0.10            Standard PC (i440FX + PIIX, 1996)
q35                Standard PC (Q35 + ICH9, 2009) (alias of pc-q35-2.3)
pc-q35-2.3         Standard PC (Q35 + ICH9, 2009)
pc-q35-2.2         Standard PC (Q35 + ICH9, 2009)
pc-q35-2.1         Standard PC (Q35 + ICH9, 2009)
pc-q35-2.0         Standard PC (Q35 + ICH9, 2009)
pc-q35-1.7         Standard PC (Q35 + ICH9, 2009)
pc-q35-1.6         Standard PC (Q35 + ICH9, 2009)
pc-q35-1.5         Standard PC (Q35 + ICH9, 2009)
pc-q35-1.4         Standard PC (Q35 + ICH9, 2009)
isapc              ISA-only PC
none               empty machine
xenfv              Xen Fully-virtualized PC
xenpv              Xen Para-virtualized PC
```

Note: ISA-PC

The machine type *isapc: ISA-only-PC* is unsupported.

28.2.1.2 CPU Model

To specify the type of the processor (CPU) model, run **qemu-system-ARCH -cpu** *MODEL*. Use **qemu-system-ARCH -cpu help** to view a list of supported CPU models.

```
x86            qemu64  QEMU Virtual CPU version 2.3.1
x86            phenom  AMD Phenom(tm) 9550 Quad-Core Processor
x86          core2duo  Intel(R) Core(TM)2 Duo CPU      T7700  @ 2.40GHz
x86             kvm64  Common KVM processor
x86            qemu32  QEMU Virtual CPU version 2.3.1
x86             kvm32  Common 32-bit KVM processor
x86           coreduo  Genuine Intel(R) CPU            T2600  @ 2.16GHz
x86               486
x86           pentium
x86          pentium2
x86          pentium3
x86            athlon  QEMU Virtual CPU version 2.3.1
x86              n270  Intel(R) Atom(TM) CPU N270   @ 1.60GHz
x86            Conroe  Intel Celeron_4x0 (Conroe/Merom Class Core 2)
x86            Penryn  Intel Core 2 Duo P9xxx (Penryn Class Core 2)
x86           Nehalem  Intel Core i7 9xx (Nehalem Class Core i7)
x86          Westmere  Westmere E56xx/L56xx/X56xx (Nehalem-C)
x86       SandyBridge  Intel Xeon E312xx (Sandy Bridge)
x86         IvyBridge  Intel Xeon E3-12xx v2 (Ivy Bridge)
x86      Haswell-noTSX  Intel Core Processor (Haswell, no TSX)
x86           Haswell  Intel Core Processor (Haswell)
x86    Broadwell-noTSX  Intel Core Processor (Broadwell, no TSX)
x86         Broadwell  Intel Core Processor (Broadwell)
x86        Opteron_G1  AMD Opteron 240 (Gen 1 Class Opteron)
x86        Opteron_G2  AMD Opteron 22xx (Gen 2 Class Opteron)
x86        Opteron_G3  AMD Opteron 23xx (Gen 3 Class Opteron)
x86        Opteron_G4  AMD Opteron 62xx class CPU
```

```
x86        Opteron_G5  AMD Opteron 63xx class CPU
x86              host  KVM processor with all supported host features (only available
 in KVM mode)


Recognized CPUID flags:
fpu vme de pse tsc msr pae mce cx8 apic sep mtrr pge mca cmov pat pse36 pn
clflush ds acpi mmx fxsr sse sse2 ss ht tm ia64 pbe
pni|sse3 pclmulqdq|pclmuldq dtes64 monitor ds_cpl vmx smx est tm2 ssse3 cid
fma cx16 xtpr pdcm pcid dca sse4.1|sse4_1 sse4.2|sse4_2 x2apic movbe popcnt
tsc-deadline aes xsave osxsave avx f16c rdrand hypervisor
fsgsbase tsc_adjust bmi1 hle avx2 smep bmi2 erms invpcid rtm mpx avx512f
rdseed adx smap avx512pf avx512er avx512cd
syscall nx|xd mmxext fxsr_opt|ffxsr pdpe1gb rdtscp lm|i64 3dnowext 3dnow
lahf_lm cmp_legacy svm extapic cr8legacy abm sse4a misalignsse 3dnowprefetch
osvw ibs xop skinit wdt lwp fma4 tce nodeid_msr tbm topoext perfctr_core
perfctr_nb
invtsc
xstore xstore-en xcrypt xcrypt-en ace2 ace2-en phe phe-en pmm pmm-en
kvmclock kvm_nopiodelay kvm_mmu kvmclock kvm_asyncpf kvm_steal_time
kvm_pv_eoi kvm_pv_unhalt kvmclock-stable-bit
npt lbrv svm_lock nrip_save tsc_scale vmcb_clean flushbyasid decodeassists
pause_filter pfthreshold
xsaveopt xsavec xgetbv1 xsaves
```

CPU flags information can be found at CPUID Wikipedia [http://en.wikipedia.org/wiki/CPUID].

28.2.1.3   Other Basics Options

The following is a list of most commonly used options while launching *qemu* from command line. To see all options available refer to *qemu-doc* man page.

`-m megabytes`

> Specifies how many megabytes are used for the virtual RAM size.

`-balloon virtio`

> Specifies a paravirtualized device to dynamically change the amount of virtual RAM memory assigned to VM Guest. The top limit is the amount of memory specified with `-m`.

`-smp` *number_of_cpus*

>Specifies how many CPUs will be emulated. QEMU supports up to 255 CPUs on the PC platform (up to 64 with KVM acceleration used). This option also takes other CPU-related parameters, such as number of *sockets*, number of *cores* per socket, or number of *threads* per core.

The following is an example of a working **qemu-system-ARCH** command line:

```
tux > qemu-system-x86_64 -name "SLES 11 SP3" -M pc-i440fx-2.3 -m 512 \
-machine accel=kvm -cpu kvm64 -smp 2 /images/sles.raw
```

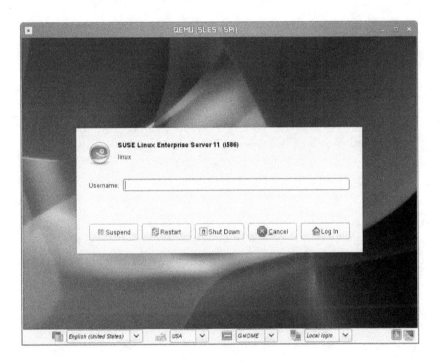

FIGURE 28.1: QEMU WINDOW WITH SLES 11 SP3 AS VM GUEST

`-no-acpi`

>Disables *ACPI* support.

`-S`

>QEMU starts with CPU stopped. To start CPU, enter `c` in QEMU monitor. For more information, see *Chapter 29, Virtual Machine Administration Using QEMU Monitor*.

Basic Virtual Hardware

28.2.2 Storing and Reading Configuration of Virtual Devices

-readconfig *cfg_file*

Instead of entering the devices configuration options on the command line each time you want to run VM Guest, **qemu-system-ARCH** can read it from a file that was either previously saved with -writeconfig or edited manually.

-writeconfig *cfg_file*

Dumps the current virtual machine's devices configuration to a text file. It can be consequently re-used with the -readconfig option.

```
tux > qemu-system-x86_64 -name "SLES 11 SP3" -machine accel=kvm -M pc-
i440fx-2.3 -m 512 -cpu kvm64 \
-smp 2 /images/sles.raw -writeconfig /images/sles.cfg
(exited)
tux > more /images/sles.cfg
# qemu config file

[drive]
  index = "0"
  media = "disk"
  file = "/images/sles_base.raw"
```

This way you can effectively manage the configuration of your virtual machines' devices in a well-arranged way.

28.2.3 Guest Real-Time Clock

-rtc *options*

Specifies the way the RTC is handled inside a VM Guest. By default, the clock of the guest is derived from that of the host system. Therefore, it is recommended that the host system clock is synchronized with an accurate external clock (for example, via NTP service).

If you need to isolate the VM Guest clock from the host one, specify clock=vm instead of the default clock=host.

You can also specify the initial time of the VM Guest's clock with the base option:

```
qemu-system-x86_64 [...] -rtc clock=vm,base=2010-12-03T01:02:00
```

Instead of a time stamp, you can specify `utc` or `localtime`. The former instructs VM Guest to start at the current UTC value (Coordinated Universal Time, see http:// en.wikipedia.org/wiki/UTC), while the latter applies the local time setting.

28.3   Using Devices in QEMU

QEMU virtual machines emulate all devices needed to run a VM Guest. QEMU supports, for example, several types of network cards, block devices (hard and removable drives), USB devices, character devices (serial and parallel ports), or multimedia devices (graphic and sound cards). This section introduces options to configure various types of supported devices.

 Tip

> If your device, such as `-drive`, needs a special driver and driver properties to be set, specify them with the `-device` option, and identify with `drive=` suboption. For example:
>
> ```
> qemu [...] -drive if=none,id=drive0,format=raw \
> -device virtio-blk-pci,drive=drive0,scsi=off ...
> ```
>
> To get help on available drivers and their properties, use `-device ?` and `-device driver,?`.

28.3.1   Block Devices

Block devices are vital for virtual machines. In general, these are fixed or removable storage media usually called *drives*. One of the connected hard disks typically holds the guest operating system to be virtualized.

Virtual Machine drives are defined with `-drive`. This option uses many sub-options, some are described in this section. For their complete list, see the manual page (**man 1 qemu**).

SUB-OPTIONS FOR THE `-drive` OPTION

`file=image_fname`

> Specifies the path to the disk image that will be used with this drive. If not specified, an empty (removable) drive is assumed.

`if=drive_interface`

> Specifies the type of interface to which the drive is connected. Currently only `floppy`, `scsi`, `ide`, or `virtio` are supported by SUSE. `virtio` defines a paravirtualized disk driver. Default is `ide`.

`index=index_of_connector`

> Specifies the index number of a connector on the disk interface (see the `if` option) where the drive is connected. If not specified, the index is automatically incremented.

`media=type`

> Specifies the type of media. Can be `disk` for hard disks, or `cdrom` for removable CD-ROM drives.

`format=img_fmt`

> Specifies the format of the connected disk image. If not specified, the format is autodetected. Currently, SUSE supports `qcow2`, `qed` and `raw` formats.

`cache=method`

> Specifies the caching method for the drive. Possible values are `unsafe`, `writethrough`, `writeback`, `directsync`, or `none`. For the `qcow2` image format, choose `writeback` if you care about performance. `none` disables the host page cache and, therefore, is the safest option. Default for image files is `writeback`. For more information, see *Chapter 14, Disk Cache Modes*.

Tip

To simplify defining block devices, QEMU understands several shortcuts which you may find handy when entering the `qemu-system-ARCH` command line.

You can use

```
qemu-system-x86_64 -cdrom /images/cdrom.iso
```

instead of

```
qemu-system-x86_64 -drive file=/images/cdrom.iso,index=2,media=cdrom
```

and

```
qemu-system-x86_64 -hda /images/imagei1.raw -hdb /images/image2.raw -hdc \
/images/image3.raw -hdd /images/image4.raw
```

instead of

```
qemu-system-x86_64 -drive file=/images/image1.raw,index=0,media=disk \
-drive file=/images/image2.raw,index=1,media=disk \
-drive file=/images/image3.raw,index=2,media=disk \
-drive file=/images/image4.raw,index=3,media=disk
```

Tip: Using Host Drives Instead of Images

As an alternative to using disk images (see *Section 27.2, "Managing Disk Images with* qemu-img*"*) you can also use existing VM Host Server disks, connect them as drives, and access them from VM Guest. Use the host disk device directly instead of disk image file names.

To access the host CD-ROM drive, use

```
qemu-system-x86_64 [...] -drive file=/dev/cdrom,media=cdrom
```

To access the host hard disk, use

```
qemu-system-x86_64 [...] -drive file=/dev/hdb,media=disk
```

A host drive used by a VM Guest must not be accessed concurrently by the VM Host Server or another VM Guest.

28.3.1.1   Freeing Unused Guest Disk Space

A *Sparse image file* is a type of disk image file that grows in size as the user adds data to it, taking up only as much disk space as is stored in it. For example, if you copy 1 GB of data inside the sparse disk image, its size grows by 1 GB. If you then delete for example 500 MB of the data, the image size does not by default decrease as expected.

That is why the `discard=on` option is introduced on the KVM command line. It tells the hypervisor to automatically free the "holes" after deleting data from the sparse guest image. Note that this option is valid only for the `if=scsi` drive interface:

```
qemu-system-x86_64 [...] -drive file=/path/to/file.img,if=scsi,discard=on
```

 Warning: Support Status

`if=scsi` is not supported. This interface does not map to *virtio-scsi*, but rather to the *lsi SCSI adapter*.

28.3.1.2   virtio-blk-data-plane

The *virtio-blk-data-plane* is a new feature for KVM. It enables a high-performance code path for I/O requests coming from VM Guests. More specifically, this feature introduces dedicated threads (one per virtual block device) to process I/O requests going through the *virtio-blk* driver. It uses the Linux AIO (asynchronous I/O) interface of the VM Host Server kernel directly—without the need to go through the QEMU block layer. Therefore, it can sustain very high I/O rates on storage setups.

The virtio-blk-data-plane feature can be enabled or disabled by the `x-data-plane=on|off` option on the **qemu** command line when starting the VM Guest:

```
tux > qemu [...] -drive if=none,id=drive0,cache=none,aio=native,\
format=raw,file=filename -device virtio-blk-pci,drive=drive0,scsi=off,\
config-wce=off,x-data-plane=on [...]
```

Currently, virtio-blk-data-plane has the following limitations:

- Only the raw image format is supported.

- No support for live migration.

- Block jobs and hot unplug operations fail with `-EBUSY`.

- I/O throttling limits are ignored.

- Only Linux VM Host Servers are supported because of the Linux AIO usage, but non-Linux VM Guests are supported.

> **(!) Important: Support Status**
>
> The virtio-blk-data-plane feature is not yet supported in SUSE Linux Enterprise Server. It is released as a technical preview only.

28.3.1.3   Bio-Based I/O Path for virtio-blk

For better performance of I/O-intensive applications, a new I/O path was introduced for the virtio-blk interface in kernel version 3.7. This bio-based block device driver skips the I/O scheduler, and thus shortens the I/O path in guest and has lower latency. It is especially useful for high-speed storage devices, such as SSD disks.

The driver is disabled by default. To use it, do the following:

1. Append **virtio_blk.use_bio=1** to the kernel command line on the guest. You can do so via *YaST* › *System* › *Boot Loader*.

   You can do it also by editing /etc/default/grub, searching for the line that contains *GRUB_CMDLINE_LINUX_DEFAULT=*, and adding the kernel parameter at the end. Then run **grub2-mkconfig >/boot/grub2/grub.cfg** to update the grub2 boot menu.

2. Reboot the guest with the new kernel command line active.

 Tip: Bio-Based Driver on Slow Devices

The bio-based virtio-blk driver does not help on slow devices such as spin hard disks. The reason is that the benefit of scheduling is larger than what the shortened bio path offers. Do not use the bio-based driver on slow devices.

28.3.2 Graphic Devices and Display Options

This section describes QEMU options affecting the type of the emulated video card and the way VM Guest graphical output is displayed.

28.3.2.1 Defining Video Cards

QEMU uses -vga to define a video card used to display VM Guest graphical output. The -vga option understands the following values:

Disables video cards on VM Guest (no video card is emulated). You can still access the running VM Guest via the serial console.

std

Emulates a standard VESA 2.0 VBE video card. Use it if you intend to use high display resolution on VM Guest.

`cirrus`

Emulates Cirrus Logic GD5446 video card. Good choice if you insist on high compatibility of the emulated video hardware. Most operating systems (even Windows 95) recognize this type of card.

 Tip

For best video performance with the `cirrus` type, use 16-bit color depth both on VM Guest and VM Host Server.

28.3.2.2   Display Options

The following options affect the way VM Guest graphical output is displayed.

`-display gtk`

Display video output in a GTK window. This interface provides drop-down menus and other UI elements to configure and control the VM during runtime.

`-display sdl`

Display video output via SDL (usually in a separate graphics window; see the SDL documentation for other possibilities).

`-spice option[,option[,...]]`

Enables the spice remote desktop protocol.

`-display vnc`

Refer to *Section 28.5, "Viewing a VM Guest with VNC"* for more information.

`-nographic`

Disables QEMU's graphical output. The emulated serial port is redirected to the console. After starting the virtual machine with `-nographic`, press Ctrl–A H in the virtual console to view the list of other useful shortcuts, for example, to toggle between the console and the QEMU monitor.

```
tux > qemu-system-x86_64 -hda /images/sles_base.raw -nographic


C-a h    print this help
C-a x    exit emulator
```

```
C-a s    save disk data back to file (if -snapshot)
C-a t    toggle console timestamps
C-a b    send break (magic sysrq)
C-a c    switch between console and monitor
C-a C-a  sends C-a
(pressed C-a c)


QEMU 2.3.1 monitor - type 'help' for more information
(qemu)
```

-no-frame

> Disables decorations for the QEMU window. Convenient for dedicated desktop work space.

-full-screen

> Starts QEMU graphical output in full screen mode.

-no-quit

> Disables the close button of the QEMU window and prevents it from being closed by force.

-alt-grab, -ctrl-grab

> By default QEMU window releases the "captured" mouse after Ctrl–Alt is pressed. You can change the key combination to either Ctrl–Alt–Shift (-alt-grab), or Right Ctrl (-ctrl-grab).

28.3.3   USB Devices

There are two ways to create USB devices usable by the VM Guest in KVM: you can either emulate new USB devices inside a VM Guest, or assign an existing host USB device to a VM Guest. To use USB devices in QEMU you first need to enable the generic USB driver with the -usb option. Then you can specify individual devices with the -usbdevice option.

28.3.3.1   Emulating USB Devices in VM Guest

SUSE currently supports the following types of USB devices: disk, host, serial, braille, net, mouse, and tablet.

disk

Emulates a mass storage device based on file. The optional `format` option is used rather than detecting the format.

```
qemu-system-x86_64 [...] -usbdevice
        disk:format=raw:/virt/usb_disk.raw
```

host

Pass through the host device (identified by bus.addr).

serial

Serial converter to a host character device.

braille

Emulates a braille device using BrlAPI to display the braille output.

net

Emulates a network adapter that supports CDC Ethernet and RNDIS protocols.

mouse

Emulates a virtual USB mouse. This option overrides the default PS/2 mouse emulation. The following example shows the hardware status of a mouse on VM Guest started with `qemu-system-ARCH [...] -usbdevice mouse`:

```
tux > sudo hwinfo --mouse
20: USB 00.0: 10503 USB Mouse
[Created at usb.122]
UDI: /org/freedesktop/Hal/devices/usb_device_627_1_1_if0
[...]
Hardware Class: mouse
Model: "Adomax QEMU USB Mouse"
Hotplug: USB
Vendor: usb 0x0627 "Adomax Technology Co., Ltd"
Device: usb 0x0001 "QEMU USB Mouse"
[...]
```

`tablet`

Emulates a pointer device that uses absolute coordinates (such as touchscreen). This option overrides the default PS/2 mouse emulation. The tablet device is useful if you are viewing VM Guest via the VNC protocol. See *Section 28.5, "Viewing a VM Guest with VNC"* for more information.

28.3.4 Character Devices

Use `-chardev` to create a new character device. The option uses the following general syntax:

```
qemu-system-x86_64 [...] -chardev backend_type,id=id_string
```

where *backend_type* can be one of `null`, `socket`, `udp`, `msmouse`, `vc`, `file`, `pipe`, `console`, `serial`, `pty`, `stdio`, `braille`, `tty`, or `parport`. All character devices must have a unique identification string up to 127 characters long. It is used to identify the device in other related directives. For the complete description of all back-end's sub-options, see the manual page (**man 1 qemu**). A brief description of the available `back-ends` follows:

`null`

Creates an empty device that outputs no data and drops any data it receives.

`stdio`

Connects to QEMU's process standard input and standard output.

`socket`

Creates a two-way stream socket. If *path* is specified, a Unix socket is created:

```
qemu-system-x86_64 [...] -chardev \
socket,id=unix_socket1,path=/tmp/unix_socket1,server
```

The *server* suboption specifies that the socket is a listening socket.
If *port* is specified, a TCP socket is created:

```
qemu-system-x86_64 [...] -chardev \
socket,id=tcp_socket1,host=localhost,port=7777,server,nowait
```

The command creates a local listening (`server`) TCP socket on port 7777. QEMU will not block waiting for a client to connect to the listening port (`nowait`).

udp

Sends all network traffic from VM Guest to a remote host over the UDP protocol.

```
qemu-system-x86_64 [...] -chardev
 udp,id=udp_fwd,host=mercury.example.com,port=7777
```

The command binds port 7777 on the remote host mercury.example.com and sends VM Guest network traffic there.

vc

Creates a new QEMU text console. You can optionally specify the dimensions of the virtual console:

```
qemu-system-x86_64 [...] -chardev vc,id=vc1,width=640,height=480 -mon
 chardev=vc1
```

The command creates a new virtual console called vc1 of the specified size, and connects the QEMU monitor to it.

file

Logs all traffic from VM Guest to a file on VM Host Server. The path is required and will be created if it does not exist.

```
qemu-system-x86_64 [...] -chardev file,id=qemu_log1,path=/var/log/qemu/
 guest1.log
```

By default QEMU creates a set of character devices for serial and parallel ports, and a special console for QEMU monitor. You can, however, create your own character devices and use them for the just mentioned purposes. The following options will help you:

-serial *char_dev*

Redirects the VM Guest's virtual serial port to a character device *char_dev* on VM Host Server. By default, it is a virtual console (vc) in graphical mode, and stdio in non-graphical mode. The -serial understands many sub-options. See the manual page **man 1 qemu** for a complete list of them.

You can emulate up to 4 serial ports. Use -serial none to disable all serial ports.

-parallel *device*

Redirects the VM Guest's parallel port to a *device*. This option supports the same devices as -serial.

Tip

With SUSE Linux Enterprise Server as a VM Host Server, you can directly use the hardware parallel port devices `/dev/parportN` where `N` is the number of the port.

You can emulate up to 3 parallel ports. Use `-parallel none` to disable all parallel ports.

`-monitor` *char_dev*

Redirects the QEMU monitor to a character device *char_dev* on VM Host Server. This option supports the same devices as `-serial`. By default, it is a virtual console (`vc`) in a graphical mode, and `stdio` in non-graphical mode.

For a complete list of available character devices back-ends, see the man page (**man 1 qemu**).

28.4 Networking in QEMU

Use the `-netdev` option in combination with `-device` to define a specific type of networking and a network interface card for your VM Guest. The syntax for the `-netdev` option is

```
-netdev type[,prop[=value][,...]]
```

Currently, SUSE supports the following network types: `user`, `bridge`, and `tap`. For a complete list of `-netdev` sub-options, see the manual page (**man 1 qemu**).

SUPPORTED `-netdev` **SUB-OPTIONS**

`bridge`

Uses a specified network helper to configure the TAP interface and attach it to a specified bridge. For more information, see *Section 28.4.3, "Bridged Networking"*.

`user`

Specifies user-mode networking. For more information, see *Section 28.4.2, "User-Mode Networking"*.

`tap`

Specifies bridged or routed networking. For more information, see *Section 28.4.3, "Bridged Networking"*.

28.4.1   Defining a Network Interface Card

Use `-netdev` together with the related `-device` option to add a new emulated network card:

```
qemu-system-x86_64 [...] \
-netdev tap❶,id=hostnet0 \
-device virtio-net-
pci❷,netdev=hostnet0,vlan=1❸,macaddr=00:16:35:AF:94:4B❹,name=ncard1
```

❶ Specifies the network device type.

❷ Specifies the model of the network card. Use `-device help` and search for the `Network devices:` section to get the list of all network card models supported by QEMU on your platform:

```
qemu-system-x86_64 -device help
[...]
Network devices:
name "e1000", bus PCI, desc "Intel Gigabit Ethernet"
name "e1000-82540em", bus PCI, desc "Intel Gigabit Ethernet"
name "e1000-82544gc", bus PCI, desc "Intel Gigabit Ethernet"
name "e1000-82545em", bus PCI, desc "Intel Gigabit Ethernet"
name "i82550", bus PCI, desc "Intel i82550 Ethernet"
name "i82551", bus PCI, desc "Intel i82551 Ethernet"
name "i82557a", bus PCI, desc "Intel i82557A Ethernet"
[...]
```

Currently, SUSE supports the models `rtl8139`, `e1000` and its variants `e1000-82540em`, `e1000-82544gc` and `e1000-82545em`, and `virtio-net-pci`. To view a list of options for a specific driver, add `help` as a driver option:

```
qemu-system-x86_64 -device e1000,help
e1000.mac=macaddr
e1000.vlan=vlan
e1000.netdev=netdev
e1000.bootindex=int32
e1000.autonegotiation=on/off
e1000.mitigation=on/off
```

```
e1000.addr=pci-devfn
e1000.romfile=str
e1000.rombar=uint32
e1000.multifunction=on/off
e1000.command_serr_enable=on/off
```

③ Connects the network interface to VLAN number 1. You can specify your own number— it is mainly useful for identification purpose. If you omit this suboption, QEMU uses the default 0.

④ Specifies the Media Access Control (MAC) address for the network card. It is a unique identifier and you are advised to always specify it. If not, QEMU supplies its own default MAC address and creates a possible MAC address conflict within the related VLAN.

28.4.2   User-Mode Networking

The `-netdev user` option instructs QEMU to use user-mode networking. This is the default if no networking mode is selected. Therefore, these command lines are equivalent:

```
qemu-system-x86_64 -hda /images/sles_base.raw
```

```
qemu-system-x86_64 -hda /images/sles_base.raw -netdev user,id=hostnet0
```

This mode is useful if you want to allow the VM Guest to access the external network resources, such as the Internet. By default, no incoming traffic is permitted and therefore, the VM Guest is not visible to other machines on the network. No administrator privileges are required in this networking mode. The user-mode is also useful for doing a network boot on your VM Guest from a local directory on VM Host Server.

The VM Guest allocates an IP address from a virtual DHCP server. VM Host Server (the DHCP server) is reachable at 10.0.2.2, while the IP address range for allocation starts from 10.0.2.15. You can use **ssh** to connect to VM Host Server at 10.0.2.2, and **scp** to copy files back and forth.

28.4.2.1   Command Line Examples

This section shows several examples on how to set up user-mode networking with QEMU.

```
qemu-system-x86_64 [...] \
-netdev user❶,id=hostnet0 \
-device virtio-net-pci,netdev=hostnet0,vlan=1❷,name=user_net1❸,restrict=yes❹
```

❶ Specifies user-mode networking.

❷ Connects to VLAN number 1. If omitted, defaults to 0.

❸ Specifies a human-readable name of the network stack. Useful when identifying it in the QEMU monitor.

❹ Isolates VM Guest. It will not be able to communicate with VM Host Server and no network packets will be routed to the external network.

EXAMPLE 28.2: USER-MODE NETWORKING WITH CUSTOM IP RANGE

```
qemu-system-x86_64 [...] \
-netdev user,id=hostnet0 \
-device virtio-net-
pci,netdev=hostnet0,net=10.2.0.0/8❶,host=10.2.0.6❷,dhcpstart=10.2.0.20❸,hostname=tux_kvm_guest
```

❶ Specifies the IP address of the network that VM Guest sees and optionally the netmask. Default is 10.0.2.0/8.

❷ Specifies the VM Host Server IP address that VM Guest sees. Default is 10.0.2.2.

❸ Specifies the first of the 16 IP addresses that the built-in DHCP server can assign to VM Guest. Default is 10.0.2.15.

❹ Specifies the host name that the built-in DHCP server will assign to VM Guest.

EXAMPLE 28.3: USER-MODE NETWORKING WITH NETWORK-BOOT AND TFTP

```
qemu-system-x86_64 [...] \
-netdev user,id=hostnet0 \
-device virtio-net-pci,netdev=hostnet0,tftp=/images/tftp_dir❶,bootfile=/images/
boot/pxelinux.0❷
```

❶ Activates a built-in TFTP (a file transfer protocol with the functionality of a very basic FTP) server. The files in the specified directory will be visible to a VM Guest as the root of a TFTP server.

❷ Broadcasts the specified file as a BOOTP (a network protocol that offers an IP address and a network location of a boot image, often used in diskless workstations) file. When used together with `tftp`, the VM Guest can boot from network from the local directory on the host.

EXAMPLE 28.4: USER-MODE NETWORKING WITH HOST PORT FORWARDING

```
qemu-system-x86_64 [...] \
-netdev user,id=hostnet0 \
-device virtio-net-pci,netdev=hostnet0,hostfwd=tcp::2222-:22
```

Forwards incoming TCP connections to the port 2222 on the host to the port 22 (`SSH`) on VM Guest. If `sshd` is running on VM Guest, enter

```
ssh qemu_host -p 2222
```

where `qemu_host` is the host name or IP address of the host system, to get a `SSH` prompt from VM Guest.

28.4.3   Bridged Networking

With the `-netdev tap` option, QEMU creates a network bridge by connecting the host TAP network device to a specified VLAN of VM Guest. Its network interface is then visible to the rest of the network. This method does not work by default and has to be explicitly specified.

First, create a network bridge and add a VM Host Server physical network interface (usually `eth0`) to it:

1. Start *YaST Control Center* and select *System › Network Settings*.

2. Click *Add* and select *Bridge* from the *Device Type* drop-down list in the *Hardware Dialog* window. Click *Next*.

3. Choose whether you need a dynamically or statically assigned IP address, and fill the related network settings if applicable.

4. In the *Bridged Devices* pane, select the Ethernet device to add to the bridge.

FIGURE 28.2: CONFIGURING NETWORK BRIDGE WITH YAST

Click *Next*. When asked about adapting an already configured device, click *Continue*.

5. Click *OK* to apply the changes. Check if the bridge is created:

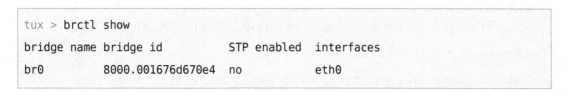

```
tux > brctl show
bridge name bridge id          STP enabled  interfaces
br0          8000.001676d670e4  no           eth0
```

28.4.3.1   Connecting to a Bridge Manually

Use the following example script to connect VM Guest to the newly created bridge interface br0. Several commands in the script are run via the **sudo** mechanism because they require root privileges.

Note: Required Packages

Make sure the `tunctl` and `bridge-utils` packages are installed on the VM Host Server. If not, install them with **`zypper in tunctl bridge-utils`**.

```
#!/bin/bash
bridge=br0 ❶
tap=$(sudo tunctl -u $(whoami) -b) ❷
sudo ip link set $tap up ❸
sleep 1s ❹
sudo brctl addif $bridge $tap ❺
qemu-system-x86_64 -machine accel=kvm -m 512 -hda /images/sles_base.raw \
-netdev tap,id=hostnet0 \
-device virtio-net-pci,netdev=hostnet0,vlan=0,macaddr=00:16:35:AF:94:4B,ifname=
$tap ❻ ,script=no ❼ ,downscript=no
sudo brctl delif $bridge $tap ❽
sudo ip link set $tap down ❾
sudo tunctl -d $tap ❿
```

❶ Name of the bridge device.

❷ Prepare a new TAP device and assign it to the user who runs the script. TAP devices are virtual network devices often used for virtualization and emulation setups.

❸ Bring up the newly created TAP network interface.

❹ Make a 1-second pause to make sure the new TAP network interface is really up.

❺ Add the new `TAP` device to the network bridge `br0`.

❻ The `ifname=` suboption specifies the name of the TAP network interface used for bridging.

❼ Before **`qemu-system-ARCH`** connects to a network bridge, it checks the `script` and `downscript` values. If it finds the specified scripts on the VM Host Server file system, it runs the `script` before it connects to the network bridge and `downscript` after it exits the network environment. You can use these scripts to first set up and bring up the bridged network devices, and then to deconfigure them. By default, `/etc/qemu-ifup` and `/etc/qemu-ifdown` are examined. If `script=no` and `downscript=no` are specified, the script execution is disabled and you need to take care of it manually.

⑧ Deletes the TAP interface from a network bridge `br0`.

⑨ Sets the state of the TAP device to `down`.

⑩ Deconfigures the TAP device.

28.4.3.2 Connecting to a Bridge with qemu-bridge-helper

Another way to connect VM Guest to a network through a network bridge is by means of the `qemu-bridge-helper` helper program. It configures the TAP interface for you, and attaches it to the specified bridge. The default helper executable is `/usr/lib/qemu-bridge-helper`. The helper executable is setuid root, which is only executable by the members of the virtualization group (`kvm`). Therefore the **qemu-system-ARCH** command itself does not need to be run under `root` privileges.

You can call the helper the following way:

```
qemu-system-x86_64 [...] \
-netdev tap,id=hostnet0 -device virtio-net-pci,netdev=hostnet0,vlan=0 \
-netdev bridge,id=hostnet1 -device virtio-net-pci,netdev=hostnet1,vlan=0,br=br0
```

You can specify your own custom helper script that will take care of the TAP device (de)configuration, with the `helper=/path/to/your/helper` option:

```
qemu-system-x86_64 [...] -netdev bridge,id=hostnet0 -device virtio-net-
pci,netdev=hostnet0,vlan=0,br=br1,helper=/path/to/bridge-helper
```

 Tip

> To define access privileges to `qemu-bridge-helper`, inspect the `/etc/qe-mu/bridge.conf` file. For example the following directive
>
> ```
> allow br0
> ```
>
> allows the **qemu-system-ARCH** command to connect its VM Guest to the network bridge `br0`.

28.5 Viewing a VM Guest with VNC

By default QEMU uses a GTK (a cross-platform toolkit library) window to display the graphical output of a VM Guest. With the `-vnc` option specified, you can make QEMU listen on a specified VNC display and redirect its graphical output to the VNC session.

 Tip

> When working with QEMU's virtual machine via VNC session, it is useful to work with the `-usbdevice tablet` option.
>
> Moreover, if you need to use another keyboard layout than the default `en-us`, specify it with the `-k` option.

The first suboption of `-vnc` must be a *display* value. The `-vnc` option understands the following display specifications:

`host:display`

> Only connections from `host` on the display number `display` will be accepted. The TCP port on which the VNC session is then running is normally a 5900 + `display` number. If you do not specify `host`, connections will be accepted from any host.

`unix:path`

> The VNC server listens for connections on Unix domain sockets. The `path` option specifies the location of the related Unix socket.

`none`

> The VNC server functionality is initialized, but the server itself is not started. You can start the VNC server later with the QEMU monitor. For more information, see *Chapter 29, Virtual Machine Administration Using QEMU Monitor*.

Following the display value there may be one or more option flags separated by commas. Valid options are:

`reverse`

> Connect to a listening VNC client via a *reverse* connection.

`websocket`

> Opens an additional TCP listening port dedicated to VNC Websocket connections. By definition the Websocket port is 5700 + display.

`password`

Require that password-based authentication is used for client connections.

`tls`

Require that clients use TLS when communicating with the VNC server.

`x509=/path/to/certificate/dir`

Valid if TLS is specified. Require that x509 credentials are used for negotiating the TLS session.

`x509verify=/path/to/certificate/dir`

Valid if TLS is specified. Require that x509 credentials are used for negotiating the TLS session.

`sasl`

Require that the client uses SASL to authenticate with the VNC server.

`acl`

Turn on access control lists for checking of the x509 client certificate and SASL party.

`lossy`

Enable lossy compression methods (gradient, JPEG, ...).

`non-adaptive`

Disable adaptive encodings. Adaptive encodings are enabled by default.

`share=[allow-exclusive|force-shared|ignore]`

Set display sharing policy.

 Note

For more details about the display options, see the *qemu-doc* man page.

An example VNC usage:

```
tux > qemu-system-x86_64 [...] -vnc :5
(on the client:)
wilber > :~>vinagre venus:5905 &
```

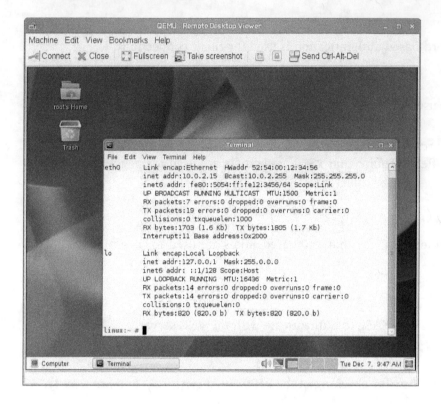

FIGURE 28.3: QEMU VNC SESSION

28.5.1 Secure VNC Connections

The default VNC server setup does not use any form of authentication. In the previous example, any user can connect and view the QEMU VNC session from any host on the network.

There are several levels of security that you can apply to your VNC client/server connection. You can either protect your connection with a password, use x509 certificates, use SASL authentication, or even combine some authentication methods in one QEMU command.

See *Section B.2, "Generating x509 Client/Server Certificates"* for more information about the x509 certificates generation. For more information about configuring x509 certificates on a VM Host Server and the client, see *Section 11.3.2, "Remote TLS/SSL Connection with x509 Certificate (*qemu+tls *or* xen+tls*)"* and *Section 11.3.2.3, "Configuring the Client and Testing the Setup"*.

The Vinagre VNC viewer supports advanced authentication mechanisms. Therefore, it will be used to view the graphical output of VM Guest in the following examples. For this example, let us assume that the server x509 certificates `ca-cert.pem`, `server-cert.pem`, and `server-key.pem` are located in the `/etc/pki/qemu` directory on the host, while the client's certificates are distributed in the following locations on the client:

```
/etc/pki/CA/cacert.pem
/etc/pki/libvirt-vnc/clientcert.pem
/etc/pki/libvirt-vnc/private/clientkey.pem
```

EXAMPLE 28.5: PASSWORD AUTHENTICATION

```
qemu-system-x86_64 [...] -vnc :5,password -monitor stdio
```

Starts the VM Guest graphical output on VNC display number 5 (usually port 5905). The `password` suboption initializes a simple password-based authentication method. There is no password set by default and you need to set one with the **change vnc password** command in QEMU monitor:

```
QEMU 2.3.1 monitor - type 'help' for more information
(qemu) change vnc password
Password: ****
```

You need the `-monitor stdio` option here, because you would not be able to manage the QEMU monitor without redirecting its input/output.

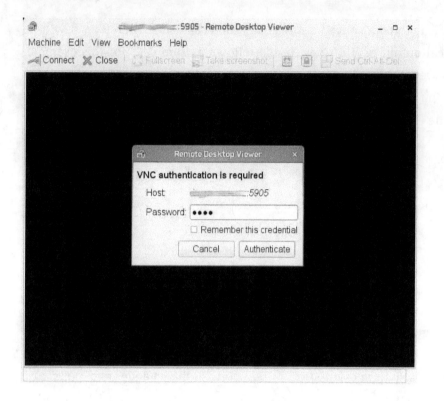

FIGURE 28.4: AUTHENTICATION DIALOG IN VINAGRE

EXAMPLE 28.6: X509 CERTIFICATE AUTHENTICATION

The QEMU VNC server can use TLS encryption for the session and x509 certificates for authentication. The server asks the client for a certificate and validates it against the CA certificate. Use this authentication type if your company provides an internal certificate authority.

```
qemu-system-x86_64 [...] -vnc :5,tls,x509verify=/etc/pki/qemu
```

EXAMPLE 28.7: X509 CERTIFICATE AND PASSWORD AUTHENTICATION

You can combine the password authentication with TLS encryption and x509 certificate authentication to create a two-layer authentication model for clients. Remember to set the password in the QEMU monitor after you run the following command:

```
qemu-system-x86_64 [...] -vnc :5,password,tls,x509verify=/etc/pki/qemu -monitor
  stdio
```

Simple Authentication and Security Layer (SASL) is a framework for authentication and data security in Internet protocols. It integrates several authentication mechanisms, like PAM, Kerberos, LDAP and more. SASL keeps its own user database, so the connecting user accounts do not need to exist on VM Host Server.

For security reasons, you are advised to combine SASL authentication with TLS encryption and x509 certificates:

```
qemu-system-x86_64 [...] -vnc :5,tls,x509,sasl -monitor stdio
```

Secure VNC Connections

29 Virtual Machine Administration Using QEMU Monitor

When QEMU is running, a monitor console is provided for performing interaction with the user. Using the commands available in the monitor console, it is possible to inspect the running operating system, change removable media, take screenshots or audio grabs and control several other aspects of the virtual machine.

 Note

The following sections list selected useful QEMU monitor commands and their purpose. To get the full list, enter **help** in the QEMU monitor command line.

29.1 Accessing Monitor Console

You can access the monitor console from QEMU window either by a keyboard shortcut—press `Ctrl`-`Alt`-`2` (to return to QEMU, press `Ctrl`-`Alt`-`1`)—or alternatively by clicking *View* in the QEMU GUI window, then *compatmonitor0*. The most convenient way is to show the QEMU window tabs with *View > Show Tabs*. Then you can easily switch between the guest screen, monitor screen, and the output of the serial and parallel console.

To get help while using the console, use **help** or **?**. To get help for a specific command, use **help** *command*.

29.2 Getting Information about the Guest System

To get information about the guest system, use **info**. If used without any option, the list of possible options is printed. Options determine which part of the system will be analyzed:

info version
> Shows the version of QEMU.

info commands
> Lists available QMP commands.

info network

Shows the network state.

info chardev

Shows the character devices.

info block

Information about block devices, such as hard disks, floppy drives, or CD-ROMs.

info blockstats

Read and write statistics on block devices.

info registers

Shows the CPU registers.

info cpus

Shows information about available CPUs.

info history

Shows the command line history.

info irq

Shows the interrupt statistics.

info pic

Shows the i8259 (PIC) state.

info pci

Shows the PCI information.

info tlb

Shows virtual to physical memory mappings.

info mem

Shows the active virtual memory mappings.

info jit

Shows dynamic compiler information.

info kvm

Shows the KVM information.

info numa

Shows the NUMA information.

Getting Information about the Guest System

info usb

Shows the guest USB devices.

info usbhost

Shows the host USB devices.

info profile

Shows the profiling information.

info capture

Shows the capture (audio grab) information.

info snapshots

Shows the currently saved virtual machine snapshots.

info status

Shows the current virtual machine status.

info pcmcia

Shows the guest PCMCIA status.

info mice

Shows which guest mice are receiving events.

info vnc

Shows the VNC server status.

info name

Shows the current virtual machine name.

info uuid

Shows the current virtual machine UUID.

info usernet

Shows the user network stack connection states.

info migrate

Shows the migration status.

info balloon

Shows the balloon device information.

info qtree

Shows the device tree.

info qdm

Shows the qdev device model list.

info roms

Shows the ROMs.

info migrate_cache_size

Shows the current migration xbzrle (= Xor Based Zero Run Length Encoding) cache size.

info migrate_capabilities

Shows the status of the various migration capabilities, such as xbzrle compression.

info mtree

Shows the VM Guest memory hierarchy.

info trace-events

Shows available trace-events and their status.

29.3 Changing VNC Password

To change the VNC password, use the **change vnc password** command and enter the new password:

```
(qemu) change vnc password
Password: ********
(qemu)
```

29.4 Managing Devices

To add a new disk while the guest is running (hotplug), use the **drive_add** and **device_add** commands. First define a new drive to be added as a device to bus 0:

```
(qemu) drive_add 0 if=none,file=/tmp/test.img,format=raw,if=disk1
OK
```

You can confirm your new device by querying the block subsystem:

```
(qemu) info block
[...]
disk1: removable=1 locked=0 tray-open=0 file=/tmp/test.img ro=0 drv=raw \
encrypted=0 bps=0 bps_rd=0 bps_wr=0 iops=0 iops_rd=0 iops_wr=0
```

After the new drive is defined, it needs to be connected to a device so that the guest can see it. The typical device would be a `virtio-blk-pci` or `scsi-disk`. To get the full list of available driver values, run:

```
(qemu) device_add ?
name "VGA", bus PCI
name "usb-storage", bus usb-bus
[...]
name "virtio-blk-pci", bus virtio-bus
```

Now add the device

```
(qemu) device_add virtio-blk-pci,drive=disk1,id=myvirtio1
```

and confirm with

```
(qemu) info pci
[...]
Bus  0, device  4, function 0:
    SCSI controller: PCI device 1af4:1001
      IRQ 0.
      BAR0: I/O at 0xffffffffffffffff [0x003e].
      BAR1: 32 bit memory at 0xffffffffffffffff [0x00000ffe].
      id "myvirtio1"
```

Tip

Devices added with the **device_add** command can be removed from the guest with **device_del**. Enter **help device_del** on the QEMU monitor command line for more information.

To release the device or file connected to the removable media device, use the **eject** *device* command. Use the optional `-f` to force ejection.

To change removable media (like CD-ROMs), use the **change** *device* command. The name of the removable media can be determined using the **info block** command:

```
(qemu) info block
ide1-cd0: type=cdrom removable=1 locked=0 file=/dev/sr0 ro=1 drv=host_device
(qemu) change ide1-cd0 /path/to/image
```

29.5 Controlling Keyboard and Mouse

It is possible to use the monitor console to emulate keyboard and mouse input if necessary. For example, if your graphical user interface intercepts some key combinations at low level (such as `Ctrl`–`Alt`–`F1` in X Window), you can still enter them using the **sendkey** *keys*:

```
sendkey ctrl-alt-f1
```

To list the key names used in the *keys* option, enter **sendkey** and press `→|`.

To control the mouse, the following commands can be used:

mouse_move *dx dy* [*dz*]

> Move the active mouse pointer to the specified coordinates dx, dy with the optional scroll axis dz.

mouse_button *val*

> Change the state of the mouse buttons (1 = left, 2 = middle, 4 = right).

mouse_set *index*

> Set which mouse device receives events. Device index numbers can be obtained with the **info mice** command.

29.6 Changing Available Memory

If the virtual machine was started with the `-balloon virtio` option and the paravirtualized balloon device that allows to dynamically change the amount of memory available is therefore enabled, it is possible to change the available memory dynamically. For more information about enabling the balloon device, see *Section 27.1, "Basic Installation with* `qemu-system-ARCH`*"*.

To get information about the balloon device in the monitor console and to determine whether the device is enabled, use the **info balloon** command:

```
(qemu) info balloon
```

If the balloon device is enabled, use the **balloon** *memory_in_MB* command to set the requested amount of memory:

```
(qemu) balloon 400
```

29.7 Dumping Virtual Machine Memory

To save the content of the virtual machine memory to a disk or console output, use the following commands:

memsave *addr size filename*

> Saves virtual memory dump starting at *addr* of size *size* to file *filename*

pmemsave *addr size filename*

> Saves physical memory dump starting at *addr* of size *size* to file *filename* -

x / *fmt addr*

> Makes a virtual memory dump starting at address *addr* and formatted according to the *fmt* string. The *fmt* string consists of three parameters *countformatsize*:
> The *count* parameter is the number of items to be dumped.
> The *format* can be x (hex), d (signed decimal), u (unsigned decimal), o (octal), c (char) or i (assembly instruction).
> The *size* parameter can be b (8 bits), h (16 bits), w (32 bits) or g (64 bits). On x86, h or w can be specified with the i format to respectively select 16 or 32-bit code instruction size.

xp / *fmt addr*

Makes a physical memory dump starting at address *addr* and formatted according to the *fmt* string. The *fmt* string consists of three parameters *countformatsize*:

The *count* parameter is the number of the items to be dumped.

The *format* can be x (hex), d (signed decimal), u (unsigned decimal), o (octal), c (char) or i (asm instruction).

The *size* parameter can be b (8 bits), h (16 bits), w (32 bits) or g (64 bits). On x86, h or w can be specified with the i format to respectively select 16 or 32-bit code instruction size.

29.8 Managing Virtual Machine Snapshots

Managing snapshots in QEMU monitor is not officially supported by SUSE yet. The information found in this section may be helpful in specific cases.

Virtual Machine snapshots are snapshots of the complete virtual machine including the state of CPU, RAM, and the content of all writable disks. To use virtual machine snapshots, you must have at least one non-removable and writable block device using the qcow2 disk image format.

Snapshots are helpful when you need to save your virtual machine in a particular state. For example, after you have configured network services on a virtualized server and want to quickly start the virtual machine in the same state that was saved last. You can also create a snapshot after the virtual machine has been powered off to create a backup state before you try something experimental and possibly make VM Guest unstable. This section introduces the former case, while the latter is described in *Section 27.2.3, "Managing Snapshots of Virtual Machines with qemu-img"*.

The following commands are available for managing snapshots in QEMU monitor:

savevm *name*

Creates a new virtual machine snapshot under the tag *name* or replaces an existing snapshot.

loadvm *name*

Loads a virtual machine snapshot tagged *name*.

delvm

Deletes a virtual machine snapshot.

info snapshots

Prints information about available snapshots.

```
(qemu) info snapshots
Snapshot list:
ID❶        TAG❷               VM SIZE❸        DATE❹           VM CLOCK❺
1          booting            4.4M 2013-11-22 10:51:10        00:00:20.476
2          booted             184M 2013-11-22 10:53:03        00:02:05.394
3          logged_in          273M 2013-11-22 11:00:25        00:04:34.843
4          ff_and_term_running 372M 2013-11-22 11:12:27       00:08:44.965
```

❶ Unique identification number of the snapshot. Usually auto-incremented.

❷ Unique description string of the snapshot. It is meant as a human readable version of the ID.

❸ The disk space occupied by the snapshot. Note that the more memory is consumed by running applications, the bigger the snapshot is.

❹ Time and date the snapshot was created.

❺ The current state of the virtual machine's clock.

29.9 Suspending and Resuming Virtual Machine Execution

The following commands are available for suspending and resuming virtual machines:

stop

Suspends the execution of the virtual machine.

cont

Resumes the execution of the virtual machine.

system_reset

Resets the virtual machine. The effect is similar to the reset button on a physical machine. This may leave the file system in an unclean state.

system_powerdown

Sends an *ACPI* shutdown request to the machine. The effect is similar to the power button on a physical machine.

q or quit

> Terminates QEMU immediately.

29.10 Live Migration

The live migration process allows to transmit any virtual machine from one host system to another host system without any interruption in availability. It is possible to change hosts permanently or just during maintenance.

The requirements for live migration:

- All requirements from *Section 10.7.1, "Migration Requirements"* are applicable.

- Live migration is only possible between VM Host Servers with the same CPU features.

- *AHCI* interface, *VirtFS* feature, and the `-mem-path` command line option are not compatible with migration.

- The guest on the source and destination hosts must be started in the same way.

- `-snapshot` qemu command line option should not be used for migration (and this **qemu** command line option is not supported).

More recommendations can be found at the following Web site: http://www.linux-kvm.org/page/Migration

The live migration process has the following steps:

1. The virtual machine instance is running on the source host.

2. The virtual machine is started on the destination host in the frozen listening mode. The parameters used are the same as on the source host plus the `-incoming tcp:`*ip*`:`*port* parameter, where *ip* specifies the IP address and *port* specifies the port for listening to the incoming migration. If 0 is set as IP address, the virtual machine listens on all interfaces.

3. On the source host, switch to the monitor console and use the **migrate -d tcp:** *destination_ip*`:`*port* command to initiate the migration.

4. To determine the state of the migration, use the **info migrate** command in the monitor console on the source host.

5. To cancel the migration, use the **migrate_cancel** command in the monitor console on the source host.

6. To set the maximum tolerable downtime for migration in seconds, use the **migrate_set_downtime** *number_of_seconds* command.

7. To set the maximum speed for migration in bytes per second, use the **migrate_set_speed** *bytes_per_second* command.

29.11 QMP - QEMU Machine Protocol

QMP is a JSON-based protocol that allows applications—such as `libvirt`—to communicate with a running QEMU instance. There are several ways you can access the QEMU monitor using QMP commands.

29.11.1 Access QMP via Standard Input/Output

The most flexible way to use QMP is by specifying the `-mon` option. The following example creates a QMP instance using standard input/output. Note that in the following examples, `->` marks lines with commands sent from client to the running QEMU instance, while `<-` marks lines with the output returned from QEMU.

```
# qemu-system-x86_64 [...] \
-chardev stdio,id=mon0 \
-mon chardev=mon0,mode=control,pretty=on


<- {
    "QMP": {
        "version": {
            "qemu": {
                "micro": 0,
                "minor": 0,
                "major": 2
            },
            "package": ""
        },
```

```
        "capabilities": [
        ]
    }
}
```

When a new QMP connection is established, QMP sends its greeting message and enters capabilities negotiation mode. In this mode, only the **qmp_capabilities** command works. To exit capabilities negotiation mode and enter command mode, the **qmp_capabilities** command must be issued first:

```
-> { "execute": "qmp_capabilities" }
<- {
    "return": {
    }
}
```

Note that `"return": {}` is a QMP's success response.

QMP's commands can have arguments. For example to eject a CD-ROM drive, enter the following:

```
->{ "execute": "eject", "arguments": { "device": "ide1-cd0" } }
<- {
    "timestamp": {
        "seconds": 1410353381,
        "microseconds": 763480
    },
    "event": "DEVICE_TRAY_MOVED",
    "data": {
        "device": "ide1-cd0",
        "tray-open": true
    }
}
{
    "return": {
    }
}
```

29.11.2 Access QMP via Telnet

Instead of the standard input/output, you can connect the QMP interface to a network socket and communicate with it via a specified port:

```
# qemu-system-x86_64 [...] \
-chardev socket,id=mon0,host=localhost,port=4444,server,nowait \
-mon chardev=mon0,mode=control,pretty=on
```

And then run telnet to connect to port 4444:

```
# telnet localhost 4444
Trying ::1...
Connected to localhost.
Escape character is '^]'.
<- {
    "QMP": {
        "version": {
            "qemu": {
                "micro": 0,
                "minor": 0,
                "major": 2
            },
            "package": ""
        },
        "capabilities": [
        ]
    }
}
```

You can create several monitor interfaces at the same time. The following example creates one HMP instance—human monitor which understands 'normal' QEMU monitor's commands—on the standard input/output, and one QMP instance on localhost port 4444:

```
# qemu-system-x86_64 [...] \
-chardev stdio,id=mon0 -mon chardev=mon0,mode=readline \
-chardev socket,id=mon1,host=localhost,port=4444,server,nowait \
```

```
-mon chardev=mon1,mode=control,pretty=on
```

29.11.3 Access QMP via Unix Socket

Invoke QEMU using the `-qmp` option, and create a unix socket:

```
# qemu-system-x86_64 [...] \
-qmp unix:/tmp/qmp-sock,server --monitor stdio


QEMU waiting for connection on: unix:./qmp-sock,server
```

To communicate with the QEMU instance via the `/tmp/qmp-sock` socket, use **nc** (see **man 1 nc** for more information) from another terminal on the same host:

```
# nc -U /tmp/qmp-sock
<- {"QMP": {"version": {"qemu": {"micro": 0, "minor": 0, "major": 2} [...]
```

29.11.4 Access QMP via `libvirt`'s **virsh** Command

If you run your virtual machines under `libvirt` (see *Part II, "Managing Virtual Machines with libvirt"*), you can communicate with its running guests by running the **virsh qemu-monitor-command**:

```
# virsh qemu-monitor-command vm_guest1 \
--pretty '{"execute":"query-kvm"}'
<- {
    "return": {
        "enabled": true,
        "present": true
    },
    "id": "libvirt-8"
}
```

In the above example, we ran the simple command **query-kvm** which checks if the host is capable of running KVM and if KVM is enabled.

Tip

If you want to use the standard 'human readable' way of QEMU commands instead of the JSON format, use the `--hmp` option:

```
# virsh qemu-monitor-command vm_guest1 --hmp "query-kvm"
```

VI Managing Virtual Machines with LXC

30 Linux Containers

30.1 Setting Up LXC Distribution Containers

A container is a kind of "virtual machine" that can be started, stopped, frozen, or cloned (to name but a few tasks). To set up an LXC container, you first need to create a root file system containing the guest distribution:

PROCEDURE 30.1: CREATING A ROOT FILE SYSTEM

There is currently no GUI to create a root file system. You will thus need to open a terminal and use **virt-create-rootfs** as root to populate the new root file system. In the following steps, the new root file system will be created in */path/to/rootfs*.

Note that **virt-create-rootfs** needs a registration code to set up a SLE-12 root file system.

1. Run the **virt-create-rootfs** command:

   ```
   virt-create-rootfs --root /path/to/rootfs --distro SLES-12.0 -c registration
    code
   ```

2. Change the root path to the root file system with the **chroot** command:

   ```
   chroot /path/to/rootfs
   ```

3. Change the password for user root with **passwd**.

4. Create an operator user without root privileges:

   ```
   useradd -m operator
   ```

5. Change the operator's password:

   ```
   passwd operator
   ```

6. Leave the chroot environment with **exit**.

PROCEDURE 30.2: DEFINING THE CONTAINER USING YAST

1. Open YaST and go to *Virtualization* › *Create Virtual Machines* to open the Virtual Machine Manager.

2. If not already present, add a local LXC connection by clicking *File, Add Connection*. Select *LXC (Linux Containers)* as hypervisor and click the *Connect* button.

3. Select the *localhost (LXC)* connection and click *File New Virtual Machine* menu. Select the *Operating system container* option and click the *Forward* button.

4. Type the path to the root file system from *Procedure 30.1, "Creating a Root File System"* and click the *Forward* button.

5. Choose the maximum amount of memory and CPUs to allocate to the container. Then click the *Forward* button.

6. Type in a name for the container. This name will be used for all **virsh** commands on the container.
   Click *Advanced options*. Select the network to connect the container to and click the *Finish* button: the container will then be created and started. A console will also be automatically opened.

> **⊘ Warning: Container Network**
>
> To configure the container network, edit the `/etc/sysconfig/network/ifcfg-*` files. Make sure not to change the IPv6 setting: this would lead to errors while starting the network.

30.2 Setting Up LXC Application Containers

Libvirt also allows to run single applications instead of full blown Linux distributions in containers. In this example, **bash** will be started in its own container.

PROCEDURE 30.3: DEFINING AN APPLICATION CONTAINER USING YAST

1. Open YaST and go to the Virtual Machine Manager module.

2. If not already present, add the LXC connection by clicking *File, Add Connection* menu. Select *LXC (Linux Containers)* as hypervisor and click *Connect*.

3. Select the *localhost (LXC)* connection and click *File › New Virtual Machine*.

   Select the *Application container* option and click *Forward*.

   Set the patch to the application to be launched. As an example, the field is filled with /
   bin/sh, which is fine to create a first container. Click *Forward*.

4. Choose the maximum amount of memory and CPUs to allocate to the container. Click
   Forward.

5. Type in a name for the container. This name will be used for all **virsh** commands on
   the container.

   Click *Advanced options*. Select the network to connect the container to and click *Finish*.
   The container will be created and started. A console will be opened automatically.
   Note that the container will be destroyed after the application has finished running.

30.3   Securing a Container Using AppArmor

By default, containers are not secured using AppArmor or SELinux. There is no graphical user
interface to change the security model for a libvirt domain, but **virsh** will help.

1. Edit the container XML configuration using virsh:

```
virsh -c lxc:/// edit mycontainer
```

2. Add the following to the XML configuration, save it and exit the editor.

```
<domain>
    ...
    <seclabel type="dynamic" model="apparmor"/>
    ...
</domain>
```

3. With this configuration, an AppArmor profile for the container will be created in the /
   etc/apparmor.d/libvirt directory. The default profile only allows the minimum applications to run in the container. This can be changed by modifying the libvirt-contain-
   er-uuid file: this file is not overwritten by libvirt.

30.4 Differences Between the libvirt LXC Driver and LXC

SUSE Linux Enterprise Server 11 SP3 was shipping LXC, while SUSE Linux Enterprise Server 12 comes with the libvirt LXC driver, sometimes named libvirt-lxc to avoid confusion. The containers are not managed or configured in the same way in these tools. Here is a non-exhaustive list of differences.

The main difference comes from the fact that domain configuration in libvirt is an XML file, while LXC configuration is a properties file. Most of the LXC properties can be mapped to the domain XML. The properties that cannot be migrated are:

- *lxc.network.script.up*: this script can be implemented using the `/etc/libvirt/hooks/network` libvirt hook, though the script will need to be adapted.

- *lxc.network.ipv**: libvirt cannot set the container network configuration from the domain configuration.

- *lxc.network.name*: libvirt cannot set the container network card name.

- *lxc.devttydir*: libvirt does not allow changing the location of the console devices.

- *lxc.console*: there is currently no way to log the output of the console into a file on the host for libvirt LXC containers.

- *lxc.pivotdir*: libvirt does not allow to fine-tune the directory used for the **pivot_root**. `/.olroot` is used.

- *lxc.rootfs.mount*: libvirt does not allow to fine-tune this.

LXC VLAN networks automatically create the VLAN interface on the host and then move it into the guest namespace. libvirt-lxc configuration can mention a VLAN tag ID only for openvSwitch tap devices or PCI pass-through of SRIOV VF. The conversion tool actually needs the user to manually create the VLAN interface on the host side.

LXC rootfs can also be an image file, but LXC brute-forces the mount to try to detect the proper file system format. libvirt-lxc can mount image files of several formats, but the 'auto' value for the format parameter is explicitly not supported. This means that the generated configuration will need to be tweaked by the user to get a proper match in that case.

LXC can support any cgroup configuration, even future ones, while libvirt domain configuration, needs to map each of them.

LXC can mount block devices in the rootfs, but it cannot mount raw partition files: the file needs to be manually attached to a loop device. On the other hand libvirt-lxc can mount block devices, but also partition files of any format.

30.5 For More Information

LXC Container Driver

http://libvirt.org/drvlxc.html

31 Migration from LXC to `libvirt-lxc`

Since SUSE Linux Enterprise Server 12, LXC is integrated into `libvirt` library. This decision has several advantages over using LXC as a separate solution—such as a unified approach with other virtualization solutions or independence on the kernel used. This chapter describes steps needed to migrate an existing LXC environment for use with the `libvirt` library.

31.1 Host Migration

The migration itself has two phases. You first need to migrate the host, then the LXC containers. After that, you can run the original containers as VM Guests in the `libvirt` environment.

PROCEDURE 31.1: HOST MIGRATION

1. Upgrade the host to SUSE Linux Enterprise Server 12 using the official DVD media.

2. After the upgrade, install the `libvirt-daemon-lxc` and `libvirt-daemon-config-network` packages.

3. Create a `libvirt` XML configuration `lxc_container.xml` from the existing container `lxc_container`:

   ```
   # virt-lxc-convert /etc/lxc/lxc_container/config > lxc_container.xml
   ```

4. Check if the network configuration on the host is the same as in the container configuration file, and fix it if needed.

5. Check the `lxc_container.xml` file for any weird or missing configuration. Note that some LXC configuration options cannot be mapped to `libvirt` configuration. Although the conversion should usually be fine, check *Section 30.4, "Differences Between the libvirt LXC Driver and LXC"* for more details.

6. Define the container in `libvirt` based on the created XML definition:

   ```
   # virsh -c lxc:/// define lxc_container.xml
   ```

31.2 Container Migration

After the host is migrated, the LXC container in `libvirt` will not boot. It needs to be migrated to SUSE Linux Enterprise Server 12 as well to get everything working.

PROCEDURE 31.2: CONTAINER MIGRATION

1. The `baseproduct` file is missing (and **zypper** keeps complaining about it). Create the relevant symbolic link:

```
# ROOTFS=/var/lib/lxc/lxc_container/rootfs
# ln -s $ROOTFS/etc/products.d/SUSE_SLES.prod $ROOTFS/etc/products.d/
baseproduct
```

2. Add the DVD repository. Note that you need to replace the DVD device with the one attached to your container:

```
# zypper --root $ROOTFS ar \
cd:///?devices=/dev/dvd SLES12-12
```

3. Disable or remove previous repositories:

```
# zypper --root $ROOTFS lr
  | Alias                      | Name                        | Enabled |
 Refresh
 --+-----------------------------+----------------------------------+---------
 +--------
 1 | SLES12-12                  | SLES12-12                   | Yes     | No
 2 | SUSE-[...]-Server-11-SP3 38 | SUSE-[...]-Server-11-SP3 138 | Yes     | No

# zypper --root $ROOTFS rr 2
```

4. Upgrade the container:

```
# zypper --root $ROOTFS dup
```

5. Install the *Minimal* pattern to make sure everything required is installed:

```
# zypper --root $ROOTFS in -t pattern Minimal
```

31.3 Starting the Container

After the host and container migration is complete, the container can be started:

```
# virsh -c lxc:/// start lxc_container
```

If you need to get a console to view the logging messages produced by the container, run:

```
# virsh -c lxc:/// console lxc_container
```

Glossary

General

Create Virtual Machine Wizard

A software program available in YaST and Virtual Machine Manager that provides a graphical interface to guide you through the steps to create virtual machines. It can also be run in text mode by entering `virt-install` at a command prompt in the host environment.

Dom0

The term is used in Xen environments, and refers to a virtual machine. The host operating system is actually a virtual machine running in a privileged domain and can be called Dom0. All other virtual machines on the host run in unprivileged domains and can be called domain U's.

hardware-assisted

Intel* and AMD* provide virtualization hardware-assisted technology. This reduces frequency of VM IN/OUT (fewer VM traps), because software is a major source of overhead, and increases the efficiency (the execution is done by the hardware). Moreover this reduces the memory footprint, provides better resource control, and allows secure assignment of specific I/O devices.

Host Environment

The desktop or command line environment that allows interaction with the host computer's environment. It provides a command line environment and can also include a graphical desktop, such as GNOME or IceWM. The host environment runs as a special type of virtual machine that has privileges to control and manage other virtual machines. Other commonly used terms include *Dom0*, privileged domain, and host operating system.

Hypervisor

The software that coordinates the low-level interaction between virtual machines and the underlying physical computer hardware.

KVM

See *Chapter 3, Introduction to KVM Virtualization*

Paravirtualized Frame Buffer

The video output device that drives a video display from a memory buffer containing a complete frame of data for virtual machine displays running in paravirtual mode.

VHS

Virtualization Host Server

The physical computer running a SUSE virtualization platform software. The virtualization environment consists of the hypervisor, the host environment, virtual machines, and associated tools, commands, and configuration files. Other commonly used terms include host, Host Computer, Host Machine (HM), Virtual Server (VS), Virtual Machine Host (VMH), and VM Host Server (VHS).

VirtFS

VirtFS is a new paravirtualized file system interface designed for improving pass-through technologies in the KVM environment. It is based on the VirtIO framework.

Virtual Machine

A virtualized PC environment (VM) capable of hosting a guest operating system and associated applications. Could be also called a VM Guest.

Virtual Machine Manager

A software program that provides a graphical user interface for creating and managing virtual machines.

Virtualized

A guest operating system or application running on a virtual machine.

Xen

See *Chapter 2, Introduction to Xen Virtualization*

xl

A set of commands for Xen that lets administrators manage virtual machines from a command prompt on the host computer. It replaced the deprecated **xm** toolstack.

CPU

CPU capping

Virtual CPU capping allows you to set vCPU capacity to 1–100 percent of the physical CPU capacity.

CPU hotplugging

CPU hotplugging is used to describe the functions of replacing/adding/removing a CPU without shutting down the system.

CPU over-commitment

Virtual CPU over-commitment is the ability to assign more virtual CPUs to VMs than the actual number of physical CPUs present in the physical system. This procedure does not increase the overall performance of the system, but might be useful for testing purposes.

CPU pinning

Processor affinity, or CPU pinning enables the binding and unbinding of a process or a thread to a central processing unit (CPU) or a range of CPUs.

Network

Bridged Networking

A type of network connection that lets a virtual machine be identified on an external network as a unique identity that is separate from and unrelated to its host computer.

Empty Bridge

A type of network bridge that has no physical network device or virtual network device provided by the host. This lets virtual machines communicate with other virtual machines on the same host but not with the host or on an external network.

External Network

The network outside a host's internal network environment.

Internal Network

A type of network configuration that restricts virtual machines to their host environment.

Local Bridge

A type of network bridge that has a virtual network device but no physical network device provided by the host. This lets virtual machines communicate with the host and other virtual machines on the host. Virtual machines can communicate on an external network through the host.

Network Address Translation (NAT)

A type of network connection that lets a virtual machine use the IP address and MAC address of the host.

No Host Bridge

A type of network bridge that has a physical network device but no virtual network device provided by the host. This lets virtual machines communicate on an external network but not with the host. This lets you separate virtual machine network communications from the host environment.

Traditional Bridge

A type of network bridge that has both a physical network device and a virtual network device provided by the host.

Storage

AHCI

The Advanced Host Controller Interface (AHCI) is a technical standard defined by Intel* that specifies the operation of Serial ATA (SATA) host bus adapters in a non-implementation-specific manner.

Block Device

Data storage devices, such as CD-ROM drives or disk drives, that move data in the form of blocks. Partitions and volumes are also considered block devices.

File-Backed Virtual Disk

A virtual disk based on a file, also called a disk image file.

Raw Disk

A method of accessing data on a disk at the individual byte level instead of through its file system.

Sparse image file

A disk image file that does not reserve its entire amount of disk space but expands as data is written to it.

xvda

The drive designation given to the first virtual disk on a paravirtual machine.

Linux Containers

cgroups

Kernel Control Groups (commonly just called "cgroups") are a Kernel feature that allows aggregating or partitioning tasks (processes) and all their children into hierarchical organized groups to isolate resources.

See also Book *"System Analysis and Tuning Guide", Chapter 9 "Kernel Control Groups"*.

chroot

A *change root* (chroot, or change root jail) is a section in the file system that is isolated from the rest of the file system. For this purpose, the **chroot** or **pivot_root** command is used to change the root of the file system. A program that is executed in such a "chroot jail" cannot access files outside the designated directory tree.

container

Can be seen as a kind of "virtual machine" on the host server that can run any Linux system, for example openSUSE, SUSE Linux Enterprise Desktop, or SUSE Linux Enterprise Server. The main difference with a normal virtual machine is that the container shares its kernel with the host it runs on.

Kernel namespaces

A Kernel feature to isolate some resources like network, users, and others for a group of processes.

Acronyms

ACPI

Advanced Configuration and Power Interface (ACPI) specification provides an open standard for device configuration and power management by the operating system.

AER

Advanced Error Reporting

AER is a capability provided by the PCI Express specification which allows for reporting of PCI errors and recovery from some of them.

APIC

Advanced Programmable Interrupt Controller (APIC) is a family of interrupt controllers.

BDF

Bus:Device:Function

Notation used to succinctly describe PCI and PCIe devices.

CG

Control Groups

Feature to limit, account and isolate resource usage (CPU, memory, disk I/O, etc.).

EDF

Earliest Deadline First

This scheduler provides weighted CPU sharing in an intuitive way and uses realtime-algorithms to ensure time guarantees.

EPT

Extended Page Tables

Performance in a virtualized environment is close to that in a native environment. Virtualization does create some overheads, however. These come from the virtualization of the CPU, the *MMU*, and the I/O devices. In some recent x86 processors AMD and Intel have begun to provide hardware extensions to help bridge this performance gap. In 2006, both vendors introduced their first generation hardware support for x86 virtualization with AMD-VirtualizationTM (AMD-VTM) and Intel® VT-x technologies. Recently Intel introduced its second generation of hardware support that incorporates MMU-virtualization, called Extended Page

Tables (EPT). EPT-enabled systems can improve performance compared to using shadow paging for *MMU* virtualization. EPT increases memory access latencies for a few workloads. This cost can be reduced by effectively using large pages in the guest and the hypervisor.

FLASK

Flux Advanced Security Kernel

Xen implements a type of mandatory access control via a security architecture called FLASK using a module of the same name.

HAP

High Assurance Platform

HAP combines hardware and software technologies to improve workstation and network security.

HVM

Hardware Virtual Machine (commonly called like this by Xen).

IOMMU

Input/Output Memory Management Unit

IOMMU (AMD* technology) is a memory management unit (*MMU*) that connects a direct memory access-capable (DMA-capable) I/O bus to the main memory.

KSM

Kernel Samepage Merging

KSM allows for automatic sharing of identical memory pages between guests to save host memory. KVM is optimized to use KSM if enabled on the VM Host Server.

MMU

Memory Management Unit

is a computer hardware component responsible for handling accesses to memory requested by the CPU. Its functions include translation of virtual addresses to physical addresses (i.e., virtual memory management), memory protection, cache control, bus arbitration and in simpler computer architectures (especially 8-bit systems) bank switching.

PAE

Physical Address Extension

32-bit x86 operating systems use Physical Address Extension (PAE) mode to enable addressing of more than 4 GB of physical memory. In PAE mode, page table entries (PTEs) are 64 bits in size.

PCID

Process-context identifiers

These are a facility by which a logical processor may cache information for multiple linear-address spaces so that the processor may retain cached information when software switches to a different linear address space. INVPCID instruction is used for fine-grained *TLB* flush, which is benefit for kernel.

PCIe

Peripheral Component Interconnect Express

PCIe was designed to replace older PCI, PCI-X and AGP bus standards. PCIe has numerous improvements including a higher maximum system bus throughput, a lower I/O pin count and smaller physical footprint. Moreover it also has a more detailed error detection and reporting mechanism (*AER*), and a native hotplug functionality. It is also backward compatible with PCI.

PSE and PSE36

Page Size Extended

PSE refers to a feature of x86 processors that allows for pages larger than the traditional 4 KiB size. PSE-36 capability offers 4 more bits, in addition to the normal 10 bits, which are used inside a page directory entry pointing to a large page. This allows a large page to be located in 36-bit address space.

PT

Page Table

A page table is the data structure used by a virtual memory system in a computer operating system to store the mapping between virtual addresses and physical addresses. Virtual addresses are those unique to the accessing process. Physical addresses are those unique to the hardware (RAM).

QXL

QXL is a cirrus VGA framebuffer (8M) driver for virtualized environment.

RVI or NPT

Rapid Virtualization Indexing, Nested Page Tables

An AMD second generation hardware-assisted virtualization technology for the processor memory management unit (*MMU*).

SATA

Serial ATA

SATA is a computer bus interface that connects host bus adapters to mass storage devices such as hard disks and optical drives.

Seccomp2-based sandboxing

Sandboxed environment where only predetermined system calls are permitted for added protection against malicious behavior.

SMEP

Supervisor Mode Execution Protection

This prevents the execution of user-mode pages by the Xen hypervisor, making many application-to-hypervisor exploits much harder.

SPICE

Simple Protocol for Independent Computing Environments

SXP

An SXP file is a Xen Configuration File.

TCG

Tiny Code Generator

Instructions are emulated rather than executed by the CPU.

THP

Transparent Huge Pages

This allows CPUs to address memory using pages larger than the default 4 KB. This helps reduce memory consumption and CPU cache usage. KVM is optimized to use THP (via madvise and opportunistic methods) if enabled on the VM Host Server.

TLB

Translation Lookaside Buffer

TLB is a cache that memory management hardware uses to improve virtual address translation speed. All current desktop, notebook, and server processors use a TLB to map virtual and physical address spaces, and it is nearly always present in any hardware that uses virtual memory.

VCPU

A scheduling entity, containing each state for virtualized CPU.

VDI

Virtual Desktop Infrastructure

VFIO

Since kernel v3.6; a new method of accessing PCI devices from userspace called VFIO.

VHS

Virtualization Host Server

VM root

VMM will run in *VMX* root operation and guest software will run in *VMX* non-root operation. Transitions between *VMX* root operation and *VMX* non-root operation are called *VMX* transitions.

VMCS

Virtual Machine Control Structure

VMX non-root operation and VMX transitions are controlled by a data structure called a virtual-machine control structure (VMCS). Access to the VMCS is managed through a component of processor state called the VMCS pointer (one per logical processor). The value of the VMCS pointer is the 64-bit address of the VMCS. The VMCS pointer is read and written using the instructions VMPTRST and VMPTRLD. The *VMM* configures a VMCS using the VMREAD, VMWRITE, and VMCLEAR instructions. A *VMM* could use a different VMCS for each virtual machine that it supports. For a virtual machine with multiple logical processors (virtual processors), the *VMM* could use a different VMCS for each virtual processor.

VMDq

Virtual Machine Device Queue

Multi-queue network adapters exist which support multiple VMs at the hardware level, having separate packet queues associated to the different hosted VMs (by means of the IP addresses of the VMs).

VMM

Virtual Machine Monitor (Hypervisor)

When the processor encounters an instruction or event of interest to the Hypervisor (*VMM*), it exits from guest mode back to the VMM. The VMM emulates the instruction or other event, at a fraction of native speed, and then returns to guest mode. The transitions from guest mode to the VMM and back again are high-latency operations, during which guest execution is completely stalled.

VMX

Virtual Machine eXtensions

VPID

New support for software control of *TLB* (VPID improves *TLB* performance with small *VMM* development effort).

VT-d

Virtualization Technology for Directed I/O

Like *IOMMU* for Intel* [https://software.intel.com/en-us/articles/intel-virtualization-technology-for-directed-io-vt-d-enhancing-intel-platforms-for-efficient-virtualization-of-io-devices].

vTPM

Component to establish end-to-end integrity for guests via Trusted Computing.

A Virtual Machine Drivers

Virtualization allows the consolidation of workloads on newer, more powerful, energy-efficient hardware. Paravirtualized operating systems such as SUSE® Linux Enterprise Server and other Linux distributions are aware of the underlying virtualization platform, and can therefore interact efficiently with it. Unmodified operating systems such as Microsoft Windows* are unaware of the virtualization platform and expect to interact directly with the hardware. Because this is not possible when consolidating servers, the hardware must be emulated for the operating system. Emulation can be slow, but it is especially troubling for high-throughput disk and network subsystems. Most performance loss occurs in this area.

The SUSE Linux Enterprise Virtual Machine Driver Pack (VMDP) contains 32-bit and 64-bit paravirtualized network, bus and block drivers for several Microsoft Windows operating systems. These drivers bring many of the performance advantages of paravirtualized operating systems to unmodified operating systems because only the paravirtualized device driver (not the rest of the operating system) is aware of the virtualization platform. For example, a paravirtualized disk device driver appears as a normal, physical disk to the operating system. However, the device driver interacts directly with the virtualization platform (with no emulation) to efficiently deliver disk access, allowing the disk and network subsystems to operate at near native speeds in a virtualized environment, without requiring changes to existing operating systems.

The SUSE® Linux Enterprise Virtual Machine Driver Pack is available as an add-on product for SUSE Linux Enterprise Server. For detailed information refer to http://www.suse.com/products/vmdriverpack/.

Refer to the Official VMDP Installation Guide at https://www.suse.com/documentation/sle-vmdp-22/ for more information.

B Appendix

B.1 Installing Paravirtualized Drivers

B.1.1 Installing virtio Drivers for Microsoft Windows*

SUSE has developed virtio-based drivers for Windows, which are available in the Virtual Machine Driver Pack (VMDP). See http://www.suse.com/products/vmdriverpack/ for more information on the VMDP. Installation instructions are now available in a dedicated official documentation.

B.2 Generating x509 Client/Server Certificates

To be able to create x509 client and server certificates you need to issue them by a Certificate Authority (CA). It is recommended to set up an independent CA that only issues certificates for libvirt.

1. Set up a CA as described in *Book "Security Guide", Chapter 17 "Managing X.509 Certification", Section 17.2.1 "Creating a Root CA"*.

2. Create a server and a client certificate as described in *Book "Security Guide", Chapter 17 "Managing X.509 Certification", Section 17.2.4 "Creating or Revoking User Certificates"*. The Common Name (CN) for the server certificate must be the fully qualified host name, while the Common Name for the client certificate can be freely chosen. For all other fields stick with the defaults suggested by YaST.

   Export the client and server certificates to a temporary location (for example, /tmp/x509/) by performing the following steps:

   a. Select the certificate on the *certificates* tab.

   b. Choose *Export › Export to File › Certificate and the Key Unencrypted in PEM Format*, provide the *Certificate Password* and the full path and the file name under *File Name*, for example, /tmp/x509/server.pem or /tmp/x509/client.pem.

c. Open a terminal and change to the directory where you have saved the certificate and issue the following commands to split it into certificate and key (this example splits the server key):

```
csplit -z -f s_ server.pem '/-----BEGIN/' '{1}'
     mv s_00 servercert.pem
     mv s_01 serverkey.pem
```

d. Repeat the procedure for each client and server certificate you would like to export.

3. Finally export the CA certificate by performing the following steps:

a. Switch to the *Description* tab.

b. Choose *Advanced* › *Export to File* › *Only the Certificate in PEM Format* and enter the full path and the file name under *File Name*, for example, `/tmp/x509/cacert.pem`.

C   XM, XL Toolstacks and Libvirt framework

C.1   Xen Toolstacks

Since the early Xen 2.x releases, **xend** has been the defacto toolstack for managing Xen instal-lations. In Xen 4.1, a new toolstack called libxenlight (also known as libxl) was introduced with technology preview status. libxl is a small, low-level library written in C. It has been designed to provide a simple API for all client toolstacks (XAPI [http://wiki.xen.org/wiki/XAPI], libvirt, xl). In Xen 4.2, libxl was promoted to officially supported status and **xend** was marked depre-cated. **xend** has been included in the Xen 4.3 and 4.4 series to give users ample time to convert their tooling to libxl, but it has been removed from the upstream Xen project and will no longer be provided starting with the Xen 4.5 series and SLES 12 SP1.

Although SLES11 SP3 contains Xen 4.2, SUSE retained the **xend** toolstack since making such an invasive change in a service pack would be too disruptive for SUSE Linux Enterprise cus-tomers. However, SLES12 provides a suitable opportunity to move to the new libxl toolstack and remove the deprecated, unmaintained **xend** stack. Starting with SLES 12 SP1, **xend** is no longer supported.

One of the major differences between **xend** and libxl is that the former is stateful, while the latter is stateless. With **xend**, all client applications such as **xm** and libvirt see the same system state. **xend** is responsible for maintaining state for the entire Xen host. In libxl, client applications such as **xl** or libvirt must maintain state. Thus domains created with **xl** or not visible or known to other libxl applications such as libvirt. Generally, it is discouraged to mix and match libxl applications and is preferred that a single libxl application be used to manage a Xen host. In SUSE Linux Enterprise 12 , it is recommended to use libvirt to manage Xen hosts, allowing management of the Xen system through libvirt applications such as **virt-manager**, **virt-install**, **vm-install**, **virt-viewer**, libguestfs, etc. If **xl** is used to manage the Xen host, any virtual machines under its management will not be accessible to libvirt, and hence not accessible to any of the libvirt applications.

C.1.1   Upgrading from xend/xm to xl/libxl

The **xl** application, along with its configuration format (see **man xl.cfg**), was designed to be backwards-compatible with the **xm** application and its configuration format (see **man xm.cfg**). Existing **xm** configuration should be usable with **xl**. Since libxl is stateless, and **xl** does not support the notion of managed domains, SUSE recommends using `libvirt` to manage SLES12 Xen hosts. SUSE has provided a tool called **xen2libvirt**, which provides a simple mechanism to import domains previously managed by **xend** into `libvirt`. See *Section C.2, "Import Xen Domain Configuration into* `libvirt`*"* for more information on **xen2libvirt**.

C.1.2 XL design

The basic structure of every **xl** command is:

```
xl subcommand OPTIONS DOMAIN
```

DOMAIN is the numeric domain id, or the domain name (which will be internally translated to domain id), and *OPTIONS* are subcommand specific options.

Although xl/libxl was designed to be backward-compatible with xm/xend, there are a few differences that should be noted:

- Managed or persistent domains. `libvirt` now provides this functionality.

- xl/libxl does not support Python code in the domain configuration files.

- xl/libxl does not support creating domains from SXP format configuration files (**xm create -F**).

- xl/libxl does not support sharing storage across DomU's via **w!** in domain configuration files.

xl/libxl is relatively new and under heavy development, hence a few features are still missing with respect to the xm/xend toolstack:

- SCSI LUN/Host pass-through (PVSCSI)

- USB pass-through (PVUSB)

- Support Direct Kernel Boot for fully virtualized Linux guests for Xen does not work anymore

C.1.3 Checklist before Upgrade

Before upgrading a SLES11 SP3 Xen host to SLES12

- You must remove any Python code from your xm domain configuration files.

- It is recommended to capture the libvirt domain XML from all existing virtual machines using **virsh** dumpxml *DOMAIN_NAME DOMAIN_NAME.xml* .

- It is recommended to do a backup of /etc/xen/xend-config.sxp and /boot/grub/ menu.lst files to keep references of previous parameters used for Xen.

 Note

Currently, live migrating virtual machines running on a SLES11 SP3 Xen host to a SLES12 Xen host is not supported. The **xend** and libxl toolstacks are not runtime-compatible. Virtual machine downtime will be required to move the virtual machines from SLES11 SP3 to a SLES12 host.

C.2   Import Xen Domain Configuration into lib-virt

xen2libvirt is a command line tool to import legacy Xen domain configuration into the libvirt virtualization library (see The Virtualization book for more information on libvirt). xen2libvirt provides an easy way to import domains managed by the deprecated **xm**/xend toolstack into the new libvirt/libxl toolstack. Several domains can be imported at once using its --recursive mode

xen2libvirt is included in the xen-tools package. If needed, install it with

```
zypper install xen-tools
```

xen2libvirt general syntax is

```
xen2libvirt <options> /path/to/domain/config
```

where options can be:

-h, --help

Prints short information about **xen2libvirt** usage.

-c, --convert-only

Converts the domain configuration to the `libvirt` XML format, but does not do the import to `libvirt`.

-r, --recursive

Converts and/or imports all domains configuration recursively, starting at the specified path.

-f, --format

Specifies the format of the source domain configuration. Can be either `xm`, or `sexpr` (S-expression format).

-v, --verbose

Prints more detailed information about the import process.

EXAMPLE C.1: CONVERTING XEN DOMAIN CONFIGURATION TO `libvirt`

Suppose you have a Xen domain managed with **xm** with the following configuration saved in `/etc/xen/sle12.xm`:

```
kernel = "/boot/vmlinuz-2.6-xenU"
  memory = 128
  name = "SLE12"
  root = "/dev/hda1 ro"
  disk = [ "file:/var/xen/sle12.img,hda1,w" ]
```

Convert it to `libvirt` XML without importing it, and look at its content:

```
# xen2libvirt -f xm -c /etc/xen/sle12.xm > /etc/libvirt/qemu/sles12.xml
  # cat /etc/libvirt/qemu/sles12.xml
  <domain type='xen'>
  <name>SLE12</name>
  <uuid>43e1863c-8116-469c-a253-83d8be09aa1d</uuid>
  <memory unit='KiB'>131072</memory>
  <currentMemory unit='KiB'>131072</currentMemory>
  <vcpu placement='static'>1</vcpu>
  <os>
  <type arch='x86_64' machine='xenpv'>linux</type>
  <kernel>/boot/vmlinuz-2.6-xenU</kernel>
```

```
    </os>
    <clock offset='utc' adjustment='reset'/>
    <on_poweroff>destroy</on_poweroff>
    <on_reboot>restart</on_reboot>
    <on_crash>restart</on_crash>
    <devices>
    <disk type='file' device='disk'>
    <driver name='file'/>
    <source file='/var/xen/sle12.img'/>
    <target dev='hda1' bus='xen'/>
    </disk>
    <console type='pty'>
    <target type='xen' port='0'/>
    </console>
    </devices>
    </domain>
```

To import the domain into `libvirt`, you can either run the same **xen2libvirt** command without the `-c` option, or use the exported file `/etc/libvirt/qemu/sles12.xml` and define a new Xen domain using **virsh**:

```
# sudo virsh define /etc/libvirt/qemu/sles12.xml
```

C.3 Differences Between the **xm** and **xl** Applications

The purpose of this chapter is to list all differences between **xm** and **xl** applications. Generally, **xl** is designed to be compatible with **xm**. Replacing **xm** with **xl** in custom scripts or tools is usually sufficient.

You can also use the `libvirt` framework using the **virsh** command. In this documentation only the first *OPTION* for **virsh** will be shown. To get more help on this option do a:

```
virsh help OPTION
```

C.3.1 Notation Conventions

To easily understand the difference between **xl** and **xm** commands, the following notation is used in this section:

TABLE C.1: NOTATION CONVENTIONS

Notation	Meaning
(-) minus	Option exists in **xm**, but **xl** does not include it.
(+) plus	Option exists in **xl**, but **xm** does not include it.

C.3.2 New Global Options

TABLE C.2: NEW GLOBAL OPTIONS

Options	Task
(+) -v	Verbose, increase the verbosity of the output
(+) -N	Dry run, do not actually execute the command
(+) -f	Force execution. **xl** will refuse to run some commands if it detects that **xend** is also running, this option will force the execution of those commands, even though it is unsafe

C.3.3 Unchanged Options

List of common options of **xl** and **xm**, and their `libvirt` equivalents.

TABLE C.3: COMMON OPTIONS

Options	Task	`libvirt` **equivalent**
destroy *DOMAIN*	Immediately terminate the domain	**virsh** destroy
domid *DOMAIN_NAME*	Converts a domain name to a *DOMAIN_ID*	**virsh** domid
domname *DOMAIN_ID*	Converts a *DOMAIN_ID* to a *DOMAIN_NAME*	**virsh** domname
help	Displays the short help message (i.e. common commands)	**virsh** help
pause *DOMAIN_ID*	Pause a domain. When in a paused state the domain will still consume allocated resources such as memory, but will not be eligible for scheduling by the Xen hypervisor	**virsh** suspend
unpause *DOMAIN_ID*	Moves a domain out of the paused state. This will allow a previously paused domain to be eligible for scheduling by the Xen hypervisor	**virsh** resume
rename *DOMAIN_ID* *NEW_DOMAIN_NAME*	Change the domain name of *DOMAIN_ID* to *NEW_DOMAIN_NAME*	1. `virsh dumpxml DOMAINNAME > DOMXML` 2. modify the domain's name in *DOMXML*

Options	Task	`libvirt` equivalent
		3. `virsh undefine DOMAINNAME`
		4. `virsh define DOMAINNAME`
sysrq *DOMAIN* <letter>	Send a Magic System Request to the domain, each type of request is represented by a different letter. It can be used to send SysRq requests to Linux guests, see `sysrq.txt` in your Linux Kernel sources for more information. It requires PV drivers to be installed in your guest OS	**virsh** send-keys can send Magic Sys Req only for KVM
vncviewer *OPTIONS DOMAIN*	Attach to domain's VNC server, forking a vncviewer process	**virt-view** *DOMAIN_ID* **virsh** *vncdisplay*
vcpu-set *DOMAIN_ID* <vC-PUs>	Enables the vcpu-count virtual CPUs for the domain in question. Like `mem-set`, this command can only allocate up to the maximum virtual CPU count configured at boot for the domain	**virsh** setvcpus
vcpu-list *DOMAIN_ID*	Lists VCPU information for a specific domain. If no domain is specified, VCPU information for all domains will be provided	**virsh** vcpuinfo

Options	Task	libvirt equivalent
vcpu-pin *DOMAIN_ID* <VCPU|all> <CPUs|all>	Pins the VCPU to only run on the specific CPUs. The keyword all can be used to apply the CPU list to all VCPUs in the domain	**virsh** vcpupin
dmesg [-c]	Reads the Xen message buffer, similar to dmesg on a Linux system. The buffer contains informational, warning, and error messages created during Xen's boot process	
top	Executes the **xentop** command, which provides real time monitoring of domains. Xentop is a curses interface, and reasonably self explanatory	**virsh** nodecpustats **virsh** nodememstats
uptime [-s] *DOMAIN*	Prints the current uptime of the domains running. With **xl** command the *DOMAIN* argument is mandatory	
debug-keys *KEYS*	Send debug keys to Xen. It is the same as pressing the Xen *conswitch* (Ctrl-A by default) three times and then pressing "keys"	
cpupool-migrate *DOMAIN* *CPU_POOL*	Moves a domain specified by *DOMAIN_ID* or *DOMAIN* into a *CPU_POOL*	

Options	Task	libvirt equivalent
cpupool-destroy *CPU_POOL*	Deactivates a cpu pool. This is possible only if no domain is active in the cpu-pool	
block-detach *DOMAIN_ID DevId*	Detach a domain's virtual block device. *devid* may be the symbolic name or the numeric device id given to the device by Dom0. You will need to run **xl** `block-list` to determine that number	**virsh** `detach-disk`
network-attach *DOMAIN_ID NETWORK_DEVICE*	Creates a new network device in the domain specified by *DOMAIN_ID*. network-device describes the device to attach, using the same format as the vif string in the domain configuration file	**virsh** `attach-interface` **virsh** `attach-device`
pci-attach *DOMAIN* <BDF> [Virtual Slot]	Hot-plug a new pass-through PCI device to the specified domain. *BDF* is the PCI Bus/Device/Function of the physical device to be passed through	**virsh** `attach-device`
pci-list *DOMAIN_ID*	List pass-through PCI devices for a domain	
getenforce	Determine if the *FLASK* security module is loaded and enforcing its policy	

Options	Task	`libvirt` **equivalent**
setenforce <1|0|Enforc-ing|Permissive>	Enable or disable enforcing of the *FLASK* access controls. The default is permissive and can be changed using the flask_enforcing option on the hypervisor's command line	

C.3.4   Removed Options

List of **xm** `options` which are no more available with the XL toolstack and a replacement solution if available.

C.3.4.1   Domain Management

The list of Domain management removed command and their replacement.

TABLE C.4: DOMAIN MANAGEMENT REMOVED OPTIONS

Domain Management Removed Options		
Options	**Task**	**Equivalent**
(-) `log`	Print out the Xend log.	This log file can be found in `/var/log/xend.log`
(-) `delete`	Remove a domain from Xend domain management. The `list` option shows the domain names	**virsh** `undefine`
(-) `new`	Adds a domain to Xend domain management	**virsh** `define`
(-) `start`	Start a Xend managed domain that was added using the **xm** `new` command	**virsh** `start`

Domain Management Removed Options		
Options	**Task**	**Equivalent**
(-) `dryrun`	Dry run - prints the resulting configuration in *SXP* but does not create the domain	`xl -N`
(-) `reset`	Reset a domain	`virsh reset`
(-) `domstate`	Show domain state	`virsh domstate`
(-) `serve`	Proxy Xend XMLRPC over stdio	
(-) `resume DOMAIN OPTIONS`	Moves a domain out of the suspended state and back into memory	`virsh resume`
(-) `suspend DOMAIN`	Suspend a domain to a state file so that it can be later resumed using the `resume` subcommand. Similar to the `save` subcommand although the state file may not be specified	`virsh managedsave` `virsh suspend`

C.3.4.2 USB Devices

USB `options` are not available with xl/libxl toolstack. **virsh** has the `attach-device` and `detach-device` options but it does not work yet with `USB`.

TABLE C.5: USB DEVICES MANAGEMENT REMOVED OPTIONS

USB Devices Management Removed Options	
Options	**Task**
(-) `usb-add`	Add a new USB physical bus to a domain

USB Devices Management Removed Options	
Options	**Task**
(-) `usb-del`	Delete a USB physical bus from a domain
(-) `usb-attach`	Attach a new USB physical bus to domain's virtual port
(-) `usb-detach`	Detach a USB physical bus from domain's virtual port
(-) `usb-list`	List domain's attachment state of all virtual port
(-) `usb-list-assignable-devices`	List all the assignable USB devices
(-) `usb-hc-create`	Create a domain's new virtual USB host controller
(-) `usb-hc-destroy`	Destroy a domain's virtual USB host controller

C.3.4.3 CPU Management

CPU management options has changed. New options are available, see: *Section C.3.5.10, "xl cpupool-*"*

TABLE C.6: CPU MANAGEMENT REMOVED OPTIONS

CPU Management Removed Options	
Options	**Task**
(-) `cpupool-new`	Adds a CPU pool to Xend CPU pool management
(-) `cpupool-start`	Starts a Xend CPU pool

CPU Management Removed Options	
Options	**Task**
(-) `cpupool-delete`	Removes a CPU pool from Xend management

C.3.4.4   Other Options

TABLE C.7: OTHER OPTIONS

Other Removed Options	
Options	**Task**
(-) `shell`	Launch an interactive shell
(-) `change-vnc-passwd`	Change vnc password
(-) `vtpm-list`	List virtual TPM devices
(-) `block-configure`	Change block device configuration

C.3.5   Changed Options

C.3.5.1   create

xl create *CONFIG_FILE* *OPTIONS* *VARS*

 Note: `libvirt` **Equivalent:**
virsh create

TABLE C.8: `xl create` CHANGED OPTIONS

`create` Changed Options	
Options	*Task*
(*) -f = *FILE*, --defconfig = *FILE*	Use the given configuration file

TABLE C.9: `xm create` REMOVED OPTIONS

`create` Removed Options	
Options	*Task*
(-) -s, --skipdtd	Skip DTD checking - skips checks on XML before creating
(-) -x, --xmldryrun	XML dry run
(-) -F=*FILE*, --config=*FILE*	Use the given *SXP* formatted configuration script
(-) --path	Search path for configuration scripts
(-) --help_config	Print the available configuration variables (vars) for the configuration script
(-) -n, --dryrun	Dry run — prints the configuration in *SXP* but does not create the domain
(-) -c, --console_autoconnect	Connect to the console after the domain is created
(-) -q, --quiet	Quiet mode
(-) -p, --paused	Leave the domain paused after it is created

Changed Options

create **Added Options**	
Options	*Task*
(+) -V, --vncviewer	Attach to domain's VNC server, forking a vncviewer process
(+) -A, --vncviewer-autopass	Pass VNC password to vncviewer via stdin

C.3.5.2   console

xl console *OPTIONS DOMAIN*

 Note: libvirt **Equivalent**

virsh console

TABLE C.11: xl console ADDED OPTIONS

console **Added Option**	
Option	*Task*
(+) -t [pv|serial]	Connect to a PV console or connect to an emulated serial console. PV consoles are the only consoles available for PV domains while HVM domains can have both

C.3.5.3   info

xl info

TABLE C.12: xm info REMOVED OPTIONS

info **Removed Options**	
Options	*Task*
(-) `-n, --numa`	Numa info
(-) `-c, --config`	List Xend configuration parameters

C.3.5.4 `dump-core`

`xl` dump-core *DOMAIN* *FILENAME*

 Note: `libvirt` **Equivalent**

  `virsh` dump

TABLE C.13: xm dump-core REMOVED OPTIONS

dump-core **Removed Options**	
Options	*Task*
(-) `-L, --live`	Dump core without pausing the domain
(-) `-C, --crash`	Crash domain after dumping core
(-) `-R, --reset`	Reset domain after dumping core

C.3.5.5 `list`

`xl` **list** options *DOMAIN*

 Note: `libvirt` **Equivalent**

  `virsh` list --all

Changed Options

list **Removed Options**	
Options	*Task*
(-) -l, --long	The output for **xm list** presents the data in *SXP* format
(-) --state==*STATE*	Output information for VMs in the specified state

TABLE C.15: xl list ADDED OPTIONS

list **Added Options**	
Options	*Task*
(+) -Z, --context	Also prints the security labels
(+) -v, --verbose	Also prints the domain UUIDs, the shutdown reason and security labels

C.3.5.6 mem-*

 Note: libvirt **Equivalent**

> **virsh** setmem
>
> **virsh** setmaxmem

TABLE C.16: xl mem-* CHANGED OPTIONS

mem-* **Changed Options**	
Options	*Task*
mem-max *DOMAIN_ID MEM*	Appending t for terabytes, g for gigabytes, m for megabytes, k for kilobytes and b for bytes. Specify the maximum amount of memory the domain can use.

mem-* **Changed Options**	
Options	*Task*
mem-set *DOMAIN_ID MEM*	Set the domain's used memory using the balloon driver

C.3.5.7 migrate

xl migrate *OPTIONS DOMAIN HOST*

 Note: libvirt **Equivalent**

> **virsh migrate --live hvm-sles11-qcow2 xen+** *CONNECTOR*:// *USER* @ *IP_ADDRESS* /

TABLE C.17: xm migrate REMOVED OPTIONS

migrate **Removed Options**	
Options	*Task*
(-) -l, --live	Use live migration. This will migrate the domain between hosts without shutting down the domain
(-) -r, --resource *Mbs*	Set maximum Mbs allowed for migrating the domain
(-) -c, --change_home_server	Change home server for managed domains
(-) --max_iters= *MAX_ITERS*	Number of iterations before final suspend (default:30)
(-) --max_factor= *MAX_FACTOR*	Max amount of memory to transfer before final suspend (default: 3*RAM).
(-) --min_remaining= *MIN_REMAINING*	Number of dirty pages before final suspend (default:50)

migrate **Removed Options**	
Options	*Task*
(-) --abort_if_busy	Abort migration instead of doing final suspend
(-) --log_progress	Log progress of migration to xend.log
(-) -s, --ssl	Use ssl connection for migration

TABLE C.18: xl migrate ADDED OPTIONS

migrate **Added Options**	
Options	*Task*
(+) -s *SSHCOMMAND*	Use <sshcommand> instead of **ssh**
(+) -e	On the new host, do not wait in the background (on <host>) for the death of the domain
(+) -C *config*	Send <config> instead of config file from creation

C.3.5.8 Domain Management

xl reboot *OPTIONS DOMAIN*

 Note: libvirt **Equivalent**

virsh reboot

TABLE C.19: xm reboot REMOVED OPTIONS

reboot **Removed Options**	
Options	*Task*
(-) -a, --all	Reboot all domains

reboot **Removed Options**	
Options	*Task*
(-) `-w, --wait`	Wait for reboot to complete before returning. This may take a while, as all services in the domain need to be shut down cleanly

TABLE C.20: xl reboot ADDED OPTIONS

reboot **Added Options**	
Option	*Task*
(+) `-F`	Fallback to ACPI reset event for HVM guests with no PV drivers

`xl` save *OPTIONS DOMAIN CHECK_POINT_FILE CONFIG_FILE*

 Note: `libvirt` **Equivalent**

`virsh` save

TABLE C.21: xl save ADDED OPTIONS

save **Added Options**	
Option	*Task*
(+) `-c`	Leave domain running after creating the snapshot

`xl` restore *OPTIONS CONFIG_FILE CHECK_POINT_FILE*

 Note: `libvirt` **Equivalent**

`virsh` restore

`restore` **Added Options**	
Options	*Task*
(+) `-p`	Do not unpause domain after restoring it
(+) `-e`	Do not wait in the background for the death of the domain on the new host
(+) `-d`	Enable debug messages
(+) `-V, --vncviewer`	Attach to domain's VNC server, forking a vncviewer process
(+) `-A, --vncviewer-autopass`	Pass VNC password to vncviewer via stdin

xl `shutdown` *OPTIONS DOMAIN*

 Note: `libvirt` **Equivalent**

virsh `shutdown`

TABLE C.23: `xm shutdown` REMOVED OPTIONS

`shutdown` **Removed Options**	
Options	*Task*
(-) `-w, --wait`	Wait for the domain to complete shutdown before returning
(-) `-a`	Shutdown all guest domains
(-) `-R`	
(-) `-H`	

Changed Options

TABLE C.24: `xl shutdown` **ADDED OPTIONS**

shutdown **Added Options**	
Option	*Task*
(+) -F	If the guest does not support PV shutdown control then fallback to sending an ACPI power event

TABLE C.25: `xl trigger` **CHANGED OPTIONS**

trigger **Changed Options**	
Option	*Task*
trigger *DOMAIN* <nmi|reset|init|power|sleep|s3resume> *VCPU*	Send a trigger to a domain. Only available for HVM domains

C.3.5.9 xl sched-*

xl sched-credit *OPTIONS*

 Note: libvirt **equivalent**

virsh schedinfo

TABLE C.26: xm sched-credit **REMOVED OPTIONS**

sched-credit **Removed Options**	
Options	*Task*
-d *DOMAIN*, --domain= *DOMAIN*	Domain
-w *WEIGHT*, --weight= *WEIGHT*	A domain with a weight of 512 will get twice as much CPU as a domain with a weight of 256 on a contended host. Legal weights range from 1 to 65535 and the default is 256

Changed Options

sched-credit **Removed Options**	
Options	*Task*
-c *CAP*, --cap= *CAP*	The CAP optionally fixes the maximum amount of CPU a domain can consume

TABLE C.27: xl sched-credit **ADDED OPTIONS**

sched-credit **Added Options**	
Options	*Task*
(+) -p *CPUPOOL*, --cpupool= *CPUPOOL*	Restrict output to domains in the specified cpupool
(+) -s, --schedparam	Specify to list or set pool-wide scheduler parameters
(+) -t *TSLICE*, --tslice_ms= *TSLICE*	Timeslice tells the scheduler how long to allow VMs to run before pre-empting
(+) -r *RLIMIT*, --ratelimit_us= *RLIMIT*	Ratelimit attempts to limit the number of schedules per second

xl sched-credit2 *OPTIONS*

 Note: libvirt **status**

> **virsh** only supports credit scheduler, not credit2 scheduler

TABLE C.28: xm sched-credit2 **REMOVED OPTIONS**

sched-credit2 **Removed Options**	
Options	*Task*
-d *DOMAIN*, --domain= *DOMAIN*	Domain
-w *WEIGHT*, --weight= *WEIGHT*	Legal weights range from 1 to 65535 and the default is 256

sched-credit2 **Added Options**	
Option	*Task*
(+) -p *CPUPOOL*, --cpupool= *CPUPOOL*	Restrict output to domains in the specified cpupool

xl sched-sedf *OPTIONS*

sched-sedf **Removed Options**	
Options	*Task*
-p *PERIOD*, --period= *PERIOD*	The normal *EDF* scheduling usage in milliseconds
-s *SLICE*, --slice= *SLICE*	The normal *EDF* scheduling usage in milliseconds
-l *LATENCY*, --latency= *LATENCY*	Scaled period if domain is doing heavy I/O
-e *EXTRA*, --extra= *EXTRA*	Flag for allowing domain to run in extra time (0 or 1)
-w *WEIGHT*, --weight= *WEIGHT*	Another way of setting CPU slice

sched-sedf **Added Options**	
Options	*Task*
(+) -c *CPUPOOL*, --cpupool= *CPUPOOL*	Restrict output to domains in the specified cpupool
(+) -d *DOMAIN*, --domain= *DOMAIN*	Domain

C.3.5.10 `xl` cpupool-*

`xl` cpupool-cpu-remove *CPU_POOL* <CPU nr> | node: <node nr>

`xl` cpupool-list [-c | --cpus] *CPU_POOL*

TABLE C.32: xm cpupool-list **REMOVED OPTIONS**

cpupool-* **Removed Options**	
Option	**Task**
(-) -l, --long	Output all CPU pool details in *SXP* format

`xl` cpupool-cpu-add *CPU_POOL* cpu-nr | node:node-nr

`xl` cpupool-create *OPTIONS CONFIG_FILE* [Variable = Value ...]

TABLE C.33: xm cpupool-create **REMOVED OPTIONS**

cpupool-create **Removed Options**	
Options	**Task**
(-) -f *FILE*, --defconfig = *FILE*	Use the given Python configuration script. The configuration script is loaded after arguments have been processed
(-) -n, --dryrun	Dry run - prints the resulting configuration in *SXP* but does not create the CPU pool
(-) --help_config	Print the available configuration variables (vars) for the configuration script
(-) --path= *PATH*	Search path for configuration scripts. The value of PATH is a colon-separated directory list
(-) -F= *FILE*, --config = *FILE*	CPU pool configuration to use (*SXP*)

C.3.5.11 PCI and Block Devices

`xl` pci-detach [-f] *DOMAIN_ID* <BDF>

> **Note: libvirt Equivalent**
>
> `virsh` detach-device

TABLE C.34: `xl` `pci-detach` **ADDED OPTIONS**

`pci-detach` **Added Options**	
Option	*Task*
(+) `-f`	If `-f` is specified, **xl** is going to forcefully remove the device even without guest's collaboration

TABLE C.35: `xm` `block-list` **REMOVED OPTIONS**

`block-list` **Removed Options**	
Option	*Task*
(-) `-l`, `--long`	List virtual block devices for a domain

TABLE C.36: OTHER OPTIONS

Option	`libvirt` **equivalent**
xl `block-attach` *DOMAIN* <disk-spec-component(s)>	**virsh** `attach-disk/attach-device`
xl `block-list` *DOMAIN_ID*	**virsh** `domblklist`

C.3.5.12   Network

TABLE C.37: NETWORK OPTIONS

Option	`libvirt` **equivalent**
xl `network-list` *DOMAIN(s)*	**virsh** `domiflist`
xl `network-detach` *DOMAIN_ID* devid|mac	**virsh** `detach-interface`

Option	`libvirt` equivalent
xl `network-attach DOMAIN(s)`	**virsh** `attach-interface/attach-device`

TABLE C.38: `xl network-attach` **REMOVED OPTIONS**

Removed Options	
Option	*Task*
(-) `-l, --long`	

C.3.6 New Options

TABLE C.39: NEW OPTIONS

Options	Task
`config-update DOMAIN CONFIG_FILE OPTIONS VARS`	Update the saved configuration for a running domain. This has no immediate effect but will be applied when the guest is next restarted. This command is useful to ensure that runtime modifications made to the guest will be preserved when the guest is restarted
`migrate-receive`	
`sharing DOMAIN`	List count of shared pages.List specifically for that domain. Otherwise, list for all domains
`vm-list`	Prints information about guests. This list excludes information about service or auxiliary domains such as Dom0 and stubdoms
`cpupool-rename CPU_POOL NEWNAME`	Renames a cpu-pool to newname
`cpupool-numa-split`	Splits up the machine into one cpu-pool per numa node

Options	Task
cd-insert *DOMAIN* <VirtualDevice> <type:path>	Insert a CD-ROM into a guest domain's existing virtual CD drive. The virtual drive must already exist but can be current empty
cd-eject *DOMAIN* <VirtualDevice>	Eject a CD-ROM from a guest's virtual CD drive. Only works with HVM domains
pci-assignable-list	List all the assignable PCI devices. These are devices in the system which are configured to be available for pass-through and are bound to a suitable PCI back-end driver in Dom0 rather than a real driver
pci-assignable-add <BDF>	Make the device at PCI Bus/Device/Function *BDF* assignable to guests.This will bind the device to the pciback driver
pci-assignable-remove *OPTIONS* <BDF>	Make the device at PCI Bus/Device/Function *BDF* assignable to guests. This will at least unbind the device from pciback
loadpolicy *POLICY_FILE*	Load *FLASK* policy from the given policy file. The initial policy is provided to the hypervisor as a multiboot module; this command allows runtime updates to the policy. Loading new security policy will reset runtime changes to device labels

C.4   External links

For more information on Xen toolstacks refer to the following online resources:

XL in Xen

XL in Xen 4.2 [http://wiki.xenproject.org/wiki/XL_in_Xen_4.2]

xl command

XL [http://xenbits.xen.org/docs/unstable/man/xl.1.html] command line.

xl.cfg

xl.cfg [http://xenbits.xen.org/docs/unstable/man/xl.cfg.5.html] domain configuration file syntax.

xl disk

xl disk [http://xenbits.xen.org/docs/unstable/misc/xl-disk-configuration.txt] configuration option.

XL vs Xend

XL vs Xend [http://wiki.xenproject.org/wiki/XL_vs_Xend_Feature_Comparison] feature comparison.

BDF doc

BDF documentation [http://wiki.xen.org/wiki/Bus:Device.Function_%28BDF%29_Notation].

libvirt

virsh [http://libvirt.org/virshcmdref.html] command.

C.5 Saving a Xen Guest Configuration in an **xm** Compatible Format

Although **xl** is now the current toolkit for managing Xen guests (apart from the preferred libvirt), you may need to export the guest configuration to the previously used **xm** format. To do this, follow these steps:

1. First export the guest configuration to a file:

   ```
   virsh dumpxml guest_id > guest_cfg.xml
   ```

2. Then convert the configuration to the **xm** format:

   ```
   virsh domxml-to-native xen-xm guest_cfg.xml > guest_xm_cfg
   ```

D Documentation Updates

This chapter lists content changes for this document.

This manual was updated on the following dates:

- Section D.1, "December 2015 (Initial Release of SUSE Linux Enterprise Server 12 SP1)"

- Section D.2, "February 2015 (Documentation Maintenance Update)"

- Section D.3, "October 2014 (Initial Release of SUSE Linux Enterprise Server 12)"

D.1 December 2015 (Initial Release of SUSE Linux Enterprise Server 12 SP1)

General

- *Book "Subscription Management Tool for SLES 12 SP1"* is now part of the documentation for SUSE Linux Enterprise Server.

- Add-ons provided by SUSE have been renamed to modules and extensions. The manuals have been updated to reflect this change.

- Numerous small fixes and additions to the documentation, based on technical feedback.

- The registration service has been changed from Novell Customer Center to SUSE Customer Center.

- In YaST, you will now reach *Network Settings* via the *System* group. *Network Devices* is gone (https://bugzilla.suse.com/show_bug.cgi?id=867809).

General

Rewrote large parts of the PCI Pass-Through documentation since KVM PCI Pass-Through has been replaced by VFIO.

Chapter 7, Supported Guests, Hosts and Features

Updated the lists of supported VM Guests and VM Host Servers (Fate #319284 and #319285).

Chapter 10, Basic VM Guest Management

- Refined the information about supported live migration scenarios in *Section 10.7.1, "Migration Requirements"* (Fate #319283).

- Added *Section 10.8.2, "Monitoring with* `virt-top`*"* (Fate #319422).

Chapter 12, Managing Storage

- Added *Section 12.5, "Sharing Directories between Host and Guests (File System Pass-Through)"*.

Chapter 13, Configuring Virtual Machines

- Added a note on how to add SR-IOV devices on VM Guest creation to *Section 13.15, "Adding SR-IOV Devices"* (Fate #315577).

Chapter 18, Virtual Networking

- Fixed unclear wording in *Procedure 18.1, "Configuring a routed IPv4 VM Guest"* (doc comment 28137).

Chapter 22, Administrative Tasks

- Added new list item for hosts in different subnets in *Section 22.3, "Migrating Xen VM Guest Systems"* (Fate #303927).

Chapter 26, Setting Up a KVM VM Host Server

- Added the whole chapter and moved `virtio` related KVM content to a subsidiary *Section 26.3, "KVM Host-Specific Features"*.

Chapter 28, Running Virtual Machines with qemu-system-ARCH

- Added support for e1000 network card variants in *Section 28.4.1, "Defining a Network Interface Card"*.

- Updated the NIC command line specification to the more preferred `-netdev -device` in *Section 28.4.1, "Defining a Network Interface Card"*.

Bugfixes

- VFIO related improvements to Virtualization Guide (https://bugzilla.suse.com/show_bug.cgi?id=907145).

- Added a snippet recommending only one watchdog device at a time in *Section 17.1, "Best Practices and Suggestions"* (https://bugzilla.suse.com/show_bug.cgi?id=917432).

- virsh Console Config Is Not Documented (https://bugzilla.suse.com/show_bug.cgi?id=936785).

- Wrong Table Title (https://bugzilla.suse.com/show_bug.cgi?id=938671).

- Missing Word "Virtualized" (https://bugzilla.suse.com/show_bug.cgi?id=926337).

- Added *Section 12.5, "Sharing Directories between Host and Guests (File System Pass-Through)"* (https://bugzilla.suse.com/show_bug.cgi?id=783346).

D.2 February 2015 (Documentation Maintenance Update)

Bugfixes

- FIPS: starting of openvn client on SLES 12 fails... (https://bugzilla.suse.com/show_bug.cgi?id=911390).

- Misleading Information Related to Supported Virtualization Host (CitrixXen Server) (https://bugzilla.suse.com/show_bug.cgi?id=912700).

- qemu-bridge-helper Location (https://bugzilla.suse.com/show_bug.cgi?id=912882).

- Virtualization Support Statement of OES 11 SP2 (https://bugzilla.suse.com/show_bug.cgi?id=914727).

D.3 October 2014 (Initial Release of SUSE Linux Enterprise Server 12)

General

- Removed all KDE documentation and references because KDE is no longer shipped.

- Removed all references to SuSEconfig, which is no longer supported (Fate #100011).

- Move from System V init to systemd (Fate #310421). Updated affected parts of the documentation.

- YaST Runlevel Editor has changed to Services Manager (Fate #312568). Updated affected parts of the documentation.

- Removed all references to ISDN support, as ISDN support has been removed (Fate #314594).

- Removed all references to the YaST DSL module as it is no longer shipped (Fate #316264).

- Removed all references to the YaST Modem module as it is no longer shipped (Fate #316264).

- Btrfs has become the default file system for the root partition (Fate #315901). Updated affected parts of the documentation.

- The `dmesg` now provides human-readable time stamps in `ctime()`-like format (Fate #316056). Updated affected parts of the documentation.

- syslog and syslog-ng have been replaced by rsyslog (Fate #316175). Updated affected parts of the documentation.

- MariaDB is now shipped as the relational database instead of MySQL (Fate #313595). Updated affected parts of the documentation.

- SUSE-related products are no longer available from http://download.novell.com but from http://download.suse.com. Adjusted links accordingly.

- Novell Customer Center has been replaced with SUSE Customer Center. Updated affected parts of the documentation.

- `/var/run` is mounted as tmpfs (Fate #303793). Updated affected parts of the documentation.

- The following architectures are no longer supported: Itanium and x86. Updated affected parts of the documentation.

- The traditional method for setting up the network with `ifconfig` has been replaced by `wicked`. Updated affected parts of the documentation.

- A lot of networking commands are deprecated and have been replaced by newer commands (usually `ip`). Updated affected parts of the documentation.

  `arp: ip neighbor`

```
ifconfig: ip addr, ip link
iptunnel: ip tunnel
iwconfig: iw
nameif: ip link, ifrename
netstat: ss, ip route, ip -s link, ip maddr
route: ip route
```

- Numerous small fixes and additions to the documentation, based on technical feed-back.

Part I, "Introduction"

- Added *Chapter 7, Supported Guests, Hosts and Features*.

- Updated *Section 7.1, "Supported VM Guests"*.

- Updated *Section 7.2, " Supported VM Host Servers for SUSE Linux Enterprise Server 12 SP1 VM Guests "*.

Chapter 8, Starting and Stopping `libvirtd`

- Added introductory paragraph on **virt-install**.

Chapter 9, Guest Installation

- Updated *Section 9.1, "GUI-Based Guest Installation"* to match SUSE Linux Enterprise Server 12 state.

- Added *Section 9.2, "Installing from the Command Line with* **virt-install***"*.

Chapter 12, Managing Storage

- **Added** *Section 12.4, "Online Resizing of Guest Block Devices".*

Chapter 13, Configuring Virtual Machines

- **Added** *Section 13.15.4, "Dynamic Allocation of VFs from a Pool".*

Chapter 10, Basic VM Guest Management

- **Added tip in** *Section 10.4.2, "Saving and Restoring with* `virsh`*".*

Part IV, "Managing Virtual Machines with Xen"

- Migrated from Xend/xm toolkit to xl.

Chapter 21, Virtualization: Configuration Options and Settings

- **Added** *Section 21.6.3, "Increasing the Number of PCI-IRQs".*

Chapter 27, Guest Installation

- **Added a tip on** `nocow` **option in** *Section 27.2.2, "Creating, Converting and Checking Disk Images".*

Chapter 28, Running Virtual Machines with qemu-system-ARCH

- **Added** *Section 28.3.1.3, "Bio-Based I/O Path for virtio-blk".*

- **Added** *Section 26.3.3, "Scaling Network Performance with Multiqueue virtio-net".*

- **Added** *Section 28.3.1.1, "Freeing Unused Guest Disk Space".*

Chapter 29, Virtual Machine Administration Using QEMU Monitor

- Added **device_add** and **device_del** commands.

- **Added** *Section 29.11, "QMP - QEMU Machine Protocol".*

Part VI, "Managing Virtual Machines with LXC"

- **Added** *Chapter 31, Migration from LXC to* `libvirt-lxc`.

Bugfixes

-

E GNU Licenses

This appendix contains the GNU Free Documentation License version 1.2.

GNU Free Documentation License

Copyright (C) 2000, 2001, 2002 Free Software Foundation, Inc. 51 Franklin St, Fifth Floor, Boston, MA 02110-1301 USA. Everyone is permitted to copy and distribute verbatim copies of this license document, but changing it is not allowed.

0. PREAMBLE

The purpose of this License is to make a manual, textbook, or other functional and useful document "free" in the sense of freedom: to assure everyone the effective freedom to copy and redistribute it, with or without modifying it, either commercially or non-commercially. Secondarily, this License preserves for the author and publisher a way to get credit for their work, while not being considered responsible for modifications made by others.

This License is a kind of "copyleft", which means that derivative works of the document must themselves be free in the same sense. It complements the GNU General Public License, which is a copyleft license designed for free software.

We have designed this License to use it for manuals for free software, because free software needs free documentation: a free program should come with manuals providing the same freedoms that the software does. But this License is not limited to software manuals; it can be used for any textual work, regardless of subject matter or whether it is published as a printed book. We recommend this License principally for works whose purpose is instruction or reference.

1. APPLICABILITY AND DEFINITIONS

This License applies to any manual or other work, in any medium, that contains a notice placed by the copyright holder saying it can be distributed under the terms of this License. Such a notice grants a world-wide, royalty-free license, unlimited in duration, to use that work under the conditions stated herein. The "Document", below, refers to any such manual or work. Any member of the public is a licensee, and is addressed as "you". You accept the license if you copy, modify or distribute the work in a way requiring permission under copyright law.

A "Modified Version" of the Document means any work containing the Document or a portion of it, either copied verbatim, or with modifications and/or translated into another language.

A "Secondary Section" is a named appendix or a front-matter section of the Document that deals exclusively with the relationship of the publishers or authors of the Document to the Document's overall subject (or to related matters) and contains nothing that could fall directly within that overall subject. (Thus, if the Document is in part a textbook of mathematics, a Secondary Section may not explain any mathematics.) The relationship could be a matter of historical connection with the subject or with related matters, or of legal, commercial, philosophical, ethical or political position regarding them.

The "Invariant Sections" are certain Secondary Sections whose titles are designated, as being those of Invariant Sections, in the notice that says that the Document is released under this License. If a section does not fit the above definition of Secondary then it is not allowed to be designated as Invariant. The Document may contain zero Invariant Sections. If the Document does not identify any Invariant Sections then there are none.

The "Cover Texts" are certain short passages of text that are listed, as Front-Cover Texts or Back-Cover Texts, in the notice that says that the Document is released under this License. A Front-Cover Text may be at most 5 words, and a Back-Cover Text may be at most 25 words.

A "Transparent" copy of the Document means a machine-readable copy, represented in a format whose specification is available to the general public, that is suitable for revising the document straightforwardly with generic text editors or (for images composed of pixels) generic paint programs or (for drawings) some widely available draw-

ing editor, and that is suitable for input to text formatters or for automatic translation to a variety of formats suitable for input to text formatters. A copy made in an otherwise Transparent file format whose markup, or absence of markup, has been arranged to thwart or discourage subsequent modification by readers is not Transparent. An image format is not Transparent if used for any substantial amount of text. A copy that is not "Transparent" is called "Opaque".

Examples of suitable formats for Transparent copies include plain ASCII without markup, Texinfo input format, LaTeX input format, SGML or XML using a publicly available DTD, and standard-conforming simple HTML, PostScript or PDF designed for human modification. Examples of transparent image formats include PNG, XCF and JPG. Opaque formats include proprietary formats that can be read and edited only by proprietary word processors, SGML or XML for which the DTD and/or processing tools are not generally available, and the machine-generated HTML, PostScript or PDF produced by some word processors for output purposes only.

The "Title Page" means, for a printed book, the title page itself, plus such following pages as are needed to hold, legibly, the material this License requires to appear in the title page. For works in formats which do not have any title page as such, "Title Page" means the text near the most prominent appearance of the work's title, preceding the beginning of the body of the text.

A section "Entitled XYZ" means a named subunit of the Document whose title either is precisely XYZ or contains XYZ in parentheses following text that translates XYZ in another language. (Here XYZ stands for a specific section name mentioned below, such as "Acknowledgements", "Dedications", "Endorsements", or "History".) To "Preserve the Title" of such a section when you modify the Document means that it remains a section "Entitled XYZ" according to this definition.

The Document may include Warranty Disclaimers next to the notice which states that this License applies to the Document. These Warranty Disclaimers are considered to be included by reference in this License, but only as regards disclaiming warranties: any other implication that these Warranty Disclaimers may have is void and has no effect on the meaning of this License.

2. VERBATIM COPYING

You may copy and distribute the Document in any medium, either commercially or noncommercially, provided that this License, the copyright notices, and the license notice saying this License applies to the Document are reproduced in all copies, and that you add no other conditions whatsoever to those of this License. You may not use technical measures to obstruct or control the reading or further copying of the copies you make or distribute. However, you may accept compensation in exchange for copies. If you distribute a large enough number of copies you must also follow the conditions in section 3.

You may also lend copies, under the same conditions stated above, and you may publicly display copies.

3. COPYING IN QUANTITY

If you publish printed copies (or copies in media that commonly have printed covers) of the Document, numbering more than 100, and the Document's license notice requires Cover Texts, you must enclose the copies in covers that carry, clearly and legibly, all these Cover Texts: Front-Cover Texts on the front cover, and Back-Cover Texts on the back cover. Both covers must also clearly and legibly identify you as the publisher of these copies. The front cover must present the full title with all words of the title equally prominent and visible. You may add other material on the covers in addition. Copying with changes limited to the covers, as long as they preserve the title of the Document and satisfy these conditions, can be treated as verbatim copying in other respects.

If the required texts for either cover are too voluminous to fit legibly, you should put the first ones listed (as many as fit reasonably) on the actual cover, and continue the rest onto adjacent pages.

If you publish or distribute Opaque copies of the Document numbering more than 100, you must either include a machine-readable Transparent copy along with each Opaque copy, or state in or with each Opaque copy a computer-network location from which the general network-using public has access to download using public-standard network protocols a complete Transparent copy of the Document, free of added material. If you use the latter option, you must take reasonably prudent steps, when you begin distribution of Opaque copies in quantity, to ensure that this Transparent copy will remain thus accessible at the stated location until at least one year after the last time you distribute an Opaque copy (directly or through your agents or retailers) of that edition to the public.

It is requested, but not required, that you contact the authors of the Document well before redistributing any large number of copies, to give them a chance to provide you with an updated version of the Document.

4. MODIFICATIONS

You may copy and distribute a Modified Version of the Document under the conditions of sections 2 and 3 above, provided that you release the Modified Version under precisely this License, with the Modified Version filling the role of the Document, thus licensing distribution and modification of the Modified Version to whoever possesses a copy of it. In addition, you must do these things in the Modified Version:

A. Use in the Title Page (and on the covers, if any) a title distinct from that of the Document, and from those of previous versions (which should, if there were any, be listed in the History section of the Document). You may use the same title as a previous version if the original publisher of that version gives permission.

B. List on the Title Page, as authors, one or more persons or entities responsible for authorship of the modifications in the Modified Version, together with at least five of the principal authors of the Document (all of its principal authors, if it has fewer than five), unless they release you from this requirement.

C. State on the Title page the name of the publisher of the Modified Version, as the publisher.

D. Preserve all the copyright notices of the Document.

E. Add an appropriate copyright notice for your modifications adjacent to the other copyright notices.

F. Include, immediately after the copyright notices, a license notice giving the public permission to use the Modified Version under the terms of this License, in the form shown in the Addendum below.

G. Preserve in that license notice the full lists of Invariant Sections and required Cover Texts given in the Document's license notice.

H. Include an unaltered copy of this License.

I. Preserve the section Entitled "History", Preserve its Title, and add to it an item stating at least the title, year, new authors, and publisher of the Modified Version as given on the Title Page. If there is no section Entitled "History" in the Document, create one stating the title, year, authors, and publisher of the Document as given on its Title Page, then add an item describing the Modified Version as stated in the previous sentence.

J. Preserve the network location, if any, given in the Document for public access to a Transparent copy of the Document, and likewise the network locations given in the Document for previous versions it was based on. These may be placed in the "History" section. You may omit a network location for a work that was published at least four years before the Document itself, or if the original publisher of the version it refers to gives permission.

K. For any section Entitled "Acknowledgements" or "Dedications", Preserve the Title of the section, and preserve in the section all the substance and tone of each of the contributor acknowledgements and/or dedications given therein.

L. Preserve all the Invariant Sections of the Document, unaltered in their text and in their titles. Section numbers or the equivalent are not considered part of the section titles.

M. Delete any section Entitled "Endorsements". Such a section may not be included in the Modified Version.

N. Do not retitle any existing section to be Entitled "Endorsements" or to conflict in title with any Invariant Section.

O. Preserve any Warranty Disclaimers.

If the Modified Version includes new front-matter sections or appendices that qualify as Secondary Sections and contain no material copied from the Document, you may at your option designate some or all of these sections as invariant. To do this, add their titles to the list of Invariant Sections in the Modified Version's license notice. These titles must be distinct from any other section titles.

You may add a section Entitled "Endorsements", provided it contains nothing but endorsements of your Modified Version by various parties--for example, statements of peer review or that the text has been approved by an organization as the authoritative definition of a standard.

You may add a passage of up to five words as a Front-Cover Text, and a passage of up to 25 words as a Back-Cover Text, to the end of the list of Cover Texts in the Modified Version. Only one passage of Front-Cover Text and one of Back-Cover Text may be added by (or through arrangements made by) any one entity. If the Document already includes a cover text for the same cover, previously added by you or by arrangement made by the same entity you are acting on behalf of, you may not add another; but you may replace the old one, on explicit permission from the previous publisher that added the old one.

The author(s) and publisher(s) of the Document do not by this License give permission to use their names for publicity for or to assert or imply endorsement of any Modified Version.

5. COMBINING DOCUMENTS

You may combine the Document with other documents released under this License, under the terms defined in section 4 above for modified versions, provided that you include in the combination all of the Invariant Sections of all of the original documents, unmodified, and list them all as Invariant Sections of your combined work in its license notice, and that you preserve all their Warranty Disclaimers.

The combined work need only contain one copy of this License, and multiple identical Invariant Sections may be replaced with a single copy. If there are multiple Invariant Sections with the same name but different contents, make the title of each such section unique by adding at the end of it, in parentheses, the name of the original author or publisher of that section if known, or else a unique number. Make the same adjustment to the section titles in the list of Invariant Sections in the license notice of the combined work.

In the combination, you must combine any sections Entitled "History" in the various original documents, forming one section Entitled "History"; likewise combine any sections Entitled "Acknowledgements", and any sections Entitled "Dedications". You must delete all sections Entitled "Endorsements".

6. COLLECTIONS OF DOCUMENTS

You may make a collection consisting of the Document and other documents released under this License, and replace the individual copies of this License in the various documents with a single copy that is included in the collection, provided that you follow the rules of this License for verbatim copying of each of the documents in all other respects.

You may extract a single document from such a collection, and distribute it individually under this License, provided you insert a copy of this License into the extracted document, and follow this License in all other respects regarding verbatim copying of that document.

7. AGGREGATION WITH INDEPENDENT WORKS

A compilation of the Document or its derivatives with other separate and independent documents or works, in or on a volume of a storage or distribution medium, is called an "aggregate" if the copyright resulting from the compilation is not used to limit the legal rights of the compilation's users beyond what the individual works permit. When the Document is included in an aggregate, this License does not apply to the other works in the aggregate which are not themselves derivative works of the Document.

If the Cover Text requirement of section 3 is applicable to these copies of the Document, then if the Document is less than one half of the entire aggregate, the Document's Cover Texts may be placed on covers that bracket the Document within the aggregate, or the electronic equivalent of covers if the Document is in electronic form. Otherwise they must appear on printed covers that bracket the whole aggregate.

8. TRANSLATION

Translation is considered a kind of modification, so you may distribute translations of the Document under the terms of section 4. Replacing Invariant Sections with translations requires special permission from their copyright holders, but you may include translations of some or all Invariant Sections in addition to the original versions of these Invariant Sections. You may include a translation of this License, and all the license notices in the Document, and any Warranty Disclaimers, provided that you also include the original English version of this License and the original versions of those notices and disclaimers. In case of a disagreement between the translation and the original version of this License or a notice or disclaimer, the original version will prevail.

If a section in the Document is Entitled "Acknowledgements", "Dedications", or "History", the requirement (section 4) to Preserve its Title (section 1) will typically require changing the actual title.

9. TERMINATION

You may not copy, modify, sublicense, or distribute the Document except as expressly provided for under this License. Any other attempt to copy, modify, sublicense or distribute the Document is void, and will automatically terminate your rights under this License. However, parties who have received copies, or rights, from you under this License will not have their licenses terminated so long as such parties remain in full compliance.

10. FUTURE REVISIONS OF THIS LICENSE

The Free Software Foundation may publish new, revised versions of the GNU Free Documentation License from time to time. Such new versions will be similar in spirit to the present version, but may differ in detail to address new problems or concerns. See http://www.gnu.org/copyleft/.

Each version of the License is given a distinguishing version number. If the Document specifies that a particular numbered version of this License "or any later version" applies to it, you have the option of following the terms and conditions either of that specified version or of any later version that has been published (not as a draft) by the Free Software Foundation. If the Document does not specify a version number of this License, you may choose any version ever published (not as a draft) by the Free Software Foundation.

ADDENDUM: How to use this License for your documents

```
Copyright (c) YEAR YOUR NAME.

Permission is granted to copy, distribute and/or modify this document

under the terms of the GNU Free Documentation License, Version 1.2

or any later version published by the Free Software Foundation;

with no Invariant Sections, no Front-Cover Texts, and no Back-Cover

 Texts.

A copy of the license is included in the section entitled "GNU

Free Documentation License".
```

If you have Invariant Sections, Front-Cover Texts and Back-Cover Texts, replace the "with...Texts." line with this:

```
with the Invariant Sections being LIST THEIR TITLES, with the

Front-Cover Texts being LIST, and with the Back-Cover Texts being LIST.
```

If you have Invariant Sections without Cover Texts, or some other combination of the three, merge those two alternatives to suit the situation.

If your document contains nontrivial examples of program code, we recommend releasing these examples in parallel under your choice of free software license, such as the GNU General Public License, to permit their use in free software.

www.ingramcontent.com/pod-product-compliance
Lightning Source LLC
LaVergne TN
LVHW060134070326
832902LV00018B/2795